TEN PERSONAL STUDIES

The Right Hon. Arthur J. Balfour, M.P.
From a painting by Philip László.

TEN PERSONAL STUDIES

A. J. BALFOUR
J. T. DELANE
R. H. HUTTON
SIR J. KNOWLES
HENRY SIDGWICK
LORD LYTTON
FATHER I. RYDER

SIR M. E. GRANT DUFF
LEO XIII
CARDINAL WISEMAN
JOHN HENRY NEWMAN
CARDINALS NEWMAN and
MANNING

BY

WILFRID PHILIP WARD

WITH TEN PORTRAITS

Essay Index Reprint Series

 BOOKS FOR LIBRARIES PRESS
FREEPORT, NEW YORK

First Published 1908
Reprinted 1970

STANDARD BOOK NUMBER:
8369-1584-4

LIBRARY OF CONGRESS CATALOG CARD NUMBER:
73-107742

PRINTED IN THE UNITED STATES OF AMERICA

PREFACE

I HAVE to thank the Editors and Proprietors of the 'Quarterly Review,' the 'Nineteenth Century and After,' and the 'Fortnightly Review' for their permission to publish such portions of the following Essays as appeared originally in those periodicals.

I have also to thank Canon Gildea for his assistance in revising my Oxford address on Cardinal Newman, delivered in the summer of 1907, and here printed for the first time, with a view to the greater care and accuracy of expression desirable before publication. Some changes have also, with the same object, been made in the Essay on Cardinals Newman and Manning, written in 1906.

The first Essay, 'Arthur James Balfour, a political Fabius Maximus,' was written in 1905, and, except for verbal changes, I have left it unaltered—a word spoken at a very critical moment. I have, however, added a postscript written in the light of the events of the three years following.

The Essay on Leo XIII. contains personal reminiscences of Rome in 1878 which were not in the original article.

The reader is asked to remember that the Oxford address on Cardinal Newman was delivered before an audience belonging to various religious communions, while the listeners to the Ushaw address on Cardinal Wiseman were nearly all Catholics.

W. W.

November 1908.

ANALYTICAL CONTENTS

I

ARTHUR JAMES BALFOUR: A POLITICAL FABIUS MAXIMUS

II

THREE NOTABLE EDITORS: DELANE, HUTTON, KNOWLES

III

SOME CHARACTERISTICS OF HENRY SIDGWICK

Sidgwick's Memoir mainly interesting as a character-study—A relentless
critic and destroyer of all theories of life—Yet a most stimulating companion—This unusual combination accounted for (1) by his gift of
sympathy in conversation, (2) by his passion for truth—Contrast between
his conversation and Jowett's—Jowett's douches of cold water—Illustrative instances—My first meeting with Sidgwick—His recitation of 'In
Memoriam'—His analysis of it on that occasion largely reproduced in
a letter published in Tennyson's Life—Influence on him of J. S. Mill
and Tennyson—Sidgwick's love of self-analysis—Illustrative instances
—His theoretic pessimism and practical optimism—His contentment contrasted with Jowett's—His wide interests—Letter on the Fioretti of St.
Francis—His grief at Tennyson's death—His letter on Fawcett's death—

VI

SIR M. E. GRANT DUFF'S DIARIES

VII

LEO XIII

VIII

THE GENIUS OF CARDINAL WISEMAN

IX

JOHN HENRY NEWMAN: AN ADDRESS

X

NEWMAN AND MANNING

LIST OF PORTRAITS

TEN PERSONAL STUDIES

ARTHUR JAMES BALFOUR
A POLITICAL FABIUS MAXIMUS [1]

THE years 1903 to 1905 were very remarkable ones in
our political history.   And they were years especially
interesting to those who watch with sympathy the
career of Arthur James Balfour, philosopher and statesman.   On October 3, 1903, 'The Spectator,' reviewing
Mr. Balfour's policy of the previous four months,
immediately after the Sheffield speech, declared *ex
cathedra* that Mr. Balfour's political reputation was for
ever at an end.   He was only a 'feeble shadow of
Mr. Chamberlain,' who agreed with Mr. Chamberlain
intellectually, but lacked the courage of his convictions.
He had allowed himself to forget the maxim that 'on
a grave and burning question it is absolutely essential
for an effective politician to be clearly and definitely on

[1] This study was written in May 1905.   Any truth it may have as a
psychological study remains now what it then was.   Of the bearing of
more recent events on the account it contains of Mr. Balfour's attitude on
the fiscal question I have added a few words in a Postscript (p. 38).
The essay itself is here given, except for a few verbal alterations, as it was
written.   In the Appendix (p. 299) will be found some particulars of the
leading political incidents referred to in the essay and in the postscript.

one side or the other.' The writer was very sad, but very positive :

> We cannot help a deep feeling of personal chagrin [he wrote] at Mr. Balfour's failure. *Sunt lachrymæ rerum*, and, being mortal, we cannot but grieve at the overthrow of a personality in many ways so attractive as that of Mr. Balfour. We are using no hyperbole—an overthrow it is. Whatever else may happen, Mr. Balfour's day as a great British states-man is over. No turn in the political kaleidoscope can restore to him the confidence of the country.

Day after day the witty caricaturist of 'The West-minster Gazette' represented the Prime Minister as a *roi fainéant*, and Mr. Chamberlain as the Mayor of the Palace—the real leader of the party ; and such manifestations in the Press represented a very wide-spread feeling. Nay, it was a feeling which seriously infected the Unionist party itself in the House of Commons and in the country. A *doctor dubitantium* was not an effective figure in a moment of excitement, when placed in competition with the positive, sanguine, enthusiastic Secretary for the Colonies. The man who was occupied in delineating with delicate hand fine shades and subtle lines of distinction and graduation in a picture as yet avowedly incomplete, which was to represent faithfully the anomalies and complexities of the actual world of commerce, seemed insignificant by the side of the painter who, unhampered by close regard to the practicable or the actual, depicted the broad scenic effects of the Glasgow programme.

Yet, as the drama developed itself, time had its revenges. We witnessed the change of fortunes which so often comes in a competition between fine and

calculating perception on the one hand and undis-
criminating and passionate energy on the other. It
can scarcely be questioned that, so far as pre-eminence
in the House of Commons was concerned, the positions
of Mr. Balfour and Mr. Chamberlain were in the
succeeding twelve months reversed. It was a case of
FitzJames and Roderick Dhu ; the cool perception and
the rapier thrust of criticism were in reality steadily
telling for victory, while to the average onlooker sheer
strength and vigour seemed to be carrying all before
them. And the space of a year brought the contrast
between the night when the Prime Minister had to be
content to risk defeat rather than press the Wharton
amendment [1]—which was identical with his own policy
—against the threatened mutiny of the Chamberlainites,
whose excesses it disowned, and the night when the
throroughgoing Chamberlainites had become numeri-
cally so weak that they gladly agreed to decline the
combat on Mr. Ainsworth's resolution. The contrast
was faithfully depicted by Sir F. C. Gould, and he gave
us Mr. Chamberlain, no longer as the real leader of
the party, but as a suppliant before the gates of Pope
Balfour's castle at Canossa.

This change in the situation was brought about by
some very remarkable qualities in the Prime Minister.
Far from being a shadow of Mr. Chamberlain, or
feebly echoing his views, two more different intellectual
attitudes towards a great problem could hardly be
conceived. Mr. Balfour with sure instinct noted at
the outset that Mr. Chamberlain's views had not

[1] *Vide infra*, p. 24.

attained that practical precision which could either
evoke an echo or call for an unequivocal disclaimer
in a really accurate mind.   In the first Parliamentary
debate of May 28, 1903, indeed, they were avowedly
undefined.[1] Yet the Prime Minister could not treat
them lightly.   Mr. Chamberlain was a colleague and
friend : Mr. Balfour naturally had confidence in his
insight into the necessities of the Colonies ; and he
had raised questions of importance.   Colonial preference had already appealed to Mr. Balfour as a
possible instrument of political value in cementing our
union with the Colonies—*if it should be workable.*
Retaliation,[2] as opposed to complete *laisser faire*,
had long been among the modifications of the existing
fiscal system which he had contemplated as desirable.
He had ever deprecated burking discussion on such
subjects in the name of the *a priori* dogmas of Free
Trade.   To reject Mr. Chamberlain's policy wholesale, or to accept it wholesale, was equally impossible
in the circumstances.   The first obvious duty was
to plead that we should think, examine, discriminate
before we decide, instead of deciding in a complex
matter before it is thought out at all.   Yet the multitude loves to be addressed in tones loud and positive.
Well-balanced thought ever seems to it a shadow.
Strong statements mean strength ; guarded statements,

[1] 'Nothing in the nature of a complete plan can be put before the
country,' Mr. Chamberlain said, in reply to Mr. Lough, who urged that
' the right honourable gentleman should tell us his plan' (*Hansard*, May
28, p. 184).
[2] See, on this subject, his speech in the House of Commons on June
24, 1880 (*Hansard*, vol. ccliii. p. 772).

weakness. Thus 'The Spectator' writer did express accurately the impression produced on the masses by the only possible attitude of a thoughtful man who was suddenly called upon to decide on a problem not ripe for decision, and to formulate a large policy on a subject which he did not consider to have as yet reached such definite issues as could justify concrete proposals suitable for the basis of a large policy.

Mr. Balfour had deprecated at the outset (in his speech of May 28, 1903) the attitude of complacent orthodoxy assumed by extreme Free Traders, and the charges of 'heresy' which they preferred against all who called their formulæ in question ; and, indeed, the situation was curiously similar to that which we see in the sphere to which such phrases primarily belong—that of divinity. Thinkers in all religious communions are just now very busy discussing the modifications in long-current theological opinions which are called for by the advance of the positive sciences. On the one hand we have the liberal thinkers, flushed with the most adventurous theories of the modern critics, and with speculations suggested by researches in the early Christian history, clamorously calling upon those in authority to transform the received teaching, and to bring it into accord with these bold and vivid speculations as though they were accurately ascertained facts. On the other hand, we have those who stand in the ancient ways, and condemn as heresy—as subversive of dogma—any attempt to call in question any detail of its customary exposition and illustration. The wise ruler yields to

neither party.   He considers the received dogma and
its explanatory theology as being in possession.   He
regards the latter as something far more sacred than
the changeable speculations of the irresponsible reason.
Even apart from all question of Divine guidance in
the Christian Church, it is largely the outcome of
great crises of thought in the past, in which the broad
outlines of Christian revelation have been rescued
from danger and explained in their relation to burning
controversies.   Its main outlines represent serious
and corporate decisions of the Church.   They have
ministered to the faith and religious life of multitudes.
To change them suddenly and materially would be
to introduce doubt and discord, and to impair the
effectiveness of theology as a bond of union in the
Church and the support of consistent religious conduct.   While some changes may be necessary in
deference to accurately ascertained historical facts,
change is in itself an evil.   To be over-ready in writing
amended theological propositions, and this in conditions in which they may have to be retracted before
the ink is dry (as Newman has expressed it), is to
forget the function of theology as a stable principle of
union and action.   On the other hand, prematurely to
close the questions raised by historians and critics,
and brand all the liberals as heretics, is also disastrous,
and tends to sheer obscurantism.   To speculate on and
discuss problems touching even the most sacred and
certain truths is not to tamper with those truths.
There are many things we may usefully think which
we would not speak ; many we would say which we

would not write ; many we would write which we would not print. There is such a thing as action in thought. And a change in the theological text-books partakes of the nature of action. Mature judgment as to when thought is ripe enough and sufficiently assured to be made the basis of action, as to when it is wise to take a step, is a process undertaken by the whole man. It needs, on the one hand, an open mind and active inquiry, and, on the other, a deep sense of the responsibility and consequences attaching to a practical move taken in deference to the results of speculation. Quickness to think and to criticise and revise thought, and slowness to act, are its two momenta. Therefore the wise ruler, with whom it lies to decide when a practical step should be taken, inevitably angers extremists on both sides. He will not, apart from the case of an exceptional crisis, silence the liberals. He knows that it is they who have hold of the materials out of which the true developments in theological exposition are to be effected. Their trade is in novelty ; and even if a dozen novel theories are started and come to naught, it is probable that their keen adventurous intellectual criticism and researches will detect the really weak points in the present text-books, and ultimately bring to the front what is needed by way of amendment. On the other hand, he will have none of the dogmatism of the obscurantists. To treat all speculative inquiry as heresy is as bad as to treat its suggestions as newly won dogma.

The analogy is obvious. The Chamberlainites are

the liberals. The blind Free Traders who will not hear of Retaliation, of the smallest tax on food, of Colonial preference, not on grounds of reason, but because they contradict the received shibboleths of Free Trade, are the theological obscurantists. Mr. Balfour's course, preserved amid kicks from all sides, has been that of the responsible ruler who knows that a change in the received fiscal system of a great commercial country is a most serious thing. He stands for the moment in the ancient ways, but at the same time recognises that those sanguine reformers who realise most keenly new conditions produced by our Colonial Empire, who are most alive to the shortcomings which time has made evident in the workings of our fiscal system, may be the pioneers of needed reform. They should be allowed to talk, though by no means as yet permitted to take decisive action. The necessary dualism of the intellect of the wise official mind, whether in theology or in politics, is brought into striking relief. His intellectual sympathy is probably, at starting, largely with those who raise, however crudely, new and urgent problems, and suggest, however rashly and unpractically, schemes for their solution. He gives these men every chance of framing a wise and workable scheme. His practical course as a ruler remains for the time with the upholders of the existing system. To change it is to take a most serious step, and radical change in any system where habit has made very elaborate machinery work even fairly well, is an evil. Change can only be safely made by very gradual steps, the wisdom of which is

completely ascertained. It is only thus that its dislocating effect can be avoided. Yet the nature of
these very steps can be satisfactorily ascertained only
by the freest discussion. Provisionally, the dogmas of
Free Trade must be largely disregarded in the discussion. That such dogma exists and is sound he
does not doubt. But he remembers the incurable
tendency of the human mind to identify the true
dogma with some current and non-final statement as
to its exact import. A return to pre-Cobdenite Protection would, indeed, be to attack an irreformable
decision in economic orthodoxy. But to condemn
measures as Protectionist, in the sense in which
Protection is disastrous, before their nature and consequences have been fully sifted, is obscurantism, and not
orthodoxy. The Chamberlainites (Mr. Balfour seems
to have argued) should be given the fullest opportunity
to show how far their schemes are thought out, are
economically sound, and are reducible to practice ;
their critics should have the fullest opportunity to
point out what will work and what will not. And
probably, after a survey of all things on earth and in
heaven, one little corner will be found for substantial
improvement which is immediately practicable and
wise. Thus, to combine a wide and daring speculative
activity and sympathy with cautious and very limited
action is in the circumstances the height of statesmanship. It is the dictate of the spirit of Edmund Burke
—of jealous loyalty to the Constitution and zeal for
reform. Yet limited action is obviously but a faint
shadow of daring thought. Thus, those who ignore

the true *modus operandi* in politics or in theology will ever regard the wise as poltroons.

One further point. The word 'leader' has been used freely, and Mr. Balfour was at first taunted with allowing the leadership to pass into the hands of Mr. Chamberlain. But here again the considerations above indicated help us to make a necessary distinction. It is quite true that where the desirable forward step is clear, it is for the leader of the party to point it out. But to say, as the writer in 'The Spectator' seems to say, that in *any* burning question the leader should pass a definite and final intellectual judgment is surely the greatest of fallacies. His line should be firm as to what is or is not now practicable; but to offer a speculative decision, on proposals which are not yet finally formulated, is the special province either of a rash and inaccurate mind or of a bigot. The latter says 'no' because they are new. The former says 'yes' because he loves adventure and novelty. If the leader means the irresponsible man who will start new hares and go far in their pursuit, or the obstinate one who is blind and won't move, Mr. Balfour has been no leader. But if by leader we understand the ruler (and this is what the leader of a party is), his very moderation, his speculative hesitation as to the unknown possibilities of the future, his practical caution and slowness to move in the present, mark him out as a reliable leader. Moreover, the leader has not only to ascertain what is wise, but to carry it out; and this entails regard for opinion in his party as well as inquiry into fact. For a policy can only be realised by the party vote. The party has to be kept together that it may act together. The Jesuits used to be taunted with saying, ' The good of our Society, is the good of the Church ' ; but there was a time when they had such a monopoly of the best energy of Catholicism that they might be excused for the sentiment. And so, too, to say that the prosperity of the Unionist party was essential to that of the country was, at a moment when the Opposition was hopelessly disunited, when its members were agreed neither on a leader nor on a policy, a pardonable and not obviously false statement. In such circumstances Mr. Balfour's devotion to his party might claim to be true patriotism.

The division of parts sketched above is inherent to the structure of a polity ; it is based on natural laws of political philosophy. And if we break a law of nature, pain and suffering are the consequence. Mr. Chamberlain did break such a law, for he, a Cabinet Minister, placed in the position of a definite policy, of practical as distinct from speculative thought, what was not ripe to be so placed. *Hinc illæ lachrymæ* ; hence the troubles from which we have not yet recovered. It was because he gave a ' bold lead '—a thing so delightful to the multitude—where he had not knowledge to justify it that the party was placed in an impossible position. He gave us all the rhetoric, all the personal influence, all the party enthusiasm which were wanted to carry out a policy so matured as to be thoroughly workable ; and when his soldiers were all at fever heat and ready for the fray, they found that it was not time to fight, for the field of campaign was not yet adequately surveyed. He aroused party feeling and gave the signal for strife not only before his colleagues had agreed that the war was wise or practical, but before he himself had seen how it could be carried on.

In this trying position Mr. Balfour showed virtues truly Roman. He did not despair of the republic. And he saw that the only hope lay in a Fabian policy of delay. Tantalising and irritating though it inevitably was, ineffective necessarily before the public eye, he persevered in it. When people shrieked for a positive policy,[1] he advocated the only step of whose complete safety he was at the moment certain—a return to Lord Salisbury's old policy of retaliation, or freedom of negotiation, of which, as we have already seen, Mr. Balfour himself had long been an advocate. For the rest, he regarded it as still under the criticism of that speculative reason which, as a great thinker has said, is ever undecided. Time was needed for Chamberlainites to prove how far their schemes were workable. Time was needed to ascertain how far the conditions of production in the several Colonies made a scheme of Colonial preference advantageous. Time was needed to find out the wishes and views of the Colonies themselves, and to ascertain what the British electorate would tolerate. Time was needed to reduce the scheme to such detail as to be able to forecast whether it would, indeed, be a bond of political

[1] See Mr. Balfour's speech of June 10, 1903 : ' I have been told in every tone, from menace to entreaty, that the position of the Government is absolutely impossible, that it is humiliating. . . . that it is unfair to the party,' &c.

union—apart from its economic merits—or whether it would not prove rather a source of contentious negotiations, or, again, of jealousy among the several Colonies, thus leading to further contention. It needed time also to bring the Free Traders to justify by argument what was sound in their criticisms, and to come down from the unpractical heights of *a priori* dogmatism and invective. During all that time it was essential that the Prime Minister should not identify himself with either extreme party. The position of balancing, so hard to support with dignity, was inevitable. It was a position which no man would have chosen. It was necessary, because the laws of political philosophy had been broken, and a number of vague and unmanageable proposals had been thrown pell-mell into the party programme which should never have been allowed to get there. We sacrifice our dignity and simply do our best when there has been a great breakage or other disastrous accident. We do not hope to pick up and put away the broken pieces with the dignity we might attempt in carrying the unbroken vase ; and so Mr. Balfour worked like a man, with no thought but how best to undo the damage done by the invader who had entered his political china-shop.

Let us recall the course of the well-known events in justification of what has been said above. So little was Mr. Balfour contemplating, as an element in the immediate party programme, any attack on Free Trade orthodoxy, that he had consented to Mr. Ritchie's proposal of repealing the existing shilling tax on corn. On

May 15, 1903, speaking at Birmingham, Mr. Chamberlain first sounded the alarm, and indicated the nature of his views on Colonial preference. It was quite evident to Mr. Balfour that the question would be taken up in the House of Commons, and it was all-important there and then to prevent Chamberlainism from being regarded as officially put forward by the Cabinet. The only way of obviating hopeless disunion was to contend that Mr. Chamberlain had been raising an interesting and important question, to which all would do well to turn their minds, and had propounded in its regard his own personal views, much as Mr. Balfour himself had in earlier days propounded his views on Irish university education, without in any way committing the Cabinet. It is generally supposed that this line of explanation was agreed upon between the two leaders; and when the eventful debate of May 28 came on, and Sir C. Dilke raised the question, this is the line which Mr. Balfour took in his reply. Mr. Chamberlain, however, instead of thus watering down the significance of the Birmingham programme, expounded it in a speech which conveyed the impression that he distinctly meant to force it on the party, and even raised in many minds the supposition that he wished to bid for the leadership. Subsequent events have shown this supposition to be false, and the alternative one to be true—that, in spite of his great gifts, his mental peculiarities have included a singular inability to gauge the effect of strong expressions or to foresee the inevitable results of his words. The words had been said, however, and the inevitable results followed. A question which the Prime Minister had earnestly wished to be an open one, which might, indeed, be ventilated, but with no view to immediate legislation, was made intensely prominent and inevitably contentious. There had always been Protectionists in the party, but they had lived at peace with their colleagues ; now they were summoned into the battlefield by a semi-official proposal on which all were called upon to take sides, and which soon became the great dividing issue both before Parliament and before the country. In this almost impossible position many Prime Ministers—probably most—would have resigned, and left the party hopelessly disunited, an easy prey to their antagonists. To do so would have meant not only the destruction of a party, but the surrender of so beneficent a measure as Mr. Wyndham's Irish Land Bill, serious risk to the success of the recently passed Education Act, and the abandonment of the Prime Minister's own cherished work for Imperial defence. Here Mr. Balfour's extraordinary staying power came in. In his memorable speech of June 10, on the repeal of the corn tax, a measure which made the confusion introduced by Mr. Chamberlain particularly conspicuous, he defined his position. In the first place, he emphatically denied that it was his duty to make an explicit pronouncement as to matters not in any sense put forward by the Government officially, but brought to the front in unofficial speeches. His own desire had been, as we have seen, to leave the whole fiscal question simply an open one.[1] As to

[1] Even in November, in the Bristol speech, Mr. Balfour recalled this earnest desire ' that the old position should be maintained in which the

what might prove some day practicable, the problem was very complex, and he could not judge before it was thrashed out. He could not profess a settled conviction which he had not yet formed. He could neither reject the proposals on the ground of *a priori* Free Trade dogma—with those who regarded the present fiscal system as perfect—nor could he stifle inquiry and discussion on new and important developments. But he did pledge himself not to interfere with the existing system without most thorough inquiry. He tried again to reduce the significance of Mr. Chamberlain's programme to the mere initiation of an inquiry rather than a declaration of policy. And, so understood, he argued in its favour. Discussion would enable the party to compare notes and act together. Peel in 1845 and Gladstone in 1886 had matured their opinions on Free Trade and Home Rule respectively in silence, and then sprang them suddenly upon their colleagues. Mr. Balfour, on the contrary, argued that a policy of discussion with colleagues and the House of Commons was far more satisfactory, as enabling the party to move together. But in weighty words he denounced as 'folly and rashness' all attempt 'to interfere with a great system, which has been in operation all these years, without a most careful examination of every side of the problem.' He pledged himself to respect the traditions of the past, but at the same time to examine the new

fiscal question was regarded as open in our ranks.' But he added, 'It was not possible, because the country would not have it, the House of Commons would not have it, and the Cabinet itself would not have it.'

problems presented by the 'ever-changing phases of industrial life.'

It is plain that the policy set forth in this speech was a policy of delay. The extraordinary difficulty of the situation consisted in this—that the party was acutely divided owing to the storm raised by Mr. Chamberlain's speeches, and a policy of delay, which meant postponement of a decision, was exactly what in such circumstances lashed both sides into a frenzy. The Free Fooders stiffened their dogmas and blazoned on their banners 'No taxation except for revenue,' 'No taxation of food,' 'No preferential tariffs,' and in some cases 'No retaliation'; the 'whole-hoggers' pressed for the 10 per cent. on manufactured goods and Colonial preference unrestricted by the commandment, 'Thou shalt not tax food.' The clamour levelled at Mr. Balfour for 'a definite lead' became overpowering.

Mr. Balfour had to create such machinery as would render possible a policy of delay—the only remedy for excited passions, the only means to give time for the experts to perform the operation of inquiry on the complicated issues involved. In response to the cry for a definite lead he had to formulate a programme as a sop to Cerberus. But his real policy was one of delay. In cases of overwrought nerves morphia is often the only immediate remedy. Other medicines cannot be used until the system is sufficiently normal to retain them. Nothing is a better anæsthetic for passion than to force men to grapple with a tough intellectual problem which is beyond their comprehension, especially if the treatment offered is abstract, the reasoning well balanced, and the practical conclusions somewhat doubtful.   Such reading absorbs all the energies.   The writer's fine distinctions destroy the food for passion—the broad, ill-defined issues which have been made into war-cries.   Such well-prepared morphia Mr. Balfour administered to the public in his ' Economic Notes.'   For the experts, indeed, they were a valuable contribution to the study of economic principles and their application ; but for the many they were a dose of calming medicine.   Their effect on heated partisans reminded the present writer in some respects of the effect on Mr. Thomas Mozley of the first session of the Vatican Council, which, as ' Times ' correspondent, he was in Rome to read and criticise. With feverish eagerness he seized on the first printed utterance of the idolatrous assembly, hoping to find propositions deifying the Pope or the Virgin and con- demning the commonplaces of modern civilisation. But instead of this he read to the following effect : ' If anyone deny that there is one God, let him be anathema ; if anyone deny that in this one God are three persons, let him be anathema.'   He found the principles and root doctrines of Christianity where he looked for the contentious utterances of controversial theology ; and the readers of the ' Economic Notes ' found the first principles of Free Trade, and the con- ditions limiting their practical efficiency, in place of the specific contentious applications thereof for which they looked.

The next step was so to remodel the Government

that it would support a policy of delay with a
minimum of practical programme.   Freedom of negotiation—and even that not defined or applied—was
the programme.   As to further proposals for fiscal
reform, they were distinctly eliminated from the practical field during the lifetime of the existing Parliament ; but they were not condemned—nay, they were
rather treated as containing probably the germ of
something that might prove practicable.   Thus members of the Cabinet who insisted that a pronouncement
professing to be final should be made on the reform
proposals, and this on the ground that they were
inconsistent with the dogmas of Free Trade, had
necessarily to go.   And Mr. Chamberlain, who could
not, as a Cabinet Minister, continue to urge his proposals on the country, had also to leave.   The surgical
operation on the Cabinet was, indeed, an alarming one ;
and, owing largely to the passionate feelings of the
time and the acute division into parties, was found to
involve the loss of the Duke of Devonshire.   Sir
Michael Hicks-Beach (afterwards Lord St. Aldwyn),
whose views were identical with the Duke's, persevered
in giving Mr. Balfour his full support ; [1] but the rhetoric
of Mr. Balfour's speech to a Protectionist audience at
Sheffield, at a crisis when the 'clash of yes and no'
was the order of the day, and everyone was flying
party banners and taking sides, proved to be the turning-point in the Duke's course at a moment of irreso-
lution ; and he thenceforth definitely threw in his lot
with that of his friends who had left the Ministry.

[1] I do not forget that Sir Michael had left the Cabinet in 1902.

The blow was indeed heavy, and the world held it impossible that the Cabinet could survive the removal of its strongest members. The loss of the prestige attaching to great names was appalling. Nevertheless, Mr. Balfour faced the situation as the alternative to the death of the party, and carried his policy through.

In some respects any action which is brief, decisive, irrevocable, is easier than the prolonged maintenance of a situation of intense difficulty. A merely impulsive man may decide to lead the life of a recluse or anchorite, but it takes a strong man to persevere in such a resolve; and the work of Mr. Balfour in the months following the Sheffield speech was one of quite extraordinary difficulty. In the first place, he had to give the effect—both in the Sheffield speech and afterwards—that he was propounding a great policy. Nothing less would gain him a hearing. Yet though, no doubt, freedom of negotiation might issue in unforeseen circumstances in a great policy, it could not, as Mr. Balfour at first propounded it, amount to a great policy. This was the Duke of Devonshire's criticism, and a sound one. Still, the policy was the best as yet available. Moreover, it had received high sanction, finding, as it did, its source in the Conservative programme of 1885—which included Retaliation, until the absorbing controversy on Home Rule in 1886 drove this element into the background.

This was Mr. Balfour's difficulty at starting, and it long haunted him. The immediately practical official policy remained before the public as a *ridiculus mus*, and Chamberlainism remained before it also—a birth far more suitable to the labour of the mountains. Then, again, quite inevitably, Mr. Balfour was reproached for his ambiguity. To be non-committal was of the very essence of his policy. Yet when the Chamberlain proposals loomed so large before the country, to remain non-committal on such a matter appeared to the heated imagination of the public to be treason. The public could not see or realise that the real position of Mr. Balfour was that the idea of a great birth immediately imminent was a false alarm ; that Mr. Chamberlain's proposals had become prematurely prominent—fatally prominent ; that unless they could be made less prominent for a time the country would be plunged into disastrous debate on immature plans, and the Unionist party be broken up ; that time alone, bringing calm to heated controversialists, could force the fiscal proposals back into their natural position of roughly outlined suggestions, to be further sifted before being brought forward. It was essential that the Chamberlain autumn campaign should test public opinion in the country, and should make the Tariff Reformers' programme more definite. There were fires which would burn themselves out if given time to do so. The attempt to extinguish them, on the other hand, would be dangerous—might prove even fatal. Meanwhile the Premier must refrain from alienating those whose extreme views reflection would gradually cure, and yet at the same time refrain from accepting their views. This inevitably brought the charge of ambiguity. The present writer, conversing with a Liberal leader, commented on the extraordinary cleverness of one of Mr. Balfour's non-committal speeches. 'So much too clever,' was the reply. 'Admirable for a debating society, but for a Minister who has to take the lead in a great and definite policy such subtleties and distinctions are most unsuitable.' This view would have been indisputable had Mr. Balfour brought the policy forward on his own account; but he did not. He desired that the question should remain at the debating stage. It had been pressed beyond it, and he strove to force it back, and used with this object the language and treatment best calculated to force it back.

The official practical programme had to be maintained—namely, that of the Sheffield speech. It consisted solely in freedom of negotiation, with a view to retaliation (not by hostile tariffs,[1] but by temporary retaliatory duties), taxation of food being formally abandoned, and Colonial preference postponed, at least until Colonial opinion had been further ascertained. The substance of these proposals could not satisfy the reformers, who were hungering for a great policy. Yet the rhetoric of the speech, designed to make it tolerable to the Sheffield audience, angered the Free Traders. Mr. Balfour at this stage could just retain his hold on both parties; he could thoroughly please neither. This double attitude was preserved by Mr. Balfour throughout the autumn of 1903 and the early spring of 1904. To relax either his rhetorical sympathy with the reformers or the rigid meagreness of his practical programme would be fatal. The rhetorical sympathy

[1] On Mr. Balfour's subsequent development on this point see p. 44.

with the reformers could only be safely modified when
Mr. Chamberlain had learned for himself the severe
limitations imposed both by public opinion and by
expert criticism on the policy which he had conceived
so vaguely, and as containing such great possibilities.
The autumn did something towards this.   Mr. Chamberlain, though at first arousing considerable enthusiasm, in the end wholly failed to sweep the
country.   His cause did not gain.   People were
disappointed at finding how little he had thought the
matter out.   A real defect in his character as a statesman became very apparent—namely, a vagueness of
thought in matters absolutely demanding the greatest
precision.   At Glasgow and Greenock he did, indeed,
to some extent define his programme.   But it left out
of account many important considerations.   Probably
Mr. Balfour himself had expected something better
from so great an authority on English trade and on
Colonial affairs.   Mr. Chamberlain formed a Commission of experts to improve it and make it workable.
But the impression left on a large section of the
public mind was that he had advanced a startling
policy before thinking it out ; that the very proposals
in his speeches were afterthoughts ; and that the
Commission was formed to find a way of doing his
will rather than to ascertain what was wise.   *Stet pro
ratione voluntas.*   Still, when Parliament met the
Chamberlainites were strong and sanguine.[1]

[1] The capture of the local associations by the 'whole-hoggers'
doubtless contributed to this.   It certainly testified to the difficulty of
keeping the party within the bounds of the official policy.

Mr. Balfour's illness early in the session of 1904 brought out the fact that no one but he could support effectively or with dignity the singularly difficult policy suited to the situation. The combination of sympathy for the *ideas* of the Tariff Reformers with Free Trade principles and firm insistence for the time on the limited official programme was quite beyond his colleagues. Only Mr. Wyndham had the subtlety and strength to sustain the attitude. Mr. Gerald Balfour made what was accepted as a Free Trade speech. Mr. Lyttelton was thought to speak as a Protectionist, and others followed suit. Things improved on Mr. Balfour's return, but any heart but his would have sunk at the incident of the Wharton amendment. The Chamberlainites resolutely encouraged the view that Mr. Balfour's reserve in the official programme was only temporary and diplomatic ; that at heart he was with them ; that the two leaders were partners at whist, who played into each other's hands. There were, undoubtedly, devoted followers of Mr. Balfour who favoured the extreme programme from a similar persuasion. Then Mr. Wharton, with the sanction of the Chief Whip, proposed an amendment to a vote of censure on the Government emphasising the Sheffield programme and disowning the excesses of the 'whole-hoggers.' So strong, however, and so confident still were the Chamberlainites that 112 members intimated that they would vote against the Government unless the amendment was withdrawn. And Mr. Balfour consented that it should be dropped. 'It was little more than five months,' commented a 'Quarterly Reviewer' on the situation, 'since Mr. Balfour had proclaimed at Sheffield that while he was leader he would lead, and a prophet in the audience had cried out, "How about Joe?"'

But it is probable that at this moment, when the outsider could most easily ridicule Mr. Balfour and his official programme as proved failures, Mr. Balfour's own keen vision saw that the day was really his. It is said that Napoleon, at a moment when the battle in his vicinity seemed to be going hopelessly against the French, would suddenly put down his field-glasses and say, 'The day is won.' He had seen that certain manœuvres had been executed at a distance from which victory must follow in a few hours, though it would take that time for the necessary sequence of events. The events of the autumn had really been decisive against any revolutionary reform; but time was needed to bring home their results to the House of Commons and the country. From the Wharton amendment to the night of Mr. Winston Churchill's vote of censure, which Mr. Balfour met by moving the previous question, a year passed, and in that time, so far as the House of Commons was concerned, the victory was won. So far, at all events, as the restoration of Mr. Balfour's effectual leadership in the House was concerned there can be no doubt in the matter. The House realised—what Mr. Balfour had already seen—that Mr. Chamberlain's proposals, so far as they went beyond what Mr. Balfour had sanctioned, were wholly outside the ken of responsible legislators of the hour. The Free Trade sentiment in the country proved very deep. The only possible means of safely determining on any scheme of Colonial preference was a Colonial Conference unfettered in its proceedings, and to this Mr. Balfour consented. The feeling in the House of Commons as to which of the leaders was really reliable was reversed. The idea of one as a statesman who knew his own mind and acted on it, in competition with his irresolute and timid shadow, gave place to a sense that the former had measured accurately neither public opinion nor practical politics ; while the latter had been cautious solely in deference to the necessities of the case—'Fools rush in where angels fear to tread.' I do not mean to characterise Mr. Chamberlain's unpractical optimism as mere folly ; but Mr. Balfour had certainly been, like a great predecessor of his, 'on the side of the angels.'

And as confidence in Mr. Balfour increased he felt able, without the risk of fatal disunion, to emphasise, as he did at Edinburgh, those elements in his own view as to possible fiscal reform, which were quite incompatible with a policy of sheer Protection, to which Chamberlainism in its original form would inevitably have led. Had he forced the note earlier, disruption would have come, just as it would have come had he insisted on the Wharton amendment.

In the House of Commons I have said the Balfour policy prevailed. And a good deal was done in the same direction even in the constituencies. The intense feeling in the country on behalf of Free Trade found voice—a feeling which Mr. Chamberlain had not at all adequately realised. The dream that he would

sweep the country was early dispelled.   His proposals
were elaborated and received close criticism, with the
result that a revolution in our fiscal system was more
and more felt to be out of the question.   Steps gradual
and tentative in the direction of Colonial preference
remained possible.   But the scale of the controversy
was reduced.   A good deal was done to bring the two
wings of the party nearer together, to form a moderate
centre party of Balfourians by recruits from both
extreme camps.   Indeed, Mr. Chamberlain soon found
that he must, to win any hearing, advocate Free Trade
as an ideal and ultimate end, and avow his opposition
to the old Protectionist system which Peel abolished
for ever.   The Free Fooders, on their side, became
more moderate.   Even Lord Hugh Cecil declared
himself not opposed to Retaliation.   The Duke of
Devonshire admitted that the Free Trade dogmas
must not be pressed too absolutely.   As in applied
mathematics, the world of fact must somewhat disturb
a priori calculations.   And so Mr. Balfour's contention,
that Free Trade principles are not best secured by
their extremest advocates, received more consideration.
It remained to be seen if the experiment of taxing
food, which troubled no Conservative in the case of
the shilling duty on corn, would be generally assented
to on a somewhat larger scale.   The Promised Land
(be it observed), the ideal too good to be realised, but
which had to be approached before *any* fiscal changes
were practicable, was to return for a time to that
atmosphere, suited to calm and dispassionate inquiry,
which had existed in the party before May 15, 1903.

Thus the country had been convulsed, a strong Ministry dismembered, and the time of the House of Commons largely wasted for two years through the use of ill-considered words in two speeches on May 15 and May 28. For a time it appeared that the Unionist party was simply shattered—and such a breach is in most cases irreparable. ' All the king's horses and all the king's men ' may be unable to mend what a few rash words can effectually break. Probably no other man living except Mr. Balfour could have effected even the partial reconstitution of the party.

The gifts which enabled him to do so afford a remarkable psychological study. Men of, in some ways, greater strength and greater constructive ability would not even have attempted it, and could not have effected it.

Let me make some brief attempt to indicate the qualities which have been brought into play. Some of them so permeate his personality that they appear in his philosophy as well as in his political action— nay, they are visible in the well-known traits of his social character. Such qualities, though at first sight superficial, are not so. The student of psychology cannot ignore them, for it is just because they appear in every aspect of his life and action that they are seen to be so intimately a part of himself.

His aloofness and imperturbability, in the first place, enable him to carry out the decisions of an acute and highly critical intellect undistracted by any disturbing force, either from the undue influence

of others or from unregulated impulses in himself.
His aloofness is the quality of one who does not wear
his heart on his sleeve, who is not expansive, who
does not readily unbosom himself, who is naturally
fastidious, who has few, if any, friends with whom he
is quite unreserved. In this quality he somewhat
resembles William Pitt. Kindness and gentleness in
his intercourse with others are not at all inconsistent
with this trait. But he is probably never exactly genial.
His natural aloofness is never quite forgotten by those
who converse with him, though he can on occasion be
most excellent company, charming everyone by his
manner, which possesses a suavity which Pitt's had not.
Pitt said of a rather pushing aspirant for honours,
'I had rather make him a Privy Councillor than
speak to him.' This attitude would, perhaps, be an
impossible one in the present age and in the existing
House of Commons. And the last thing that could
be alleged against Mr. Balfour is that he is unapproach-
able. Nevertheless, the fastidious temper the anecdote
betokens is common to the two men.

Mr. Balfour's power of attracting personal devotion
is also like Pitt's, and has been an important factor in his
success. Personal influence must have had much to say
in the apparently impossible feat of September 1903,
when he parted from Mr. Chamberlain without breaking
with him, and all but succeeded in retaining the Duke
of Devonshire when the other Free Traders left the
Cabinet. Personal charm, again, not improbably had
its share in the retention of Sir Michael Hicks-Beach
after their intercourse at Bristol. In the House of

Commons his absence, in the beginning of 1904 bore stronger testimony to his personal influence than anything his presence could have effected.

A certain leisureliness in his manner, which might at first sight be only the leisureliness of a man of fashion, is really a most significant trait. The leisureliness of his manner is symptomatic of a certain leisureliness in his diplomatic method. The late Lord Lyons used to say, ' Never write to-day what you can put off until to-morrow,' because things may settle themselves. The complications caused by unnecessary initiative Mr. Balfour instinctively avoids, aided perhaps by a certain constitutional indolence.

His perception of public opinion is as accurate as is possible concomitantly with a certain deficiency in emotional sympathy—an aspect of what I have called his aloofness. This deficiency gives him an indifference which is a great source of strength. A more sensitive man could hardly have preserved for so many months a policy hardly understood even by his friends, and derided by his critics, or patiently worked at creating the public opinion by which alone it could be understood and approved. His aloofness and indifference, however, tell at times against success. They make him fail at times in full perception, as in his public utterances at the time of the war in South Africa.

He follows instinctively Polonius's maxim, and is slow to begin a fight, but steady in carrying it through when once it is begun. Drive him into a corner, and with his back to the wall he will do battle with a vigour and pertinacity astonishing to those who are accustomed to his normal imperturbability.

The net result is great insight, tenacity, and persistence, and the strength arising from these qualities. The main aim is never lost sight of. He acts on the motto, ' More haste, less speed.' There is remarkable readiness to note and take account of the least breath of public opinion, but no disturbance of his course from the mere clamour of the mob, or, again, from his own ungoverned emotion ; carefully measured adaptability to external conditions, but no distracting influence from within. The absence of excitement or passion which makes his movement so deliberate keeps his course perfectly coherent. If he seems sometimes to ' dawdle,' it is not the dawdling of an idler, but of one who constitutionally dislikes hurry, and has no need to hurry in order to make sure of keeping to his purpose. Though an acute thinker, he is essentially a great man of action, and such men are seldom in a hurry —for he seldom hurries who is quite at ease.

He is marked by great tenacity in friendships, alliances, undertakings. He knows well the value of small things, as answering letters or a kind word, and measures out such gifts with care and judgment.

In early years it was said that his social fastidiousness used at times to give offence. This result is probably now reduced to a minimum by his experience and philosophy, which make him realise that larger and cherished aims may suffer from any such form of self-indulgence. But the fastidiousness remains in his nature, and shows itself on occasion.

A touch of pessimism runs through his thought and work, yet not the profound pessimism which leads to inaction. Rather, his pessimism goes with a certain philosophic contentment ; for he looks in this imperfect world for no great results, and is, therefore, not easily disappointed. This holds in his philosophy of religious faith. His argument is, ' You criticise the reasons as inadequate. Yet how inadequate are our reasons for the primary beliefs which we all necessarily accept— in the outward world, in nature's uniformity ! Be therefore content to act in religion, as in other things, on imperfect philosophical proofs. Philosophy is a poor thing.' So, too, as to theology. ' True enough, the old theological formulæ do not take account of the latest science and criticism. But what an inadequate instrument at best are human ideas for the expression of things divine ! The boasted new theology of the future, theology amended to suit the brand-new speculations of the critics, will not be *much* nearer the truth than the old. Theology is a poor thing.'

This relentless and cold criticism implies, doubtless, a certain lack of lively enthusiasm. But there is deep down a strenuous desire to do his best to help the machine to work as well as it can, whether the machine be philosophy, theology, or politics. *Fais ce que dois, advienne que pourra.* There is, then, an underlying pessimism which helps to resignation ; but also an accompanying tenacity of purpose which leads to victory.

His aloofness and fastidiousness, I may add, greatly affect his style in writing. They give it distinction. But they bring also a certain deficiency in volume and humanity.

Nearly all these qualities appear to me to have had their share in Mr. Balfour's conduct of affairs during the past two years. The critical intellect carefully discounted the value of Mr. Chamberlain's rhetoric and noted the vagueness of his proposals. The same gift saw in the invectives of the Free Traders something far beyond the rational outcome of Cobden's principles. The policy of dawdling with a purpose, to give time for excitement to subside, needed all his passionless aloofness, steadiness of aim, leisureliness of action, imperturbable confidence ; while the constant intellectual fencing in debate demanded by the situation—which had to be at once successful and non-committal—called for all his acuteness and perception of the forces of opinion with which he had to deal.

His pessimism, again, has helped to keep him aloof from both extreme parties. Neither the optimism of Chamberlain nor the optimism of the extreme Free Traders was possible to him. Neither the future nor the present was ever in his eyes golden. Yet the peculiar limitation of his pessimism made him work with a certain enthusiasm for the practicable—for making the best of things. What other keen man of action among our public men can dispense with the idealising tendency, and see things simply as they are ? What other pessimist, on the other hand, would work, endeavouring to make the best of a rather bad job, as hard as an optimist who hopes to realise golden dreams ? Again, we have our sensitive politicians who are alive to every breath of opinion and are swayed by it, and our imperturbable politicians who calmly carry through their policy regardless of opinion. But where else but in Mr. Balfour have we the useful quality that belongs to sensitiveness—namely, fine perception—without its defect of impressionableness? Where else have we the strength of indifference without its defect of insensibility? A merely sensitive politician would have resigned in the circumstances. A merely determined one would have persevered and broken the party to bits. Nothing but the finest and most accurate perception of feeling and opinion, coupled with the calmest persistence, could have prolonged the life of the last Unionist ministry without absolute catastrophe. And here the tenacity of his friendships, which survived in spite of greater tenacity to principles which tried friendship, helped again. Mr. Chamberlain's friendship has been an asset of the most essential importance. Yet who else but Mr. Balfour could have kept it at a time when he yielded so little practically to the object on which his friend's heart was set? Probably a certain aloofness even in friendship makes this possible. A more enthusiastic temperament would beget friendships with more quarrelsome possibilities.

Note, again, how the pessimistic and critical tendencies in him, and his aloofness from passion, helped in sifting the problem—in separating Free Trade from its current shibboleths, in pointing out the share of contingent events in framing so-called necessary maxims ; for example, the share of English history in begetting the intense feeling of Englishmen against the taxation of food. And what he did in bringing to book Free Trade dogmatism he also did in reducing the optimistic declarations of the Tariff Reformers to the shape of schemes practicable in themselves and in view of public opinion. How carefully, again, has he avoided the old fallacy of the Manchester school— that men always act from self-interest! How important is the cognate distinction, which the hot-headed ever forget, between what is economically best and what is on the whole wisest! Man does not live by bread alone. If Colonial preference should prove practicable and politically very valuable, have we not a gain far outweighing even valid criticisms from an economic point of view? If countries love each other the more through attaching a mistaken value to well-meant concessions, may not the gain in love outweigh the loss due to error? Are we to eliminate illusion wholly from the sources of love? If so, the mortality among existing loves will be heavy. In all this we see Mr. Balfour's patient, passionless pessimism—not the pessimism of the impracticable sentimentalist, but that of the highly practical statesman, who tenderly reminds dreamers that they are in a hard world of fact.

To one whose views of life were more enthusiastic such labour, devoted to an object which promised so little, would have been intolerable. It was a policy in many ways of self-effacement and self-abnegation, for the many could not appreciate it. It had nothing inspiring in it, and the best of his rivals would have done no more than carry it through perfunctorily and without spirit.   Mr. Balfour, on the contrary, put his very best work into it.   The energy which others reserve for favourite schemes, urged on by visions of great results to be accomplished, Mr. Balfour devoted to this *pis-aller* policy, which he had not chosen, which he thought a mistake—though now an inevitable one—which offered no prizes and many possible blanks.

I have in the foregoing pages, emphasised the gifts shown by Mr. Balfour during two eventful years because they appear to me to be inadequately appreciated, and often confounded with qualities quite out of keeping with his intellectual character.   But no fair critic should ignore the defects of the best qualities. If his power of dealing with a situation of unparalleled difficulty has been such that one need hardly, in some directions, fear the possibility of an over-estimate, I think he had some share in creating the difficulties he has dealt with so ably.   The duality of his own mind, the aloofness which enables his own intellect to work undisturbed by his own passions, does not exist in others, and it may be questioned whether the policy of raising the fiscal question in the House of Commons and discussing it as in a debating society, would be quite practicable for any House of Commons which did not consist mainly of Balfours.   Even apart from Mr. Chamberlain's excesses the endeavour would probably have led to trouble.   The policy of Peel and Gladstone, which Mr. Balfour criticised on June 10, 1903—the policy of maturing a programme before it is ventilated in the House—is perhaps almost a necessary one, because there will always be Chamberlains to turn a judicial inquiry on a question on which feeling is in some quarters very strong, into a source of immediate disunion. I think that in his later action (in 1905), in shelving the fiscal question, Mr. Balfour showed a conscious or unconscious perception of his earlier mistake.[1] Moreover, the staying power and absolute imperturbableness which enabled him to prolong a situation to most men intolerable brings this much of Nemesis, that a prolonged crisis is a prolonged period in which even small mistakes are serious. And no one can be constantly strung up to the desirable pitch. A man may boast that he keeps awake during an all-night sitting, when his colleagues at one moment or another nod. But he will not be quite at his best all night. And so Mr. Balfour has occasionally, though rarely, at moments of fatigue or inattention, lost touch with the House's feeling. Again, his sense of what will affect his immediate audience—in which his perception goes hand-in-hand with his pessimism—sometimes makes him content on the platform with arguments unworthy of the political philosophy on which he practically acts —as when he swept away, in his speech to Protectionist Sheffield, the Cobdenist controversy as wholly without present interest, and as belonging simply to ancient history,[2] such a view is inadequate to the real convictions of one who so fully realises the organic

---

[1] On Mr. Balfour's more recent attitude in this respect see p. 43.

[2] It is 'of no interest whatever to us now, except from an historical point of view. It is over and done with. I care no more for it than I do about the Bangorian controversy.'

connection between present and past. Again, for one who sees a waiting game to be essential there are moments when the dilemma, 'Own that you have failed,' or 'Play a purely opportunist game for the present,' becomes intolerably difficult. The problem as to how far the end justifies the means is ever a hard one, and is ever haunted by the alternatives of failure owing to passing causes, or forms of compromise which the 'plain man' regards as somewhat disingenuous.

The surrender of the Wharton amendment appeared to some like a sacrifice of the official programme and an admission that the Premier was at heart with the extreme reformers. It seemed to confirm the 'two whist players' theory. And stronger instances could be given.

But when criticism has said its worst, Mr. Balfour's achievement in the two years I am reviewing was extraordinary. It has been, I think, inadequately appreciated by his contemporaries. Yet it may well be that the future historian will have to record in the story a fresh instance in which one man has at a moment of extreme difficulty restored the fortunes of the republic by a policy of delay. *Cunctando restituit rem.*

If so, the events which 'The Spectator' regarded as the downfall of a great statesman will have proved to be his opportunity.

PS.—To deal at an adequately with the developments of the fiscal question since the above study was written would need another essay equally long. I will here only set down very briefly what I take to be their outcome in relation to Mr. Balfour's policy. The fundamental views which I have ascribed to Mr. Balfour are—(1) That changes—even desirable changes—in the fiscal system of a great commercial country must be made very cautiously and gradually—while some of Mr. Chamberlain's followers desired a sudden and ill-considered revolution; (2) that fiscal reform is desirable and quite consistent with Free-Trade principles, Protection forming no part of his policy; (3) that before any legislation should be decided on public opinion, both at home and in the Colonies, must be carefully weighed, and that the preservation of the unity of the party was essential, for with its ranks divided and its majority destroyed no legislation on the subject could be effected at all.

I have maintained that by a Fabian policy of delay he so far calmed the dangerous agitation raging in 1903 and 1904 as to prevent the party from committing itself to premature schemes which would have been disastrous, and saved its substantial unity by winning the trust of the more moderate members of each camp for his method and his judgment. The large majority of the party became, therefore, ready to fall in with such a modified programme of tariff reform as, after the period of deliberation and inquiry for which he asked, he should formulate.

Against such a view of the case it has been urged in some quarters that, on the contrary, he later on surrendered to the 'whole-hoggers,' renounced his cautious programme, and committed himself to the very re-volutionary and Protectionist policy which he at first resisted.

On behalf of this view three main proofs are adduced. :—(1) The 'Valentine' letter, which was popularly regarded as a surrender to Mr. Chamberlain ; (2) the fact that tariff reform, which at the time with which the above article deals he desired to leave an open question, urging it himself only so far as the necessities of retaliation demanded, has now been placed by him first on the constructive programme of the party ; (3) the Albert Hall meeting, followed by the Birmingham speech, which appeared to fore-cast Colonial preference based on taxation of food, and a general tariff—both proposals being innovations on the Sheffield speech[1] and concessions to the 'whole-hoggers.'

That the argument deduced from the above facts is not without some *prima facie* force the present writer feels, for he himself experienced for a time a difficulty in following the course of Mr. Balfour's mind. Never-theless, he believes that the event will show Mr. Balfour's consistency, and that in the future, as in the past, he will disappoint the inveterate optimism of extremists, 'whole-hoggers' as well as Free Fooders.

The following considerations may, perhaps, help at once to account for the impression produced by the events and utterances above referred to and to vin-

[1] It should be remembered that the Leeds speech of December 1905 had already foreshadowed this development.

dicate the consistency of Mr. Balfour's development in policy :—

(1) The Valentine letter was assumed by the public to be a *fresh* declaration of policy, the announcement of an advance towards Mr. Chamberlain ; largely, doubtless, because it was read in the papers together with Mr. Chamberlain's reply, in which it was treated as accepting a policy substantially identical with his own. It was intended by Mr. Balfour himself, on the other hand, not as the declaration of a fresh policy, but as the promulgation of 'articles of peace' based on existing agreements and differences between the leaders. To prevent exaggerations as to the extent of the divergences between them Mr. Balfour formulated the conditions and reservations which his own view of the situation imposed on his acceptance of Mr. Chamberlain's proposals. Now, a fresh declaration of policy would rightly be judged by its popular—I had almost said its 'rhetorical'—effect, and the popular effect of the Valentine letter, coupled with Mr. Chamberlain's highly satisfied reply, was in some degree that of a surrender. 'Articles of peace,' on the contrary, must be interpreted strictly and logically. There is, moreover, an inevitable apparent indetermin- ateness on the face of such articles, just because they are intended as a bond between persons whose views, if precisely and quite fully stated, do diverge. The Duke of Devonshire and Mr. Chamberlain combined from opposite sides in disregarding the 'ifs' and 'whens' of the 'Valentine' letter. Mr. Balfour replied that the 'ifs' and 'whens' were essential to

his policy. The view of Mr. Chamberlain and the Duke—that the 'ifs' and 'whens' were negligible quantities—would be intelligible in the case of a *manifesto* professing to convey to the public the broad lines of a new departure in policy. Such a view is absurd in the case of 'articles of peace,' designed merely to analyse and reduce to a *minimum* the points of divergence in the existing policy of two men whose differences are an acknowledged fact. Those points are covered precisely by the 'ifs' and 'whens.' Moreover, close observers saw that Mr. Chamberlain's 'this is pretty nearly all I wanted' was susceptible of the interpretation 'this is all I shall get, and I had better be thankful for it and in future want no more.' His letter, as well as Mr. Balfour's, bore a meaning by no means identical with its rhetorical effect.

(2) The placing of tariff reform in the front rank of the party programme is certainly a change. But the real question is, Can it be viewed as a lawful development due to fresh circumstances, or does it mark the absorption of Mr. Balfour by the 'whole-hoggers'? This is the issue on which Mr. Balfour's consistency must be judged, and the answer depends, again, on the meaning of Mr. Balfour's act. To the present writer it appears to mean primarily that he sees that the clamour for tariff reform represents too influential a feeling in the party for legislation to be postponed. Moreover, the Colonial Conference of 1907 by its endorsement of Colonial preference fulfilled one of the very preliminary conditions laid down by Mr. Balfour for the adoption of one item of Chamberlainism

with which he always sympathised. Here at least an
'if' had been realised. And at the same moment
Mr. Asquith's budget startled the country by its revelation of the inadequacy of the existing system to
the growing needs of revenue. Tariff reform, then,
has come within the sphere of practical problems
owing to the Colonial Conference of 1907 and the
ever-increasing necessity of finding fresh sources of
public revenue. As to introducing a general tariff,
I do not believe that when the time comes for
formulating any practical proposal on the subject
we shall see in it anything at variance with the
general position Mr. Balfour has held throughout—
that fiscal reform in a commercial country must be
gradual, and in a sense empirical; that we must see
how small changes actually work before attempting
large ones. So far as certain violent partisans identify
the tariff reform contemplated by Mr. Balfour with
the entire Glasgow programme, I should be surprised
if such a supposition were confirmed by the event.
What Mr. Balfour has accorded to tariff reform
appears to me to be mainly a precedence in time—it
must be dealt with directly he comes to office. The
announcement of this precedence was the best way
of calming undesirable agitation, of accomplishing the
very same object he had in view of trying previously
to place tariff reform for a time in a minor position.

(3) In answering the first two objections I have
really answered the third. If the view I have indicated be true, all the Birmingham speech meant was
that full deliberation as to what is practicable and

what is desirable, in view of public opinion in the party and in the country, has brought Mr. Balfour a little way—but only a little way—beyond the Sheffield speech. He may see his way to a low general tariff which shall satisfy the needs of revenue—retaliatory and not protective in principle. And he does think, what he at first doubted, that the general desire of the Colonies, manifested at the Conference, to come to a preferential agreement has made it wise to consider seriously in detail a scheme of preferential treatment based on the readjustment of food taxation.

That Mr. Balfour now finds himself at the head of a strong party, which on these points is likely to follow him at the cost of no substantial defections, is due, I believe, to the Fabian policy of delay at a most dangerous crisis which I have attempted to outline, and to the great qualities as a statesman and leader of which I have given a very imperfect analysis.

One final word. The charge against Mr. Balfour may be summed up as that of weakness and opportunism. He is supposed to have been ultimately carried away by the current of opinion among the ' whole-hoggers.' The view taken in the above essay is that such a view of his course treats as identical two very different qualities. He has been keenly alive to opinion, both in the country and in the party, because it was a most important factor to be taken into account in deciding both what was really wise politically and how it could be achieved. This differs from mere opportunism and from weakness as the

course of a boat that drifts without a rudder differs
from that of one steered with exceptionally close knowledge of and allowance for wind, tide, and current.

He has also attached importance to public opinion
in another way. He has been anxious for discussion
from all points of view before action is taken, to aid
in forecasting what will work well economically. He
has pleaded throughout for dispassionate reasoning,
untrammelled by the shibboleths either of Protection
or of Free Trade. He has desired to delay legislation
until such comprehensive discussion should clearly
point the road as to what is wise economically, and
political opinion in the country and party should be
ripe for carrying out such a programme. He wished
to delay so long, but no longer. And history will,
I believe, judge that, if he has been more cautious
than others, it was because he realised far more accurately than they the many interests, both economical
and political, really involved, and the great circum-
spection consequently needed to make sure that the
forward step should be a wise, vital development.

> Not clinging to some ancient saw ;
>   Not mastered by some modern term ;
>   Not swift nor slow to change, but firm :
> And in its season bring the law,
>
> That from Discussion's lip may fall
>   With Life, that, working strongly, binds—
>   Set in all lights by many minds,
> To close the interests of all.

I have attempted throughout, in speaking of Mr.
Balfour's policy, not to trace a plan of action rigidly

fixed beforehand—an absurd supposition regarding
one who had to deal with each unforeseen manifestation
of fluctuating opinion as it arose—but certain statesmanlike qualities which have made each step in that
policy (to continue the metaphor used above) one of
skilful seamanship, calculated to bring the boat to port
in rough and changeable weather, and not a merely in-
genious cleverness in keeping her above water. Again,
it would be absurd to ascribe to him views on fiscal reform absolutely fixed and cut and dried from the first,
to which he meant to bend the extreme tariff reformers.
On the contrary, his plea was for time and full discussion, for himself as well as for his party, before
he could on many points decide what was wise and
practicable. That in making up his mind the opinions
of others have influenced him, while his own caution
has so strongly influenced them, is probable enough.
That in circumstances of extraordinary difficulty he
has always done the wisest thing I am not concerned
to maintain. But I believe the qualities I have de-
lineated to be such as will preserve him in the future,
as they have in the past, from any step of critical
importance which is either economically unsound or
politically unwise, and that in his hands fiscal reform
may become, what it scarcely can in those of our other
statesmen, both practicable and safe. Nearly all others
are apt to forget one of two sides of the problem.
For there are two sides, the speculative and the
practical—what is the ideally best aim if shibboleths
are disregarded and facts faced, and how that aim is to
be approached and ultimately won, things being as they

now are, without changes which would be dislocating economically, and with due regard to political opinion. Mr. Balfour, and he only, seems to me to have kept both sides of the problem—the speculative and the practical—equally in view.

THREE NOTABLE EDITORS—DELANE, HUTTON, KNOWLES

THE early months of the year 1908 witnessed the publication of the Life of John Thadeus Delane and the death of the veteran Sir James Knowles ; while the publication in Mr. A. J. Church's 'Memories of Men and Books' of his recollections of Richard Holt Hutton, of 'The Spectator,' recalled to the world at the same time another editor of great eminence.   All three were conspicuous alike for ability and for their long tenure of the editorial chair.   In the 'seventies each was at the very height of his position ; and they were in this sense contemporaries—although these years were comparatively early in Knowles's career and late in Delane's, while for Hutton they found his editorship in mid-stream.   Three men differing more from each other, alike in gifts and character, and in the nature of their success, could scarcely be imagined.

A comparison between them is hardly possible. Yet to set side by side some features of their career will, perhaps, be instructive in itself and in relation to the history of our times.

'Editors of "The Times" have existed before and since Delane,' writes Sir Algernon West in his 'Recollections,' 'but none, I will venture to say, ever filled

Photo. F. Hollyer.

R. H. HUTTON.

the place in Society that he did.   He was in the confidence of everybody of both political parties, and this
confidence he never betrayed.   No Minister would
have thought it odd if he had sent in his card and
asked to see him at any hour of the day or night.'

Delane's nephew, Mr. Dasent, has given us in two
extremely interesting volumes enough material to
justify this verdict.   'Material,' I say, for these
volumes are the material for a biography rather than
the finished biography itself.   They lack both desirable compression and literary form.   Still their reader
has no cause to complain.   Once he has begun to
peruse the book he will not readily set it down.   When
he has finished it, he will have before him very clearly
the outlines of the character and career of the very
strong journalist who was so great a power in his
generation.

What were the main sources of a power so unusual ? is the question which will at once obtrude itself
on the reader's mind.   In attempting to answer it I
must begin with a paradox.   The gifts of the great
editor appear to me not to have been primarily literary.
His letters show little sense of literary form.   His
temperament had not the sensitiveness or the fastidious
refinement of the literary artist.   We see the character
and power of the man, and something of the secret of
his success, in tastes and endowments far removed from
his life work.   He had a great love of horses and was
a constant and very plucky rider.   He and his horse
seemed to his friends to be almost inseparable.   Even
his morning calls were paid on horseback.   'Like the

E

centaurs of old he is part and parcel of his horse,' said his Oxford tutor. He was a good boxer, and a memorable scene is recorded in his undergraduate days when he found that he had to fight the 'Chicken of Wheatley'—and this without any boxing-gloves—and emerged victorious from the fray. The river also attracted him at Oxford, and deer-stalking and all forms of sport in later years. He had, too, a distinct taste for racing. Nerve, love of action, readiness of resource, courage, prompt and sound judgment, keenness, the determination to succeed and win, were apparent in these tastes ; and they contributed largely to his success as an editor.

Equally remarkable and of value in his career was Delane's sure instinct in dealing with his fellow creatures. He was in this respect essentially a man of the world. As we read we feel constantly that in his relations with his fellow-men he strikes the happy mean which so many miss. He is absolutely independent in his judgments and determined in matters of importance, yet ever considerate towards others. He respects rank and position, and yet is never in the smallest degree unduly subservient or excessive in deference.

These qualities were not the outcome of any theory as to what best befitted an editor's *rôle*. They were not, I think, cultivated deliberately, but were developed spontaneously. They formed part of his character, and they would have told for success in any field of action— in the House of Commons, at the Bar, in diplomacy. Fortune gave him 'The Times' to edit, and to the characteristics I have named rather than to any great

literary gifts is, I think, due the position which he won
for that journal. It may be objected to this that in
his work of literary revision he was quite exceptionally
careful, touching and retouching, modifying every
article, and that this needed great literary aptitudes
of a certain kind. Doubtless it did, but—again to
risk a paradox—they were not the aptitudes distinctive of a man of letters. He had none of the
brilliancy of a 'Saturday' reviewer of the 'sixties. It
was not to literary form that he gave such close
attention. It was to the effect on the public mind, on
public opinion, of the articles. And as to this he was
unsparingly critical down to a sentence, a phrase, a
word. It was the statesmanship and the diplomacy of
journalism, not its literary side, which so engrossed
him and in which he was such a master. And this required a gift akin to that shown by a great ambassador
in his despatches rather than literary brilliance.

Finally must be added to the causes of his success
that all-important driving power without which the
greatest gifts fail of effect—single-minded and entire
concentration. 'No man can serve two masters.' In
course of time many of the distractions of social success
came upon Delane : the court paid to him by Society
was an inevitable consequence of the power he came
to wield. Delane was no ascetic, and he tasted with
pleasure, though always in moderation, of the enjoy-
ments of social life. But distractions in the literal sense
they never were to him. In the last decade of his life,
when he dined out and gave dinners constantly in the
season, and his holidays were spent among the most

influential people, both socially and politically, of the
kingdom, when Royalty singled him out for marked
civilities, and the great ladies added their attentions to
those which he had long received from the leading
Ministers of the Crown, his absorption in his work for
' The Times' remained what it had always been. ' He
allowed no mundane pleasures,' writes his biographer,
'to prevent his going every night to his room at " The
Times " office at half-past ten or eleven.'   No man
could afford to be more absolutely indifferent to
Disraeli's sneer in 1858 at his increase of social engagements.   The allusion—in a speech to his consti-
tuents—was made in Dizzy's most characteristic phrase.
He spoke of ' the once stern guardians of popular
rights ' as ' now simpering in the enervated atmosphere
of gilded saloons.'   Certainly the ' gilded saloons '
were far more to Disraeli's own Oriental imagination
than they ever were to Delane.   His head was never
in the least turned or his firm and consistent course
affected by the attentions either of great Ministers
or of their wives.   He took gladly the social
recreations that came, but only on condition that
they did not interfere with his work.   It was in
his last years, those in which invitations were most
numerous, that the late Warden of Merton describes
him in terms that testify to his kindness and con-
siderateness as well as to his habits of constant work :

Always at his post by half-past ten in the evening [writes
Dr. Brodrick], never to quit it until four in the morning, he
took breakfast when others took lunch, and was busily
engaged with interviews and correspondence during all the

earlier part of the afternoon, and perhaps, during emergencies, up to dinner time. In looking through letters of his which now lie before me, I am chiefly struck by the kind consideration for my own health and feelings which some of them show. He speaks little of himself, but always cheerfully until his final breakdown. In one letter, written in September, he says : ' I have not stirred from this place since last I saw you, and I believe not a column has been published in " The Times " which had not some of my handwriting in the margin.'

Delane's political independence is strikingly illustrated by the fact that the two Ministers with whom his friendship was most intimate, and who most constantly sought his advice—Aberdeen and Palmerston— were on occasion strongly criticised or opposed by him, while the statesman for whom his expressed admiration was most unqualified—Sir Robert Peel— was hardly known to him at all. The opposition of ' The Times ' to Palmerston's foreign policy in 1850, when Aberdeen's party accused Delane of having helped to cause the overthrow of Louis Philippe's Government, was in no way mitigated by the famous Don Pacifico speech. On the other hand, when, four years later, English public opinion was deeply moved by the want of energy and competence of the responsible authorities in the conduct of the Crimean war, Delane, at the cost of attacking the Government of so firm and valued a friend as Lord Aberdeen, gave constant voice to this criticism. Kinglake's testimony to the influence of ' The Times ' at this juncture is worth recording :

No more able, more cogent appeals [he writes] were perhaps ever made than those in which its great writers insisted again and again that the despatch of reinforcements must be achieved with an exertion of will strong enough to overthrow every obstacle interposed by mere customs and forms. When the story of Inkermann reached them they uttered, if so one may speak, the very soul of a nation enraptured with the hard-won victory, and abounding in gratitude to its distant army, yet disclosing the care, the grief which sobered its joy and its pride.

And again, when, a few days later, the further accounts from our army showed the darkening of the prospect before it, the great journal assuming its leadership, and moving out to the front with opportune, resolute counsels, seemed clothed with a power to speak, nay, almost one may say, to act, in the name of a united people.

The House of Commons endorsed the verdict of 'The Times.' The Aberdeen Government fell, and Lord Palmerston, at the age of seventy, became for the first time Prime Minister. From this time to the end of his life Palmerston worked in close co-operation with Delane, and when he died, full of honours, in 1865, a very competent judge—Lord Torrington— wrote to Delane after the great funeral in Westminster Abbey this striking estimate of the value of 'The Times'' support to Palmerston's career :

I thought very much of you on the day of the funeral, and of the great manifestation which took place and the respect shown to his memory. It recalled to my mind what was his position and popularity till *you* gave him aid and support! In fact, *but for you* he would have died almost as unnoticed as I should be, and possibly quite as little regretted. *You* made the show of last Friday, and carried him in triumph through the last dozen years of his life; and yet I fear that all the set which lived round Cambridge House will hardly duly and sufficiently remember the hand who raised and made their departed friend.

There can be no doubt that it was the very independence, arising from the strong convictions of a strong man, which made Delane prepared on occasion to oppose his great political friends, which gave also such value to his support. A like independence is visible in his dealings with his contributors; and so valued a writer as Henry Reeve—Don Pomposo as Delane facetiously called him—was dismissed without a pang, in 1855, when he failed to meet the editor's views of the requirements of the dignity and honour of 'The Times.' 'Much as I hate quarrelling, I would rather quarrel with a whole parish of Reeves,' he writes to Sir George Dasent, 'than submit to such insolent assertions as his letters display. He just wanted to job the paper to his own purposes, to prove to his patrons that he was supreme, and to receive their pay in flattery and dinners while he was taking ours in hard cash.' Even so old a friend as Disraeli found that he touched very delicate ground when he infringed on the editorial prerogative and asked for Charles Greville as reviewer of his 'Life of Lord George Bentinck.' Another reviewer was at once selected by Delane, and the review was by no means enthusiastic.

The ability and independence, then, of Delane won for 'The Times' an almost unique position; and it is startling to look at the statistics of the circulation of daily papers in 1852, when, against the 40,000 sold by 'The Times,' the other London journals, taken all together, did not approach that figure—'The Morning Advertiser' coming next with 7,000, and 'The Daily

News,' 'The Morning Herald,' 'The Morning Post' and 'The Morning Chronicle' selling only about 3,000 each. Those were the days of Trollope's Tom Towers and 'the Jupiter.' The decree of 'The Times' had all the authority of great Jove's nod.

Perhaps the most graphic picture of the man at work—his determination to form first-hand judgments in matters of vital importance—is Mr. Dasent's account of Delane's journey to the seat of war at the Crimea, with his own illustrative letters written *en route*.

'The Times' prided itself on always being the first to announce any important news. Of bold and shrewd ventures made with this object, Delane's announcement of Lord Northbrook's appointment as Viceroy of India in 1872 is a good instance—on the strength only of Northbrook's having asked his doctor (a friend of Delane's) if a warm climate would suit his daughter's health. The appointment—though of course antecedently probable—was a perfect secret, and was, indeed, only accepted after the doctor's favourable reply. The divination of 'The Times' completely amazed Northbrook. Another editorial *tour de force* of a very different kind was Blowitz's accomplishment of Delane's suggestion—which to its own author seemed hardly possible—that Thiers's great speech of April, 1872, which the two men had heard together in Paris, should be reported in next day's 'Times.' Blowitz's wonderful memory served him in good stead, and he transmitted in the afternoon a report (*in extenso*) which was acknowledged to be

substantially accurate—a feat in those days most
memorable.

In spite of his complete absorption in his work, it
is interesting to know that Delane would never talk
'shop' or allude to 'The Times' in general conversation.   Among the noteworthy judgments of this acute
observer of political life we may record that he placed
Sydney Herbert—whose premature death cut short so
promising a career—higher than his fellow-Peelite,
W. E. Gladstone, whom he 'admired as a financier
and orator without feeling any enthusiasm for him as
a statesman.'

To Catholics, and the interests dear to Catholics,
The Times' was not friendly, though it opposed the
extremes of 'no Popery.'   It was too faithful an index
of English public opinion to be really just to the Roman
Catholic Church.   The outcry of 1850 against the new
Hierarchy was largely promoted by 'The Times,' and
the Italian Revolution and invasion of the Papal States
received its active support.   On the other hand, in
1867 Delane's sense of justice revolted against the
attempt to charge the Irish bishops with complicity in
the Fenian movement, and his letter to Dasent on the
subject is strongly expressed.   Equally emphatic was
his public support of the bishops on this question in
'The Times' itself.

I may add, as part of the picture left us in these
volumes, that Delane's family affections were strong ;
and his devotion to his mother is a touching and
attractive trait in his character.   Religious movements
seem to have inspired him but little, and his attendance

as an undergraduate at Newman's Oxford sermons was probably mainly due to their being the event of the hour.   He looked death in the face, but it was with the eyes of a philosopher ; and he meant to work as long as his health permitted it, not caring to live when work was past.   All his enthusiasms were those of a man of the world and a man of affairs, and in many respects he recalls to us Lord Macaulay, although he lacked Macaulay's literary genius.   The keenness of their interests, the immense extent of their general information, their strong domestic affections, the apparent absence in them both of the deeper human passions and of other-worldliness, the glow of imaginative interest with which they watched the movement of public affairs, coupled with the lack in both of the higher poet's imagination—both their powers and their limitations— were largely similar.   Delane's momentary enthusiasm for Newman meant no more than Macaulay's excitement over Ranke's ' History of the Popes.'   Both men lived for work and for success, yet ever working with conviction and public spirit ; and both passed away, at the age of threescore years, after an active life, without having to face what would have tried them so intensely—a protracted experience of life's decline.

When we turn from John Thadeus Delane to Richard Holt Hutton we pass to an absolutely different type, akin only in that secret of influence which is found in strong convictions and independence of mind. Hutton's intellectual gifts were those of a thinker

on the problems of life and a literary critic of fine
insight.   Although his judgments on politics were
weighty and often wise, and his political views strongly
held and finely expressed, they were but a small part
of the man.   His influence on the political history of
the country, of course, cannot compare with Delane's.
Yet it was considerable—largely owing to his friendship with Mr. Gladstone.   And an intimate friend of
Gladstone's told the present writer that that statesman
felt none of the separations from old allies which his
Home Rule policy caused more than the breach with
Hutton.

If, however, Hutton's political influence was small
compared with Delane's, I believe that his influence on
English public opinion was, from its range and its
momentum in so many departments, far greater.   It is
very rare that a weekly journal should be the *medium*
whereby a great thinker and spiritual leader exercises
his power over his generation.   It was so in Hutton's
case.   Much of the influence on human lives which a
great teacher of philosophy exercises in a university,
or a great preacher from his pulpit, was exerted week
by week by Richard Hutton in ' The Spectator,' for
the space of thirty-five years, on a large number of
English readers.   It was not primarily a matter of
direct teaching or preaching.   It was the treatment of
all the subjects of the day and the literature of the day,
and the utterances of public men, with earnestness and
a high standard which all felt to be absolutely sincere
and to represent the unswerving rectitude and principle
of the writer.   The effect of this would have been

great even had his gifts as a thinker and writer been less remarkable. As it was, this high standard was enforced by a really great critic and thinker. He was, indeed, a literary critic of rare insight and independence. Occasionally—as, for example, in his essays on George Eliot, Goethe, Matthew Arnold, and Browning—he rose to the very highest point in what Tennyson used to call the critic's highest function, the analysis of the genius of his author—of the secret of his greatness— as distinguished from the perception of his defects.

His power of seizing and delineating a personality, too, was very unusual. His personal studies of Newman, R. W. Church, Matthew Arnold, W. G. Ward, and many another, written at the time of their death, have well deserved to be preserved, as they have been, by posthumous publication. Of Hope-Scott—whom he never knew—he gave so faithful a portrait from the evidence contained in his biography, and appreciated that evidence so far better than did the biographer himself, that Hope-Scott's relations took the article to be the work of one of his most intimate friends.

But Hutton's work in 'The Spectator' year after year, not merely in placing before the public a serious and comprehensive view of events and persons, but in communicating to his readers some of that elevated moral atmosphere in which he himself lived, probably had a far wider and deeper effect on the country than his achievements for literature proper.

In this work he had, indeed, from the first the ablest collaboration. But the stamp of Hutton's mind

was unmistakable, and his style and spirit were caught
by his colleagues. Some people complained that
'The Spectator' was dull. There is always an
element of dulness in prolonged attention to the
duties of life. And in Hutton's view the formation
of public opinion in regard to those duties was one
chief function of journalism. In truth, those who found
'The Spectator' dull did so greatly in consequence of
an opposite view of journalism from Hutton's. His
paper had, indeed, the seriousness attaching to a
responsible formative influence on public opinion. It
consistently eschewed pettiness and personalities. On
the other hand, with humour of a certain kind Hutton
was abundantly endowed, and there were ever in 'The
Spectator,' for those who looked for them, traces of a
powerful individuality, original and often *piquant* in
its exhibitions, and constantly at war with the insincerities and frivolities of the hour. This was the
antithesis of real dulness. Hutton in one of the
numbers of 'The Spectator' described our own day
as one 'in which Society imposes its conventional
assumptions and insincerities on almost every one of
us.' He recommended his contemporaries to learn
their lesson from Dr. Johnson, who, 'whatever else he
was, was always true to himself,' who was 'more afraid
of his conscience than of all the world's opinion'; and
who 'towers above our own generation just because
he had the courage to be what so few of us are—
proudly independent of the opinion in the midst of
which he lived.' These words might be used with
absolute truth of Hutton himself. And great as were

his gifts, high as were the intellectual and moral lessons he read to his generation, it was the almost personal communication of this ethical character to the readers of ' The Spectator,' the feeling they caught from living in his company week by week that the sentiments and opinions they read were the expressions of a strong man's character, to which his special and lasting influence was due.   'The world will miss in him,' wrote Mr. Aubrey de Vere, one of Hutton's oldest friends, to the present writer at the time of his death, 'what is, perhaps, greater than what it most admires.'   And I interpret these words in the sense I have indicated. What it has missed was the constant unconscious quasi-companionship in ' The Spectator ' with his noble mind—with one whose words it had come to regard as identical with the man himself—having, therefore, the influence of example as well as of precept.

Doubtless he had the defects of his qualities, but they were literally, for the most part, defects inseparable from the qualities.   The occasional neglect of form in expression, the sentences over-pregnant with condensed and complex reflection and analysis, told unmistakably of laborious effort rather to convey genuine thought to his readers than to earn for himself a reputation for artistic workmanship.   His strong prepossessions on certain subjects—prejudices they might fairly be called—were such as are found in nearly all men of deep convictions.   Among them was his exaggerated feeling as to any pain inflicted on animals, however good the object of such infliction might

be.   ' You must generally choose,' Tennyson used
to say, ' between bigotry and flabbiness.'   But Hutton's
prejudices were generally lovable, and they were his
own.   He never helped a popular prejudice to survive
its natural lifetime, and he generally succeeded in
cutting short its career.   His championship of a great
man or of a literary genius was uncompromising—of
Mr. Gladstone, of Cardinal Newman, of Mr. Matthew
Arnold, and later on of Mr. Watson and Mr. Balfour.
It was, perhaps, now and again too unqualified.   But
that it was not blind, even when most impassioned,
was shown by his strenuous opposition from 1886
onwards to the policy of the man who had for so long
been his political prophet.

Let a word be added as to Hutton's extraordinary
kindness.   To do a kind act to a beginner or to one
in need, or, again, to one who was ill or in suffering,
was among his greatest joys.   There was often little
of the *suaviter in modo*, and the kindness would
surprise those who did not know him.   I published in
' The Nineteenth Century' a dialogue on ' The Wish
to Believe' in 1882—almost my first literary effort—
and Hutton, who had seen it in manuscript and liked it,
had growled out something which I took to mean that he
would notice it in ' The Spectator' when it appeared.
When it did come out, with the impatience of youth, I
called at the office to remind him of this, and was
greeted so gruffly that I almost repented having come.
Without looking up from his writing he said : ' Why
do you come on Thursday, my busy day ?   I can't
attend to you.'   I faltered out some words about the

appearance of my article, and he interrupted me by saying : 'The longer you keep me talking, the shorter will be my sub-leader on your article, which I am this moment writing.' I retreated with alacrity, and the sub-leader appeared on Saturday—an excellent introduction of a new-comer to the world of letters.

Hutton was quite as assiduous at his work as Delane, and as little given to distractions from what was the pursuit of his life. For 'gilded saloons' he had no taste at all, and he was never a figure in Society, as Delane was in his later years. He was by temperament as well as by virtue unworldly. The great world did not appeal to his imagination in the least. Yet Hutton's social influence was considerable in the circle of his friends. I have dined with him at the Devonshire Club in company with such men as Mr. Gladstone, Mr. W. E. Forster, Dean Church and Canon Liddon, and heard at these dinners as good talk as I have ever heard anywhere, Hutton generally taking the lead. Dean Church used to recall Hutton's power in the debates of the old Metaphysical Society of raising the tone and earnestness of the discussions ; while perhaps he was at his very best at breakfast parties of three or four persons, when his prolonged tea-drinking—of perhaps six or seven cups of excellent tea—was, I think, the only instance of keen enjoyment of anything in the way of food or drink which I ever observed in him. He enjoyed his cup of tea as a parson of the old school would enjoy his bottle of fine old port.

His conversation on literature was greatly helped

by his remarkable verbal memory. From Dickens, especially, he could quote whole pages, and I doubt if anyone was more familiar with the sayings of Mr. Pecksniff or Mrs. Gamp. I have only very rarely heard of his presence at more fashionable social gatherings. I recall meeting him at one dinner, about the year 1885, at the house of Lady Clifden—then Mrs. Leo Agar-Ellis—in Green Street, to which he was tempted by the presence of Mr. Gladstone. The late Duke of Devonshire (then Lord Hartington) was also there, and Cardinal Vaughan (then Bishop of Salford) ; and the occasion is stamped on my memory by the fact that the future Cardinal and the future Duke combined in being excessively bored by the theological discussion which Gladstone and Hutton carried on when the ladies had left us, and resolutely resisted all attempts to draw them into it, finally moving to some distance and enjoying a talk together on topics more mundane, including both shooting and racing, I think.

To Catholics there were special points of interest in Hutton's life. He certainly did very much to get rid of the old 'no-Popery' prejudices which long had so paralysing an influence on English Catholics. Ever since 1864, when his strong words aroused the public to an enthusiastic acceptance of Newman's 'Apologia,' he repeatedly said the word in season for the 'Papists' of England, and was to them a friend in need. Hutton's defence of the 'Apologia' was especially influential from his known admiration for Kingsley. He has rightly ascribed the great change of English public feeling in regard to Roman Catholics

F

mainly to the influence of Cardinal Newman, but it needed a certain relation between Newman and the public for the creation of that influence. When, in 1851, Newman lectured at the Birmingham Corn Exchange on the position of Catholics in England, the Press did its best to boycott him. It may be open to question whether Newman would ever have completely emerged from the cloud which stood between him and the English public after the events of 1845 had it not been for the outspoken and independent admiration of 'The Spectator.'

Hutton was strongly drawn towards many features in Catholic belief. I think that Mr. A. J. Church is right in saying that his devotion to Newman helped more than anything else to foster this attraction. But he had also many familiar friends among Catholics. In the days of the old Metaphysical Society, Father Dalgairns, Cardinal Manning, and the other Catholic members, were his close allies in the debates. He might be seen at Mass, Sunday by Sunday, at Twickenham during the last decade of his life, but he never could believe the Catholic Church to be more than a communion with special spiritual gifts, indeed, but advancing claims which were, in the light of modern thought and criticism, untenable.

Hutton was so regardless of fame that he published comparatively little under his own name. There are some Literary Essays, and some very valuable studies in theology, including one which is really autobiographical, on his progress from Unitarianism to belief in the Trinity and the Incarnation. He passed under the influence successively of Martineau, Frederick Denison Maurice, and Cardinal Newman. He retained to the end traces of the modes of thought of Martineau and Maurice, and these remnants of a liberalistic theology always qualified his attitude in relation to the Catholic ideals towards which Newman drew him. His love and admiration for Dean Church was one of the deepest feelings of his later years. Great, too, was his affection for Dr. Liddon. But from the latter especially he was, I think, intellectually separated by a difference of sentiment with regard to the Sacramental system traceable to his early religious Liberalism.

Hutton had intimate friends of nearly all schools of thought. And, however otherwise divided, they were united in regarding him not only as what he was often called—a great teacher—but as one who in practical sympathy with the distressed, personal holiness, and unswerving devotion to duty, had in him something of the saint. Perhaps it has never before happened that Catholics, Anglicans, and inquiring Agnostics have repaired, on occasion, to an editor's office in the Strand with feelings somewhat akin to those with which the Savoyard went to St. Francis de Sales, for advice in perplexity or a stimulus to do his duty. And the memory of the rugged face—which was sometimes compared to that of Socrates—at first sight so little encouraging, of the manner which might for a moment be mistaken for an uninviting brusqueness, will ever remain for many of us coupled with that of unfailing sympathy and high-minded counsel.

F 2

Delane and Hutton represented in different ways the high-water mark of the influence of strong men in the editorial chair who exercised the principle of 'protection' in their journals for the views they desired to urge on their fellow-countrymen.   Sir James Knowles was the most successful representative of the opposite principle—of 'free trade' for all competing opinions. Though not the originator of the signed article, he was its greatest and most successful promoter, first when he took over from Dean Alford the editorship of 'The Contemporary Review' in the later 'sixties, and afterwards when, in 1877, he founded 'The Nineteenth Century.' The system was in some sense a response to new conditions.   The increase in the number of journals and of the reading public had already made the debates in the House of Commons addresses to the country through the newspapers, and not merely to those who heard them.   But politics were, after all, but one department of public affairs.   A platform was needed from which distinguished men of all ways of thinking could address the whole reading public on all great topics of the hour.   The idea was that of public debating, in which the name and antecedents of each speaker, as well as his arguments, should have their weight, as they have in the House of Commons. Before the signed article came into fashion the clumsy system of pamphlets had been the only way of effecting this object.   But a pamphlet needed advertising, and was consequently expensive to produce, and was not in the end widely read unless the occasion or the author was exceptionally important.   'The Contemporary Review ' and ' The Nineteenth Century,' on the other hand, were read by everyone. For those who had a wish and right to claim a hearing from the public no rostrum commanded so wide an audience, except a letter to ' The Times,' as ' The Nineteenth Century.' And letters to ' The Times' were ever necessarily strictly conditioned as to length and subject, while the range of ' The Nineteenth Century' was very wide.

In the early years of his editorship Knowles obtained an immense accession of weighty contributors from his connection with the Metaphysical Society, of which he was the founder. I remember his coming with Tennyson to our house at Hampstead in April, 1869, to discuss with my father and Archbishop Manning the scheme of the proposed Society, and the idea met with such general approval that in a few months its members included nearly all the eminent thinkers of the day on the philosophy of religion ; the only notable exceptions, I think, being J. S. Mill, Cardinal Newman, and Herbert Spencer, who all three declined to join. Many statesmen were of the company, including Gladstone, the Duke of Argyll, Grant-Duff, Lord Arthur Russell, and the late Lord Selborne ; and the number of poets and men of letters and of science, in addition to the professed metaphysicians, made the Society far more representative of wide interests than its name and object promised. Aided by this powerful group of supporters Knowles, in 1877, threw off the fetters imposed by a Review of which he was not himself proprietor, and founded ' The Nineteenth Century.' Tennyson, Matthew

Arnold, the Duke of Argyll, Ruskin, Gladstone, J. A. Froude, are the names of only a few writers among others equally eminent who contributed from the very first.

Both as to what people wished to hear about and whom they wished to hear Knowles's instinct was unerring. It was, indeed, to this quality that both the foundation of the Metaphysical Society and the success of 'The Nineteenth Century' were due. Knowles was no metaphysician. The philosophy of religious belief had no special interest for him. But accident led him to discover that the subject had at that moment very special interest for a large number of exceedingly eminent and representative men. Having known Tennyson slightly, he met him accidentally when he was planning his house at Aldworth, near Haslemere. Knowles, who was an architect by profession, offered to design the house for him, and Tennyson accepted the offer.

To the intimacy which hence arose with Tennyson, who was profoundly interested in the subject of the metaphysics of religious belief, was due the foundation of the Metaphysical Society. The idea caught on with Tennyson's friends and with others. And Knowles's activity and power of organisation both brought the Society into being and secured its active and flourishing life. His peculiar quickness of perception and acquisition was once spoken of by Tennyson to the present writer in special reference to the Metaphysical Society. 'No man ever had his brain in his hand as Knowles had,' Tennyson said. 'He could learn in half an hour enough of a subject which was quite new to him to talk about it, and never talk nonsense. When we first planned the Metaphysical Society Knowles did not know a " concept " from a hippopotamus. Before we had talked of it for a month he could chatter metaphysics with the best of us.' And it was this quickness and alertness which also made his editorship so singularly successful in the years of his prime. He applied at the right moment to the right man to address the public on the right topic. He often told me that when he saw what was wanted he made it a rule to insist on having it, and would gladly pay with even excessive liberality rather than lose it. Indeed, everything was conducted on a liberal scale in the Review, and nothing was more noticeable to a contributor than the absence of petty economies and the facilities afforded for any amount of revision of contributions—a luxury for which I confess to being particularly grateful. Knowles once told me that my four revises had meant more expense than breaking up the article and resetting it, but the fact was conveyed to me without the slightest reproach. He aimed at securing the best-known representatives of competing views on subjects of the day ; but he also had an eye to the future, and was quick to recognise rising talent and give young men their chance. He always wished to be on good terms with the representatives of every department of activity, political, social and religious ; and I remember his dissatisfaction at not knowing the present Archbishop of Westminster having been intimate with both Cardinal Manning and

Cardinal Vaughan.   I brought them together at his
desire, and he was afterwards, I believe, a not infre-
quent visitor at Archbishop's House.

His gifts and his opportunities made 'The Nineteenth Century' one of the most signal immediate
successes, I suppose, in the history of reviews.   Before
starting it—so he once told me—he asked his father to
guarantee £2,000 against possible loss in setting it on
foot.   In the event not only did he never apply to his
father for a penny, but he made from the beginning
many thousands a year, and at once outstripped in
popularity all competitors in the same kind.   In the
days of the Metaphysical Society his house, like his
Review, was a great rendezvous for persons of varied
interests and different opinions.   Manning, Huxley,
J. A. Froude, and Dean Stanley were often there.
Tennyson on several occasions stayed with him, and
Gladstone was a frequent guest at his table.   After
the Home Rule Bill the story was current that Tennyson telegraphed proposing to stay with Knowles, and
found on arrival that Mr. Gladstone was dining.   After
first refusing to dine in his company, he was afterwards
prevailed upon to come down after dinner, and Gladstone's charms were too much for him.   The intended
stern reserve which was to bring home to him the
error of his Home Rule ways entirely disappeared.
Gladstone's conversation and animation completely
won the day, and acted as good wine in compelling
friendliness and fellowship.   Next day at breakfast
Tennyson was as one who in the light of the morning
headache and calm reflection repents the genial pota-

tions of the night before. 'That's the worst of Gladstone,' he said ; ' he gets round one at once if one sees him.'

Such was Sir James Knowles as an editor and as a man—a wonderful and most universal medium of communication between different men and between thinkers of all schools and the public. In conversation he had a very happy art of finding the subject on which different members of the company could and would talk freely, and of himself putting in the right word, and, as it were, winding up the clock. He used to be compared to Boswell ; but I think this comparison materially inaccurate. Knowles was a far stronger man as well as more business-like and methodical. Boswell could never have edited a review with success. On the other hand, the extraordinary intuitive perception of another man's mind and ways of thought which enabled Boswell to record Johnson's conversation with such absolute fidelity did not exist in Knowles. One feels that Boswell could do what by some unexplained power our dreams do for us—depict actions or conversations, entirely characteristic of our friends,—which have never actually occurred. Boswell could have written down a conversation between Johnson and Goldsmith which never took place, and yet which would be precisely what they would have said in given circumstances. This creative power as of the novelist was different from Knowles's gift, which was a more practical one—that of drawing out the different interlocutors in a conversation. Boswell could, perhaps, on occasion, do this also, but he entirely lacked Knowles's practical and business-like sense of what was wanted at the moment, his promptness in action, his reliable and systematic habits of work.

Although primarily the purveyor of the views of others—he never or hardly ever wrote in his Review himself—Knowles had the strong convictions of an energetic man, and he liked energy and strong convictions in others. He liked everyone to be a good party man, and once told me that he particularly appreciated his Roman Catholic and Nonconformist contributors because they could always be relied on to write when appealed to, and write strongly and definitely. He was alert and prompt to the end in asking for those contributions on matters of the hour as they arose which were necessary to sustain the character of the Review, in addition to the large mass of articles standing in type. My own last connection with him was on the occasion of M. Briand's Law of Associations. Knowles came to me at the Athenæum and asked me, at only a fortnight's notice, to write on the situation. I said it would entail going to Paris and putting off engagements, and with characteristic determination and generosity he placed the offer on so liberal a footing that my hesitation was overcome. When the Papal 'Encyclical' on Modernism appeared he was equally prompt, and went to Archbishop's House to get the best Catholic official statement of the Pope's views, and secured an article from the Canon Theologian of the Diocese, Monsignor Moyes.

Knowles loved the society of his friends and loved beautiful things. He was an excellent judge of

pictures. His collection of pictures in his house in
Queen Anne's Gate was a very fine one, including
Millais' 'Tennyson,' Leighton's 'Clytie'—the last
picture painted by the great artist—and a magnificent
'Claude,' purchased by him from the Wynne-Ellis
collection. He lived to be older than Hutton or
Delane, but kept his full powers till the last. He was
proud of the success of his Review, as he well might
be. If anyone looks through the catalogue published
by him at the end of 1901 of its contents from the
beginning, they will realise that it was for years the
mouthpiece of the representatives of all that was most
interesting in England. The roll of contributors, in
the first twenty years especially, would be hard to
rival. He regarded the extension of the signed
articles as his great achievement. In his prefatory
remarks to this published list of contents he thus
writes on the subject :

More than a quarter of a century's experience has sufficiently tested the practical efficacy of the principle upon which
'The Nineteenth Century' was founded, 'of free public discussion by writers invariably signing their own names.'

The success which has attended and continues to attend
the faithful adherence to this principle proves that it is not
only right but acceptable, and warrants the hope that it may
extend its influence over periodical literature until unsigned
contributions become quite exceptional.

No man can make an anonymous speech with his tongue,
and no brave man should desire to make one with his pen,
but, having the courage of his opinions, should be ready to
face personally all the consequences of all his utterances.
Anonymous letters are everywhere justly discredited in private
life, and the tone of public life would be raised in proportion

to the disappearance of their equivalent—anonymous articles
- -from public controversy.

In so far as 'The Nineteenth Century and After' has
helped to further that good end, it may claim for the writers
whose names are recorded in the following catalogue that they
have rendered a public service.

Delane was editor of 'The Times' for thirty-five
years ; Knowles's editorship of ' The Contemporary '
and ' The Nineteenth Century ' lasted yet longer, and
Hutton's of ' The Spectator ' about as long. Each
proved his capacity by realising possibilities which
others had failed to realise. ' The Times' was well
established when Delane took it, but Delane gave
it an influence new in kind as well as in degree.
Hutton gave to ' The Spectator '—which also was
a going concern when he took it—its distinctive
character and power. If ' The Nineteenth Century '
was Knowles's creation it was but the development of
the signed article system, which others had planned
and begun but Knowles realised. It was he who
effectively established a recognised platform for free
discussion. All three are notable figures in the annals
of editorship—the two whose views in different ways
so profoundly influenced the country, and the one who
systematised the total absence in a review of any
editorial views whatever. In mere practical success,
perhaps, the man who set a review on foot which
became from its first number one of the most successful in the country performed the greatest feat. As
a great political force in the country, swaying its
destinies, the man whom the Queen of Holland called

' le quatrième pouvoir de l'Etat Britannique ' was unrivalled.   Yet that unrivalled power died with the man.   Hutton alone of the three has left behind him in the thoughts which he published to help an earlier generation a legacy which is still prized by our own (as the sale of his republished essays from ' The Spectator ' attests), and which will descend to our children along with the tradition of the noble and austere character, which made his great thoughts so intimately part of himself.

SOME CHARACTERISTICS OF
HENRY SIDGWICK

IT is mainly as a character-study that the Memoir of Henry Sidgwick [1] is interesting. External events in his career there were next to none. But a mental history instructive for the times we do find in its pages, and the revelation, largely the self-revelation, of a profoundly interesting personality. ' An enthusiastic doubter ' is a type not easy at once to conceive. Yet I think this phrase conveys fairly well the peculiar— the almost unique—interest of Sidgwick's intellectual character. The enthusiasm was, indeed, suppressed and undemonstrative, but it was unmistakable.

A man who in written criticism or in conversation can accept no statement as satisfactory, who finds a flaw in every theory, who bores fatal holes in every intellectual structure, theological or philosophical, which has stimulated the enthusiasm of men in the past,—and who after so much destruction cannot even then offer any decided alternative, whether by way of affirmation or of negation, for the systems he has killed or mutilated—would seem likely to be a very un-stimulating individual. If he is wrong in his views,

[1] *Henry Sidgwick : A Memoir.* By A. S. and E. M. S. London : Macmillan. 1906.

Walter L. Colls, Ph.So.

Henry Sidgwick
From a painting by J.J. Shannon.

he would appear to be at once disheartening and mischievous. If he is right, he is at least disheartening; and it still remains a question whether the wholesale slaughter of helpful illusion is a gain to life. He is at best a most unwelcome prophet of ill-tidings. Destruction is ever a melancholy process; and indecision adds an element which is extremely provoking.

Yet the fact remains that Henry Sidgwick, relentless critic though he was, and concrete embodiment of intellectual indecision, was a most stimulating companion and friend, one who inspired, at least in many, real enthusiasm; and it is, as I have said, on the explanation of this apparent opposition that much of the supreme interest of Sidgwick's character depends.

I am disposed to account for the combination mainly by two characteristics. In the first place, his gift of sympathy was as remarkable in conversation as was the habit of inexorable and incisive criticism. If his companion urged a view which he could not accept, he met him in the first instance not by mere objections. On the contrary, he walked two steps with him in fullest sympathy before finding 'no road' at the third. The sympathy was quite as marked as the critical tendency. This will be remembered by all who knew him, and the quality of mind it represented is vividly shown in the second paper he read before the Synthetic Society (printed in the Appendix to the Memoir), in which he gives, with extraordinary sympathy and fidelity, an entirely original version of his opponent's argument before dissecting it.

His very scepticism in matters of theology had in it this element of sympathy.   He might almost have been the seventeenth-century sceptic gibbeted by the witty Bishop Earle in his 'Microcosmographie' as 'one that hangs in the balance with all sorts of opinions, whereof not one but stirs him and none sways him ; a man guiltier of credulity than he is taken to be, for it is out of his belief of everything that he fully believes nothing.'   This is the description of a hostile critic.   But Sidgwick had the quality, Bishop Earle thus caricatures, in its most winning form.   Thus conversation began with all the charm of sympathy, and then it was kept from flagging by the additional stimulus of what Tennyson has called 'the clash of yes and no.'

But this quality of sympathy was supplemented by something which went far deeper.   There was an ideal passion for truth, which shed a halo over all his discussion of the problems of the mind, and gave it an almost religious earnestness.   The dissecting process, so minute, so detailed, so persistent, was different, even opposite in character, from the dry word-chopping of the mere logician.   Its spirit was constructive—that of a great artist, who in his carving or sculpture fastidiously removes what deviates by a hair's breadth from fidelity to his model or ideal.   Sidgwick's delicate work on a small area of discussion was the building of an altar, or perhaps the carving of a reredos, in the great cathedral of philosophic truth.   The thought of the greatness of the ideal whole gave zest to the work of completing one portion with fastidious care.

In both these respects the present writer used to feel his qualities thrown into relief by the contrast between him and one who, as a philosopher and liberal theologian, held a somewhat similar *rôle* at Oxford. Conversation with Dr. Jowett tended at times to languish. His criticisms were intellectual snubs. He would fix on a weak point in one's argument or a point of disagreement at the very outset. He would not spare one, or help one out of a difficulty he had raised, by any suggestion that one had not been talking sheer nonsense. The consequence was that difference of view, instead of stimulating discussion, as it does between those who partly agree, often brought it to a dead halt. His criticisms were *douches* of cold water which extinguished the flame. Again, Jowett had not at all the same faith as Sidgwick in an ultimate triumph of the cause of philosophic truth. His very conformity to the Church of England was allied with a want in this respect. The stone cathedrals that were already standing were nearer to him than any prospective temple dedicated to truth and built of ideas. The consequence was that, while the two men in some respects apparently played the same *rôle*—for both were critics and representatives of broad theology, both philosophers, both independent thinkers of liberal views—it would be hard to conceive two more different men as companions. With Sidgwick conversation never ceased. His fertility was endless. From the ashes of a destroyed theory phœnix-like there arose a new one full of life—though one knew that its life would be short. Jowett's

G

sterility was at times equally remarkable—not, indeed, universally, but in conversing on similar subjects. He snubbed the man who pressed his doubt to far-reaching conclusions as much as he snubbed the dogmatist.   Conversation was often checked by his dislike of any approach to sounding the deeper depths of conviction.   Indeed, the popular conceptions of Oxford and Cambridge were almost reversed in these men, for Sidgwick talked and wrote of nothing more readily than of problems connected with the finding of a 'Weltanschauung,' while it rejoiced the heart of the Oxford don to bring his friends abruptly down from such soaring heights to the plain prose and *terra firma* of everyday life.

Everyone knows the story of the undergraduate who confided to the Master his doubts as to the existence of God, and of Jowett's reply that, unless he could find arguments to prove His existence in the course of twenty-four hours, he much regretted that it would be his duty as Master of Balliol to send him down into the country.   I remember another case, not so amusing as a story, but still more characteristic of the man, in which Jowett mistook some random talk of a Catholic friend for a serious confession of doubt, and replied with complacency : 'I am the last person to come to for answers to your doubts, but I should not advise anyone who was born a Roman Catholic to become a Protestant.'   The uncontrollable laughter which followed disconcerted him ; and he did not appear pleased, but quite the reverse, on being assured by the friend that his faith in the Catholic Church was

deep and unshaken.   In fact, he did not like too much
demonstration either of faith or of doubt.   *Ne quid
nimis* was the essence of many of his characteristic
aphorisms—as, for example, his 'never quarrel, never
explain ; never spare, never drudge.'   Anything more
unlike the spirit of Sidgwick's sympathetic and searching inquiries could not be conceived.

The two traits in Sidgwick which I am endeavouring to indicate—of sympathy and of enthusiasm—
struck the present writer on first meeting him, and
subsequent intercourse only deepened the impression.
Knowing him only from his published 'Methods of
Ethics,' destructive criticism and indecision were
qualities for which I was prepared ; and the agreeable
sense which his conversation at once brought of really
living sympathy, under which one's own ideas grew
and looked more attractive and persuasive in his re-
capitulation of them than in one's own first present-
ment, was an unexpected pleasure.   Yet at such times
Sidgwick was only fattening his ox before killing him.
The knife of relentless logic was only put in his pocket
for a while.   And when the theory had come to look
thoroughly healthy and thriving, the instrument of
destruction was produced and did its work.

The occasion was fortunate in its circumtances,
for the company was small, and he was at his best.
It was at the house in Cambridge of Baron Anatole
von Hügel, about the year 1893, and the first half-
hour of dinner passed in very varied conversation,
in which I noticed that, unlike many great talkers,
Sidgwick did not insist on choosing a subject, but, on

the contrary, took up what naturally arose with the zest with which a great operator deals with the case set before him—with a certain adventurous sense (it seemed to me) of pleasure in exercising his skill on new material.   Many remember the effect of his stammer, but on this occasion it was perhaps more marked than usual, for he was—so my host told me afterwards—unusually keen and interested.

Towards the end of dinner Tennyson's poetry was discussed, and something led us to speak of ' In Memoriam.'   There was a remarkable change in his manner.   Something of inspiration came into his face, a look which is to some extent conveyed in the photograph I have prefixed to this Essay, and the discussion passed to a higher plane.   It soon gave place by general consent to almost a monologue, and Sidgwick's stammer entirely ceased as he recited in illustration of his remarks stanza after stanza of that great poem.   I should be afraid to say how much he gave us, but he seemed to know the whole by heart ; and though I knew it well, I have read much of it with different eyes since that night.   Sidgwick's reading and comments had on me an effect very similar to my first hearing of ' Tannhäuser ' under Richter's conductorship.   In that case, too, I knew the opera well already, but Richter's wonderful power of imparting to the orchestra his own delicate perception of the beauties of the work revealed new features to me, and brought out familiar ones in a new way.   His very gestures as he wielded the baton were a commentary of the highest value.   And so Sidgwick's prose interludes, describing the effect on him of parts of the poem, led up to the stanzas in such a way as to bring newly before one the poet's mind, though I had had opportunities, and had profited by them, of asking Tennyson himself questions on passages that specially interested me.

Such conversations cannot be reproduced; but some years after my first meeting with Sidgwick he wrote a letter to the present Lord Tennyson—published later on in Tennyson's Life—in which I recognised some of the best of the points he made that evening. The letter also gave the clue to the extraordinary effect of the poem on his own mind, which showed itself in his conversation. It was just the combination of intense feeling with critical intellect that marked Sidgwick himself which he here found expressed in a great poet's verse; 'the unparalleled combination,' he tells us, 'of intensity of feeling with comprehensiveness of view and balance of judgment shown in presenting the deepest needs and perplexities of humanity.'

Of his own alternations between faith and doubt Sidgwick's letters give a very outspoken record. Perhaps, however, none is more interesting, as summing up the situation, than the following concluding lines of his letter to Lord Tennyson:

I have always felt that in a certain sense the effect of the introduction [to ' In Memoriam '] does not quite represent the effect of the poem. Faith, in the introduction, is too completely triumphant. I think this is inevitable, because, so far as the thought-debate presented by the poem is summed up, it must be summed up on the side of faith. Faith must give the last word ; but the last word is not the whole utterance of the truth. The whole truth is that assurance and doubt must alternate in the moral world in which we at present live, somewhat as night and day alternate in the physical world. The revealing visions come and go ; when they come we *feel* that we *know* ; but in the interval we must pass through states in which all is dark, and in which we can only struggle to hold the conviction that—

> . . . Power is with us in the night
> Which makes the darkness and the light,
> And dwells not in the light alone.[1]

With this should be read the following passage from the same letter :

What ' In Memoriam ' did for us—for me at least—in this struggle was to impress on us the ineffaceable and ineradicable conviction that *humanity* will not and cannot acquiesce in a godless world : the ' man in men ' will not do this, whatever individual men may do, whatever they may temporarily feel themselves driven to do, by following methods which they cannot abandon to the conclusions to which these methods at present seem to lead.

The force with which it impressed this conviction was not due to the mere *intensity* of its expression of the feelings which atheism outrages and agnosticism ignores, but rather to its expression of them along with a reverent docility to the lessons of science which also belongs to the essence of the thought of our age.

The combination in Sidgwick which I have endeavoured to indicate, of the critical temper with utter candour and rich intellectual sympathy, was doubtless fostered by the great influence of J. S. Mill. Mill's celebrated essay on Coleridge contains but few sen-

[1] *In Memoriam*, xcvi.

tences which might not have been written by a follower
of that philosopher instead of by the leader of the
opposition. And though a remarkable instance of the
quality I speak of, it does not stand alone. Tennyson,
the other great influence on Sidgwick's intellectual life,
embodied the side which made him an 'enthusiastic
doubter,' in whom faith in the cause of truth, in spite
of intellectual doubt, went with an underlying religious
faith, the inalienable birthright of the 'man in men.'

Sidgwick, however, perhaps stood almost alone in
the pleasure he took in self-analysis while passing
through many different moods—a characteristic which
makes the Memoir a remarkable illustration of Newman's saying that mere 'reason is ever undecided.'
He carried this habit further than did the author of
'In Memoriam.' His moods changed more and
extended to opposite poles. He was 'prejudiced
against his own prejudices,' said a friend. If there
were two points outside the range of his normal
sympathy, they were Voltaireanism and Roman
Catholicism; yet we find him scenting a momentary
whiff of Voltaire's spirit in himself and imagining
himself a Roman Catholic, and even a Jesuit. 'I am
haunted by a dread,' he writes, 'that it is only a wild
dream, all this scientific study of human nature, a
dream as vain and unsubstantial as alchemy. At such
moments, if I had been brought up a Roman Catholic,
I might become a Jesuit in order to get a definite
object in life.' In the prime of his life he regarded
Christianity as untenable intellectually, though irre-
placeable sociologically. Later on we find him

approaching it again, and endeavouring, in respect of
theism as held by Christians, to find some such bridge
between speculative doubt and practical conviction as
Kant built in his ethical works.

But the impression left on the present writer by
the Memoir is that the philosophic creed of Mill, with
its strong empirical element, was responsible for
Sidgwick's earlier assumption that his speculative
doubts ought also to be practical doubts ; and that he
was at all times in religion not really far removed at
heart from the other great guide of his intellectual life—
Tennyson.

Sidgwick's microscopic criticism naturally enough
employed itself on his own mental constitution, and
we find some very interesting letters in the collection
published in the Memoir dealing with some, at least, of
the characteristics I have noted above.   His absolute
candour and fidelity to fact led him not to spare himself,
and in a letter written to H. G. Dakyns in his twenty-
ninth year he appears to be intensely conscious of his
own habit of indecision.   He gives a precise account
of the fluctuations in his mental barometer during the
space of a few months, which apparently leads him to
contemplate the possibility of working towards an exceptionally comprehensive philosophical system, based
on his own alternate moods of exceptional sympathy
with very varying schools of thought :

I have not progressed since I saw you, except backwards.
At my age it is a great thing even to progress backwards ; it
shows that one is not stagnating.   I mean, in respect of
thought I feel more like a young man (in all the points in

which youth is inferior to age) than I did in June.   In the first place, I have less of a creed, philosophically speaking. I think I have more knowledge of what the thoughts of men have been, and a less conscious faculty of choosing the true and refusing the false among them.

I wonder whether I shall remain a boy all my life in this respect.   I do not say this paradoxically, but having John Grote in my mind, who certainly retained with the freshness the indecisiveness of youth till the day of his death.   I wonder whether we are coming to an age of general inde-cisiveness ; I do not mean the frivolous scepticism of modern Philistines (I almost prefer the frivolous dogmatism of ancient ditto), but the feeling of a man who will not make up his mind till mankind has.   I feel that this standpoint is ulti-mately indefensible, because mankind have never made up their mind except in consequence of some individual having done so.   Still there seems to me to be the dilemma.   In the present age an educated man must either be prophet or persistent sceptic ; there seems no *media via*.   I have sold myself to metaphysics for 'a time and half a time' ; I do not as yet regret the bargain.   Take notice that I have finally parted from Mill and Comte—not without tears and wailings and cuttings of the hair.   I am at present an eclectic.   I believe in the possibility of pursuing conflicting methods of mental philosophy side by side.   I am at any rate in travail with an idea ; whether it is worth anything remains to be seen.

Nearly twenty years later, however, he had settled down to a mental course in which, while ever bent on the search after ultimate truth, he had abandoned any optimistic hope of formulating a satisfactory system in his own lifetime.   This is recorded in a remarkable passage in his diary, in which he gives expression to his passion for clear thought and true analysis apart from all hope of immediate results on a large scale. The interest of the work and the sense of the greatness of the quest after truth, however, kept him from practical pessimism. One effect on him of this attitude of mind was that he confined himself in his lectures to giving his pupils such a habit of clear analysis of the views of others as they could eventually use in formulating their own conclusions. He taught them no system of his own, but exhibited with unrivalled clearness the various systems with which their academic course required familiarity.

The immediate occasion of the entry in his diary of which I speak is a letter of criticism, on his method as a teacher, from his friend Professor Alfred Marshall. Sidgwick's note in comment would be hard to parallel in its absolute candour and fidelity of self-analysis :—

On Tuesday I received from him a long and very impressive letter, analysing my academic career. . . . He contrasted my lecture-room, in which a handful of men are taking down what they regard as useful for examination, with that of [T. H.] Green, in which a hundred men—half of them B.A.'s—ignoring examinations, were wont to hang on the lips of the man who was sincerely anxious to teach them the truth about the universe and human life. I have left out the partly courteous, partly affectionate—for Marshall is an old friend—padding of the letter, by which he meant to soften the pressure of these hard truths, but this is the substance.

I was much interested by this letter : reflected on my own life and career, and came to the conclusion that I would write down my own view of the causes of my academic failure—I mean my failure to attract men on a large scale.

First, my character and opinions. Once, in reading Bagehot's article on Clough, I noted a few sentences which struck me as applying also to myself. As follows :

' Though without much fame, he had no envy. But he

had a strong realism. He saw what it is considered cynical to see—the absurdities of many persons, the pomposities of many creeds, the splendid zeal with which missionaries rush on to teach what they do not know ; the wonderful earnestness with which most incomplete solutions of the universe are thrust upon us as complete and satisfying.' (This represents my relation to T. H. G. and his work.) ' " Le fond de la Providence," says the French novelist, " c'est l'ironie." Mr. Clough would not have said that, but he knew . . . what was the portion of truth contained in it. Undeniably this *is* an *odd* world, whether it should have been so or no ; and all our speculations upon it should begin with some admission of its strangeness and singularity. The habit of dwelling upon such thoughts as these will not of itself make a man happy, and may make unhappy one who is inclined to be so.'

I, however, am not unhappy, for destiny, which bestowed on me the dubious gift of this *vue d'ensemble*, also gave me richly all external sources of happiness—friends, a wife, congenial occupation, freedom from material cares ; but, feeling that the deepest truth I have to tell is by no means ' good tidings,' I naturally shrink from exercising on others the personal influence which would make men [resemble] me, as much as men more optimistic and prophetic naturally aim at exercising such influence. Hence, as a teacher, I naturally desire to limit my teaching to those whose bent or deliberate choice it is to search after ultimate truth ; if such come with vaguer aims, I wish, if possible, to train their faculties without guiding their judgements. I would not if I could, and I could not if I would, say anything which would make philosophy—my philosophy—popular.

As for ' over-regulation ' [another of Marshall's charges], it seems to me that there is an element of truth in it and an element of error. I have no desire to have my own way— not knowing sufficiently what way is my own—still less to coerce others. But I have a great desire in all social relations for definite understandings ; not knowing what road is best for humanity to walk in, I want all roads that claim to be roads to be well made and hedged in. This impulse may no doubt mislead to pharisaism and mere schematism that devitalizes the courses that kind nature keeps—perhaps it has misled me.

The union of a certain speculative pessimism with practical contentment, and even optimism, is a very interesting trait in Sidgwick's character. ' I have to fight against optimism rather vigorously,' he writes; ' my individual efforts are still rather baulked in most directions. Spiritualism is *in statu quo*; I see no sound methods for attacking philosophical problems; I am growing daily more sceptical in educational methods; politics are a blind free fight. With all this I am horribly and disgracefully conscious of *bien-être*.'

It was the predominant optimism of one who feels everything in life to be intensely interesting, quite apart from personal success, although a sufficiency in this last respect no doubt helped, at least negatively, in his happiness. His keen idealisation of the German student life, which he himself tasted for a time, was symptomatic in this respect. He told his friends that he felt in Germany almost as in his own home.

The note of contentment is prominent also in the later letters of Benjamin Jowett. But with Jowett it was far more the contentment which comes of attainment. Jowett idealised his work and the position he had achieved as Master of Balliol, and saw many cherished dreams realised at Oxford. Sidgwick had rather the *joie de vivre* of the intellectual epicure—of a nature with the very keenest perceptions—a joy in pursuing and criticising apart from the joy of attainment. He exulted in his strength. His intellect was

a fine machine which was well in hand, and he revelled
in its use as a Rubinstein might rejoice in the execution
of a *tour de force* on the pianoforte. His intellectual
grasp, his critical candour, his independence of
thought, all gave pleasure in their exercise; and one
subject of admiration to the present writer in Sidgwick's
use of these gifts was his firm stand against popular
fashions in thought or criticism, as when he at once
detected the one-sidedness of the Tübingen school and
the exaggerated praise bestowed on Stephen Phillips's
' Paolo e Francesca.' His interests were almost universal, and one special charm of his letters is the wide
range of subjects on which he gives his friends
criticisms at once delicate and illuminating. The
'magnificent senility' of Tennyson's later poems—
' Vastness,' for example—is appreciated by him as
keenly as the mellow wisdom of ' In Memoriam,' the
poem of his prime. Novels, from the tragedy of
Tolstoy's ' Anna Karénina ' to the pictures of placid
home life in the pages of Miss Yonge or the sparkling
humour of the ' Dolly Dialogues,' give him keen
pleasure. Politics and economics have their full share.

To a Catholic correspondent he writes on the
' Fioretti' of St. Francis of Assisi, and though the
book was quite new to him, the students of Franciscan
literature will appreciate the acute perception shown
in his remarks :

I send back the ' Fioretti.' . . . I am ashamed of having
kept it so long . . . but I found my Italian a little more
rusty than I had supposed, and only managed to read slowly.
I am sincerely obliged to you for directing my attention to

it. It has—or, rather, the first portion of it has for me—a quite unique and remarkable charm. By the first portion I mean rather more than half the first volume, *i.e.*, the chapters that relate to St. Francis himself. When one passes in reading to the narratives relating to miracles and visions of other 'frati,' I find that the peculiar attraction of the Franciscan stories has vanished ; it seems to depend on the individuality of the man. Compare the preaching to the birds in Chapter XVI. and the preaching to the fishes in Chapter XL. I do not quite know why the effect of the former is powerful and moving, while the latter is irresistibly comic ; but so I find it.

I also much prefer the *naïveté* of the earlier chapters to the more elaborate and precise style of the ' Considerations ' in the second volume, with their somewhat insistent glorification of the saint and his order. But this is, of course, the view of an outsider, who cannot approach the topic of the stigmata without a rather definite scientific presumption.

The great variety in Sidgwick's tastes and interests removes him far from the category of the typical metaphysician. He had in this respect something in common with a thinker whom he failed to appreciate— Cardinal Newman, whose mind J. A. Froude has described as ' world-wide,' and whose perceptions, physical and artistic as well as intellectual, were so delicate and keen.

With all his lack of enthusiasm for systems Sidgwick was capable of great enthusiasm for persons. Of Tennyson he writes from Freshwater: 'The occasional contemplation of the Laureate affords one of the purest pleasures our fallen nature has to give'; and when Tennyson dies it is to Sidgwick 'like the end of a reign—only there is no concluding "Vive le roi." It is impossible,' he writes, 'that anyone's thoughts and

words should be so entwined with the best moments
of the spring and summer of our lives. To us he
seems the last.'

More characteristic still, and very touching, is his
admiration for Fawcett's heroic constancy under his
blindness. He writes as follows on hearing the news
of Fawcett's death :

Just now think most of the wonderful success and
example of this life, which is now beyond the reach of time
and change. Some lines of Tennyson run in my head :

> O well for him whose will is strong !
> He suffers, but he will not suffer long ;
> For him . . .
> Not all Calamity's hugest waves confound,
> Who seems a promontory of rock,
> Tempest-buffetted, citadel-crowned.

He was a hero of a peculiar type, without any outward air of
self-sacrifice or suggestion of idealism in his ordinary talk,
and yet one felt that his determination to live the ordinary
life of a man, and a successful man—who gives pity and aid
more than he takes it—required a continual sustained effort
which did not draw its force from self-love alone ; it con-
tinually demanded and obtained the further force given by
the consciousness of the power of serving others ; and the
needs of this struggle gave to a nature, which, though large,
healthy and generous, was not originally characterised by
high moral aspiration, an elevation it would not otherwise
have had.

In spite of all that I have read of saints and sages, I feel
that if grievous physical calamity came upon me, yet one
that left the springs of physical energy unimpaired, I should
turn for strength to this example. I wonder how many
blind feel that he has opened the door of their prison-house
and shown them the way back to ordinary life : steep, yet
one that might be trodden by a steady and trustful step.

These sentences suggest to us something of the character of Sidgwick himself. He was indeed morally, as well as mentally, one of the great academic figures of our day, strenuous in effort, rich in sympathy, with high and simple aims, combining in his intellectual life a noble ideal with unrivalled powers of analysis and criticism, and, above all, with an intense passion for truth. On the stone at his grave those who knew and loved him best have put the words, 'In Thy light he shall see light.' Few philosophers have ever desired more earnestly to see that light; yet the very multiplicity of the points of view he realised so vividly made it harder for him than for most to concentrate his gaze upon it.

G.Hollyer.Photo.   EmeryWalker.Ph.Sc.

The Earl of Lytton
From a portrait by G.F. Watts
in the National Portrait Gallery
Painted in the year 1884

ROBERT EARL OF LYTTON
STATESMAN AND POET

LADY BETTY BALFOUR has given to the world a very fascinating character - study in the two published volumes of her father's letters.[1] The reflective habit which marked the late Lord Lytton, combined with his candour, modesty and insight, makes his correspondence serve to some extent the purposes of an autobiography. From early manhood to the last years of his life Robert Lytton was haunted by the feeling that he had somehow failed in his life to realise possibilities almost within his grasp. In an early letter he maintains that he has just missed intellectual greatness, and is yet so enamoured of the things of the mind as to lose all satisfaction in the commonplace and the humdrum. 'I am too clever,' he writes to his father at thirty, 'at least have too great a sympathy with intellect, to be quite content to eat the fruit of the earth as an ordinary young man, yet not clever enough to be ever a great man, so that I remain like Mohammed's coffin suspended between heaven and earth, missing the happiness of both, and neither trust nor am satisfied with myself. A little more or a little

---

[1] *Personal and Literary Letters of Robert, first Earl of Lytton.* Edited by Lady Betty Balfour 2 vols. London : Longmans. 1906.

H

less of whatever ability I inherit from you would have
made me a complete and more cheerful man.' He
regarded himself as one who appreciated many things,
and nevertheless wanted the power of concentration
required for full achievement.

Yet there is an obvious compensation in the interest
of the individuality here presented to us for what its
peculiar combination of gifts lacked so far as the
happiness of contentment was concerned. That interest is largely due to the very fact that Lord Lytton
touched life at so many points, was so rich in sympathy,
so wide in his imaginative grasp of things. His spirit
consequently dwelt in a world of possibilities so varied
that attainment could in no man, however gifted, have
borne any considerable proportion to imaginative conception. In this he shared only in the disappointment
of the poet as such—even of the greatest. The
completest, the most unalloyed satisfaction comes of
success in that on which our imaginative ideals mainly
concentrate themselves. Thus those who limit these
ideals to the practical possibilities of the future pave
the way for contentment. The barrister, whose day-
dreaming is of the Bench ; the soldier, whose absorbing
ideal of greatness is to be one day a general ; even the
cricketer or golfer to whom a high average or to be a
'scratch' player is the chief subject of his day-dreams—
all these, by the very narrowness of their mental lives,
bid for the happiness that comes of achievement allied
with contentment. With the poet it cannot be so.
To be a great or even a true poet his imagination
must live in mental realisation of so many cravings

which can never be satisfied, that achievement in his art cannot bring contentment. His own success as an artist cannot calm the habitual unsatisfied desires which belong to the world he dreams of, for his art alone belongs to the world in which he lives. So far, then, it would seem that not the lack of the highest intellectual achievement, but the very nature of the poet's mind, largely accounted for Lytton's unrest. It was largely the 'noble discontent' of one who dreams ever of the illimitable, and who has yet to put up with achievements which are of earth.

But in a letter written thirty years later to his daughter, when his days were all but at an end, when unlooked-for success had come in public life, and he was at the same time recognised, at all events by some critics of the first rank, as a very considerable poet, he puts the defect of his own life more truly, and poses a more interesting problem. Johnson tells us in ' Rasselas' that the attainable gifts of life are grouped on the one side of our path and on the other. We may choose between the groups, but if we try to gain both we shall miss both. Lytton seems to have felt at moments that this fate had befallen him. Had he resolutely withdrawn into the life of imagination for which his poet's nature fitted him, and put away the prizes which were offered by his openings in official life, happiness of one kind might, he thought, have been attained ; or if, on the contrary, he had fixed his ambition on the career to which external circumstances pointed, and crushed the poetic and Bohemian nature which accorded with it so imperfectly, his public success

might both have been greater and have brought contentment. The letter is so excellent a specimen of
the writer's power of frank and candid analysis that
I give it almost in full :

There is a fine passage in Schopenhauer which often
haunts me ; I wish I could quote it, but it is in substance to
this effect : that as a bird can only thrive in the air, a fish in
the water, so a man can only thrive in that element of life
which is suitable to his nature ; and that as life abounds in
pursuits and attainments good in themselves, and generally
good for all, but not equally good for each, therefore every
individual should select from the throng of good things life
offers him those only which are thoroughly suitable to his
nature, and eschew the rest. But, says Schopenhauer, many
a man covets and pursues objects, because he sees them
enjoyed and coveted by others, which, when attained, he is
incapable of enjoying. The man who does this lays up for
himself endless disappointment, and his way through life,
instead of being straight to the mark, is crooked and
wandering. My physical temperament has a great tendency
to beget blue devils, and when those imps lay siege to my
soul they recall these words of Schopenhauer's, and say to
me, 'Thou art the man !' Then I reflect that if I had acted
more selfishly—I don't mean in the bad, but the best sense
of the word, with more of that self-assertion which springs
from a man's confidence in the bent of his own nature, and
is the distinguishing mark of genius—I should have resolutely
eschewed a number of good things not suitable to my nature,
and should have bent the circumstances of my life into
conformity with the natural direction of the faculties best
fitted to render life fruitful. In my inability to do this I
recognise the absence of that mission without which the
imaginative faculty is a will-o'-the-wisp. On the other hand,
I reflect further, that if I had had more talent and common-
sense, more *savoir vivre*, I should have taken the really
fortunate circumstances of my life, without repining, as they
are, cheerfully adapted myself to them, and by placing

myself in unison with them, by the rejection of all antagonistic impulses and tendencies, I should have reaped from the field of a life so richly favoured in all its external conditions a fruitful harvest of content. In either case, my blue devils whisper to me, I should have been a happier and probably a better man, of more 'reasonable soul and flesh consisting.' But when my blue devils are cast out, and I recover sanity of spirits, then I say to myself just what you, dear, say to me in your letter—that the main thing is not to do but to be ; that the work of a man is rather in what he is than in what he does ; that one may be a very fine poet yet a very poor creature ; that my life has at least been a very full one, rich in varied experiences, touching the world at many points ; that had I devoted it exclusively to the cultivation of one gift, though that the best, I might have become a poet as great at least as any of my contemporaries, but that this is by no means certain to me, for my natural disinclination to, and unfitness for, all the practical side of life is so great that I might just as likely have lapsed into a mere dreamer ; that the discipline of active life and forced contact with the world has been specially good for me, perhaps providential, and that what I have gained from it as a man may be more than compensation of whatever I may have lost by it as an artist. Besides, there is this paramount consolation. I feel no doubt whatever that my official and public life has been in all ways more beneficial than the other, or any other, could have been for those I love and to the welfare of whose lives my own can be conducive. But, O my dear *alter ego,* enough and too much of this egotistical psychology !

To a great extent the last part of this letter replies successfully to the first—to the suggestions of the ' blue devils.' But a further reply, and the only adequate reply, is to be found in these two volumes and the two which preceded them some years ago, dealing with Lord Lytton's career as Viceroy of India. Dr. Johnson used to say that it was astonishing with what little mental superiority a man could make a great figure in public life. A great official, who in social intercourse displays the qualities which belong to the aristocracy of intellect, is a rare addition to the riches of the world. Two aristocracies meet in his person. And to sacrifice distinction in one kind in order to gain something more in the other would probably mean to lose a rare combination for doubtful or slight gain. A considerable figure in public life Lord Lytton certainly was. Whether he would have been much greater had he taken the second of the alternative paths he sketches in his letter—rigidly crushed his poet's nature, and attempted to destroy or deaden by disuse his very varied æsthetic and intellectual interests—is very doubtful. He won an official position in the first rank of Imperial administrators; whether he could under any circumstances have ranked with the very few statesmen or diplomatists who stand out as landmarks in each century I question. On the other hand, he had and he cultivated what so many public men are without, what makes a man supremely interesting to his fellows, what leads us to remember him, and to live with his thoughts long after he himself is gone. Lytton, as a diplomatist or Viceroy, more successful by one degree than he was, but without half those varied interests, aspirations, nay, those very inconsistencies which made him what these pages reveal, might perhaps have been more at peace in his own life. But the peace would have been rather a step in the direction of the placidity of the oyster than of that peace which is the crown of highest attainment, and

which cannot be won on earth by those who see and
feel most, because universal attainment is not of this
world.   His life would have had more unity, and some
of that satisfaction in looking back which is sometimes
called happiness, but probably far less of joy distri-
buted throughout its course.   The verdict on the
happiness of his own career passed by a man at its
termination can never be taken as though it were the
infallible judgment of one who sees all.   Such a verdict is at all times conditioned by the existing circumstances of the mind, even of the body which reacts on
the mind, in which it is formed.   'The devil was sick,
the devil a monk would be ; the devil got well, the
devil a monk was he,' is only the cynical expression of
a psychological and philosophical truth.

Against the verdict formed when in later years
'blue devils' possess the mind, may be set the verdict
when life is at its height.   The former cannot claim to
be necessarily the true one.   And if even from the
standpoint of his own happiness there is much to be
said for the duality of Robert Lytton's life, for posterity,
and therefore for fame, there is much more.   What
removes the second Lord Lytton far from being only
the man who attained to the position of Governor-
General of India is just this many-sided nature which
the correspondence before us reveals.   To clear this
verdict from all suspicion of special pleading I will
add that I do not doubt the truth of Lord Lytton's
candid avowals of his own deficiency in strength of
will, nor do I imply that he might not have largely
kept his varied interests and yet lived more consis-

tently and with more self-restraint as one who had a
' mission ' in life—to use his own expression.   But I do
submit that the dual existence he led was to a large
degree necessary to the interest of his life and to a due
measure of self-realisation.   To adopt Goethe's most
true sentiment (which, however, Lord Lytton himself
rejects), the 'stream of the world,' with which public
life brought him in contact, not only gave him great
opportunities, but perforce disciplined his character
and diminished the Bohemian tendency to which the
poet's nature is so liable ; whereas to think of him, on
the other hand, as the mere official, is to place him on
a par with hundreds of officials whose very names will
be forgotten, while his very interesting individuality
retains its niche among the remarkable men of the
century.

As has been already intimated, these volumes and
their predecessors should be read as a whole to obtain
an adequate idea of what Robert Lord Lytton really
was.   All I propose to do here is to call attention to
some characteristic traits of a character in so many
respects both touching and interesting.   If I were to
single out one quality which marks him off from other
many-sided and brilliant men, I should say that it was
' humanity ' in the wide sense of the word, including,
but not at all confined to, the more restricted sense
in which it is sometimes used as the equivalent of
kindness.   He had a very genius for friendship.   His
own poetic inspiration was kindled by nothing more
than by the sympathy of kindred spirits.   He had a
kindly and humorous eye, open to all the varied play

of human feeling in the society in which he found himself, and the drama of his own life also found in him an appreciative spectator. His letters to Mr. John Morley, Mr. Wilfrid Blunt, Mr. Forster, and Sir James FitzJames Stephen display this sympathetic habit of observation and description. They reveal also his special gifts for friendship. He puts his whole self into his correspondence. His intimate talks would last far beyond cock-crow; and he jokingly said of himself and a friend that if ever they should have sunstroke it would be before going to bed.

None of Lord Lytton's friendships are more attractive than that for de Villers, Saxon Secretary of Embassy at Vienna. ' He was a man,' writes Lady Betty Balfour, ' in whom French wit mingled with German fancy, a poet who did not write poetry, a musician who did not write music, a scholar and a romantically devoted friend. He was a bachelor and poor, and Robert Lytton cherished dreams of a literary partnership which should prove in its results a very gold mine to them both. Dreams of an Eldorado never realised.' Lytton's own meditations on life —on his own life, on that of his friends, on that of the human race—display the quality I have referred to—a keen, a wide appreciation of all that is human; and his close and serious analysis was relieved by a boyish sense of fun. The simplicity and reality, and still more the universality, of human sympathy is the quality which is most often damaged or killed by a great worldly position, and therefore it is especially worthy of note in the instance before us.

Official rank more often than not brings with it a characteristic analogous to what is known in the universities as 'donnishness.' Of this characteristic Robert Lytton had not the faintest trace. We see in these letters the 'human' quality of mind which I am endeavouring to indicate in its many forms, and it can only be faithfully represented to the reader by preserving in the few extracts I shall give just those intimate personal touches, and those specimens of candid thinking aloud, which mark them off from literary essays written for the many.

Let us read Lord Lytton on the drama of human life and what Tennyson calls 'the passion of the past.' The following remarks in a letter to Mr. John Morley were suggested by news from his correspondent concerning the Queen of Holland, whom Lytton had known in his early youth and associated in his mind with the generation that was gone by :

Tempi passati! All this belongs to a bygone generation already. When I recall my diplomatic experiences and acquaintances I feel wondrous old. I knew intimately Clay and Webster, and I feel that between them and the American politicians of to-day there is a political century. I knew the old Prince Metternich, and this fact makes me sometimes feel as if I had actually assisted (as an unpaid attaché) at the Congress of Vienna. I remember as a boy hearing the old Duke of Wellington talk about Soult and the Peninsular War whilst warming his venerable *rear* quarters at the fireplace of the great drawing-room at Hatfield House. It is only the other day that I was listening to Guizot's reminiscences of his own youth. How weird it all seems and eerie! How little the longest life counts in the progress of anything; how far back the shortest life can reach, vicariously, in the retrospect of all things ; how fast we grow old, how soon our enthusiasms are quenched, how rapidly the march of the mass passes beyond the point at which each individual member of it halts! During the last week I have been looking over and sorting old letters from my father to myself, with the object of selecting from them those which may be available as materials for his biography. Oh dear, oh dear, what ghosts these old letters evoke! I have carefully kept every letter he ever wrote to me. When I now re-read those which I received from him while I was yet a boy at Harrow, I wince at his reproofs, blush at his reprovals, as though I were still fourteen, with a vague, ghostly consciousness of having in some quite other planet passed beyond the age of forty. And amongst those old letters I now and then come across old verses of my own, some of them written, I verily believe, when I was twelve years old! 'Oh, the pity of it, Iago, the pity of it!'

Very human, too, are his reflections to Lady Bloomfield on the welcome pause for reflection which the weeks of convalescence give now and again, when, with no distraction, we can review our own life in its entirety as spectators of the drama rather than actors in it :

I think sickness or ill-health of any kind which is enough to confine one to a sick-room for many weeks, but not enough to absorb all one's faculties during that time in the endurance of physical pain, is a most beneficent and refreshing event. I know of none which better deserves to be called a godsend. It enables one to extricate not only one's arms and legs, but also one's thoughts and feelings (often more easily tired than arms and legs!) from this noisy, eager crowd of earthly activities and needs through which we struggle to our graves. It gives us time to look before and after, to review the past, realise the present, and more clearly contemplate the future. What better place than the sick-bed, when fever has fled from it, and the body is at rest, and

the mind unemployed upon mean details of life's hourly
struggle for leave to live—what better place than this to sum
up life's results so far as life has gone—examine ourselves
and our gains and losses of love, hope, faith and courage?
It is so wholesome and, thank God! so comforting, if there
be no crime gnawing the conscience, to be able now and
then, as we journey on through its few hasty years, to look
upon life from some point of view which reduces it to its
real dimensions and proportions, showing us how little are
the things which the world in general calls great, and how
mighty, how momentous are the things which are so generally
accounted of little worth. As the perspective widens how
the objects dwindle in size which, when close before us, seem
to fill up so much of life's space! What a small thing,
in one sense, how brief at the longest, how paltry at the
mightiest, is this single phase of man's immortal, inde-
structible existence! and yet in another sense how important
every least thought, feeling or action with which the soul, as
she passes through this earthly life, defines her own image in
permanent outline on the immense background of eternity!
Thoughts like these of late, as I lie here in bed, seemingly
idle, and really very busy, have led me very, very often to
you, dear friend. For at such times there comes upon the
heart a great yearning towards those whom, at such times
more than ever, the heart instinctively calls into commune,
as its natural kindred. I wonder whether you have ever felt
me near you? You have so often seemed to be near me, and
we have had many silent talks together.

A sad note in his philosophy of life is struck in a
letter to John Forster on spring and winter: a letter
written at the age of thirty-one, before youth, so often
the period most given to pessimism, was gone by:

O Spring! Spring! the ever new! how I bless God for
thy sake! Strange! I cannot conceive, dear Forster, why
men have so universally taken Winter for the death-picture
and Spring for the life-picture in Nature. It strikes me

quite otherwise. In Winter I see, everywhere, Life as it is : the life of use and wont, and apathetic habit ; the enduring need ; the painful struggle with difficulty ; the cramped energy ; the long imprisonment ; the want of warmth. *That* is Life. But Spring? No. All that boundless emancipation, the deep, deep exultation and triumph, the wonder, the novelty, the surprise of every movement, the fresh beginning of untried things—the escape from the staled and the spoiled experience, the joy, the freedom, the confident impulse, the leaping entrance into the realm of limitless possibility, surely all this is Death—or else there is no good God in heaven ; and under the heaven of Spring who would help being sure of the goodness of God? I send you the first primrose I have seen this year. I hailed it as the star of how many pleasant hopes! Here is a fine red beetle crawling over my letter. He has put on his holiday coat—obviously quite new—a splendid vest of scarlet slashed with black—all to do honour to Spring.

Of the deeper side of his human sympathies a touching and beautiful illustration is to be found in this letter to his friend, Theodore Gomprez, on the death in England of a beloved nephew, the only child of his sister :

'Whom the gods love die young,' says the old proverb. Those souls are doubtless fortunate on whose perfect promise at the full Death sets his indelible *fecit*, thereby placing them at once amongst the Maker's completed works, manifestations of power and beauty finished by their own rare felicity of being beyond all need of the slow, tentative, defective process of life's gradual fulfilment. I can understand that. I can conceive cause to be glad—glad for all men's sake—that any human spirit should be so happily formed as to fulfil at once the purpose of man's passage through life by simply revealing itself, and having thereby proved its right *of birth* to all that others acquire only by right of *conquest*, pass lightly upward and onward without effort and without delay. But the unseen hand that strikes from the cripple the crutch to which he clings selects for special theft the poor man's one ewe lamb, and snatches the water-cup from the lips that are most parching—this staggers and stuns experience, and almost seems to leave no way through the mystery of things here, but the way of some poor beast of burden that, in obedience of a will he can neither anticipate nor comprehend, is turned about to right or left by the blows that fall on his back. . . . Perhaps life with all its various experiences is no more in the inscrutable purpose of Providence than so much stuff of different kinds for the spirit to work upon, and thereby prove its power, putting itself, as it were, in evidence before the great spirit of all—as fire shows itself, and proves its power, by burning, not by the thing it burns ; and the circumstantial result of such working of the spirit—the stuff on which it works, and the earthly residuum of its working, whether joy or sorrow, ashes or smoke—can be of no permanent con-sequence to the individual spirit, or innermost nature of man, which has worked upon it, thereby kindling, showing and setting itself free.   If that be the case, or anything like the case, in this great sorrow of your dear sister's, and in your own, dearest friend, this great sorrow and power of sorrowing, there is such great love, and power of loving, that I for one must trust, by all my trust in all things good and noble, that such sorrowing cannot be in vain.   But there is a profanation to true sorrow in all speculation as to the possibility of its spiritual profit.   Not to your sister, scarcely to yourself, dare I speak of this.   With her, and with you, dear friend, all my thoughts and feelings sympathise too closely to explore, apart from your own, any portion of that experience which is yet untraversed by your grief.   Rather must I remain with you, where you are now, on the road of life.   I honour your grief.   How should I hope to comfort it ?

It is hard to write of this sacred subject without diverging for a moment to quote Stevenson's match-less four stanzas, in case to any reader they may still be unknown :

Yet, O stricken heart, remember, O remember
How of human days he lived the better part.
April came to bloom, and never dim December
Breathed its killing chills upon the head and heart.

Doomed to know not Winter, only Spring, a being
Trod the flowery April blithely for a while,
Took his fill of music, joy of thought and seeing,
Came and stayed and went, nor ever ceased to smile.

Came and stayed and went, and now when all is
finished,
You alone have crossed the melancholy stream ;
Yours the pang, but his, O his, the undiminished,
Undecaying gladness, undeparted dream.

All that life contains of torture, toil and treason,
Shame, dishonour, death, to him were but a name.
Here, a boy, he dwelt through all the singing season,
And ere the day of sorrow departed as he came.

Lytton's sense of atmosphere and humorous appreciation of the peculiarities of the human beings with
whom he found himself—a part of the quality of
'humanity' which I am emphasising—appear in many
of his letters. Here is one written to John Forster
during Lytton's first sojourn in Paris as Secretary
to the Embassy in the days of Lord Lyons. The
year was 1873, that of Thiers's Presidency. Lytton's
admiration for Napoleon III. perhaps deepened his
sentiments as to the meanness and ignobility of the
Presidential Court. He thus writes after his first
evening at the Elysée :—

Hitherto the fact of finding myself in a palace has inspired
me with the most democratic sentiments, but then being in a
palace involved being in the presence of royalty. To-night
the aspect of this palace had certainly a contrary effect on

me, and I contemplated all my neighbours *du haut de ma grandeur de gentleman Anglais*. For a scrubbier, drearier, more ignoble set of male and female odds and ends were never, I think, gathered together in closer contact or more glaring contrast with the relics of departed grandeur. There were the old Empire tapestries and furniture, all marked with the bees, and thunder-bolts, and N's uneffaced ; and squatted upon one of those Imperial instruments of torture, a sofa as old-fashioned and inconvenient as her husband's commercial policy, there was Madame Thiers, fatly purring asleep. To her I was first presented, and in the hopes of giving her time to awake I turned my talk in the style of St. Paul, which English Greek scholars tell me is a very courtly as well as intellectual style. I crammed my sentences with parentheses each a yard long, in order to make them last. But I only succeeded in putting her into a deeper slumber. Then I tried the effect of silence, which gradually awoke her. She lifted a drowsy eyelid like the Nibelungen dragon, jerked her tail, and mumbled an excuse for the rooms being insufficiently heated, plaintively explaining that there had not been time to put calorifers in the house. In point of fact, however, the temperature of the rooms was that of a baker's oven. Then I was re-presented to Thiers, whom I had known before. He was furious with Grévy, whose resignation Madame Thiers called a *mauvais tour*. We talked about Spanish affairs. I asked him what he thought of the chances of the Carlists. This I did because the old rascal has been complaining to Bismarck of the assistance rendered (he says) by England to Don Carlos. He replied, ' I can only say what Fontenelle said of ghosts : *Je ne crois pas au revenants, mais pourtant je les crains.*' This was the only *mot* I heard this evening at a gathering of notables whose dulness would have disgraced even a London drum.

I was going to say that the rooms were full of men, but in fact they were not full at all. With the exception, however, of Madame Thiers and her sister, a thin repetition of herself, the only women present were my unfortunate Edith (with a bad headache) and a lively, affected little Princess Dolgorouky

(Russian), who luckily for me is an old acquaintance of mine. I sprang at her as a new-born babe springs from the strangeness of the world it has just entered to its mother's breast, or as a bulldog springs at the throat of its victim—and I should have stuck to her with bulldog tenacity if Lyons had not carried me off to introduce me to Léon Say, the Finance Minister, . . . who plunged at once into a technical harangue to me on the English Sugar Duties, a subject about which I need not assure you I am profoundly ignorant. I thought it prudent to assent to everything he said. But he seemed to expect me to argue each point with him, and looked disappointed each time I said *Oui*.

He notes among Frenchmen a singularly candid way of referring to their own defects in the following words—embodying, we may suppose, a slight parody — written to the same correspondent :

The tone in which the French people talk of themselves is really astonishing—in the third person, as if they were impartial or rather contemptuous spectators of their own follies.

' Voyez-vous, Monsieur ; le peuple Français est un gros enfant—qui n'a pas le sens commun. Les Français ne savent pas se gouverner—ça aime du tapage—c'est un peuple inconséquent qui n'est jamais sérieux. Croyez-moi, Monsieur, ce qu'il faut à ce pays c'est un bon despotisme.'

This is the sort of self-criticism you hear on all sides round. A workman said to me yesterday, ' L'ouvrier c'est de la canaille.' Shopkeepers say, ' Le fait est, Monsieur, que la bourgeoisie est poltronne.'

Of Lytton's treatment in his correspondence of deeper problems in relation to man's destiny in another life and religious beliefs in this, I will only say that those who differ from him most widely will recognise the absolute reality and candour of his reflections—

I

qualities very rare, and not least rare among hereditary believers, whose deficiency in this respect is doubtless responsible for Tennyson's famous lines on 'honest doubt.' At a time when insincere or only half-sincere reflection is waste of the time which might have been valuable indeed if devoted to simple and earnest thought on such subjects, this characteristic of Lytton's discussions will have its attractions for many. We see in a letter published in this collection and addressed to the present writer that, of alternative forms of fixed faith, Catholicism attracted him most :

> To my mind it is not only in her liturgy and her ritual, but far more in her real catholicity, her vast humanity, her organisation, so flexible and yet so firm, so sympathetically and sagaciously adapted to the idiosyncrasies of all her children, that the Catholic Church transcends all others, Greek or Protestant, and justifies her proud title of the Church Catholic. . . . For all sorts of reasons I shall never become a Catholic. But a Catholic I should certainly be if I could get over the initial difficulties of belief common to all the Churches. Perhaps the main reason why I shall never get over those difficulties is that I have no inclination to get over them, no 'wish to believe'— in that particular sense. I do not feel my mental attitude to be in this direction an irreligious one—at least, it is a profoundly reverential one. But the tremendous problems presented by observation of the natural world and human life do not affect me as *difficulties* but as *mysteries*—which, in this life at least, must ever so remain. I cannot bring myself to look upon the universe as a book of riddles, and dogmatic theology as a book of answers to them. Evil, pain, birth, death, the unfathomable sense of right and wrong, the constant, unappeasable yearning of the soul for the unseen substance, coupled with the inveterate inability of the mind to get beyond phenomena ; the cruel inequalities of human life, the bewildering multiplicity of accepted revelations ; the

intense suffering which our higher nature endures in contact
with circumstance, and the comparative impunity with which
our lower nature is so often indulged—all these mysteries I
contemplate with a sensation, not of terror, but of awe and
worshipful wonder.   The immensity of them, the sense of
infinitude they excite in me, does not inspire fear, but rather
a vague hopefulness, a strange sort of subdued, inarticulate,
passive conviction that in so infinite a scheme of things
nothing can be irrevocably lost or go irrevocably wrong,
nothing appear or pass without the best of all reasons in
relation to a purpose and a power that transcends reason.
I suppose that a convinced Christian would call this a
dangerous state of mind, and being asleep in sin.   But I
don't *feel* the danger of it.   If my contemplation of these
mysteries and my sense of the unknowableness of the
unknown exasperated and afflicted me—if they threw me
into a state of revolt and panic—I would turn for rescue from
such a condition, not only to Christian dogma, but to that
dogma in its most authoritative form—*the most authoritative*,
because what I should then need and hope to find in dogma
would not be a rational explanation of such things, but a compelling guide to faith in their unexplained beneficence—a
potent aid to trust and rest in the contemplation of them.

With these extracts I take leave of this book.
As it is not my object to deal with the tremendous
moral problems which the story of any life opens up,
I shall not attempt here to discuss the peculiar variety
of semi-agnosticism which the letter just cited dis-
closes.   Lord Lytton's position was halfway between
the agnosticism of all Christians who realise that God
is inscrutable, and that of the more or less aggressive
Agnostics of the school of the late Professor Tyndall.
How far his attitude towards Christianity was determined by the form in which it had been presented to
him in youth, and how far his deep reverence for

Christian ethics presupposed a creed latently, if not explicitly, believed in, we have not full material to learn with any certainty. The light thrown in his letters on such questions is merely incidental. But the collection may be heartily commended as being in reality what it professes to be—a human document, and a document of the highest interest.

FATHER IGNATIUS RYDER.

From a Photograph by C. G. Mason.

FATHER IGNATIUS RYDER

A REMINISCENCE

WITH the death of Father Henry Ignatius Dudley
Ryder in November, 1907, a distinguished figure
passed from our midst.   Father Ryder was the last of
those Oratorian Fathers whose names are immortalised
in the concluding section of the 'Apologia.'   He is
best known to students of theological literature as the
author of one of the very best pieces of controversial
polemic penned in our own time—his reply to Dr.
Littledale's ' Plain Reasons against Joining the Church
of Rome.'   His straightness, his thoroughness, his
very wide theological reading, his absolute candour—
an intellectual quality so rare among the adepts in
scholastic dialectics—his sense of humour and power of
satire, all combine to make this little volume a veritable
masterpiece in argument, and in some sense a work
of art.   Father Ryder wrote also some excellent fugi-
tive essays for 'The Nineteenth Century' and for
'The Dublin Review,' which will, it is to be hoped, be
reprinted in a collected form.   His work was kept
before the attention of the general public by the
admiration of his literary skill frequently expressed by
R. H. Hutton in 'The Spectator.'   I remember my
father speaking of him in 1881 as by far the best

theologian in England, and I do not know who could dispute the title with him up to the time when his health broke down.   His analysis of the Church's infallibility, in three pamphlets, brimful of theological learning, published just forty years ago, will always remain helpful and instructive for every theologian, whichever side he may take of the controversy of which they formed a part.

Yet those who had the privilege of knowing him always felt that his literary output bore but a small proportion to the gifts of the man, and that his controversial work represented but a minor part of his mental powers. A nearer view of him is to be obtained from a brief volume which he gave to the world a quarter of a century ago, a collection of short poems. This is less widely known than his reply to Dr. Littledale, but it presents a far truer picture of one whose whole nature and temperament were those of a poet. If, in the few pages which shall here be devoted to his memory, I adopt partly the form of reminiscence, with illustrative extracts from his letters and poems, it is because in no other way can I indicate that personal equation which is necessary to the appreciation of a remarkable man, and which his printed writings do not adequately convey. The very sensitive fastidiousness, which made him so slow to publish—which made his known works, therefore, so inadequate a representation of their author—was a part of the refinement of intellect, of the old-world hatred of advertisement, of the love of literary art for its own sake and apart from all thought of fame, which were among the qualities

which made him memorable.   If he gave us comparatively little, it was not that he had little to give, but
largely because, as the French proverb has it, 'The
better was the enemy of the good.'   His literary ideal
was so high, his self-criticism so unsparing, that much
which might have secured him a wider reputation was
set aside.   Quantity was sacrificed in preference to
letting the world see anything which he himself felt to
fall short of his own high standard in quality.

Father Ryder's name was very familiar to me forty
years ago, when he published his strictures on my
father's views, expressed in 'The Dublin Review,' as
to the exact extent of Papal infallibility.   Those were
days of great excitement in the theological and ecclesiastical world.   The invasion of the States of the
Church, a prolonged drama of iniquitous spoliation
which lasted over ten years, had aroused a sentiment
of intense loyalty to the Holy See among Catholics.
Nowhere was that loyalty more conspicuous than at
the Birmingham Oratory, in no public discourse more
eloquently expressed than in Cardinal Newman's
sermon on 'The Pope and the Revolution.'   But there
was a real danger lest the temporal power, so brutally
assailed, should be spoken of in the excitement of the
time as of right an inseparable adjunct of the Papacy
by those whose feelings were stronger than their
reason, and who seemed to forget how many centuries
the Papacy had existed without it.   And a similar
danger of exaggerated statement was apparent in
France among the friends of M. Veuillot, of 'The
Univers,' in respect of the extent of Papal infallibility.

Father Ryder was one of those who had misgivings lest this tendency might very seriously confuse the long-recognised theological teaching, and he wrote a pamphlet called 'Idealism in Theology,' very witty as well as very learned, in which he joined issue with my father's arguments—arguments which, though resting on a clear theological basis and falling short of Louis Veuillot's positions, tended in the same direction. He stamped the general line of his argument on the memory by one of those witty epigrams which were so characteristic of him, describing a prerogative of infallibility which should attach to every word of the Pope as 'a gift which, like Midas's touch of gold, would be very wonderful but very inconvenient.'

I remember the first echoes that reached me and my brothers, as boys, concerning this daring young man, brilliant indeed, but dangerous and really impertinent, who had entered the lists against our father. The first sentiment among us was horror at his audacity. Then came mollifying rumours. Some things had not been meant quite in the sense at first supposed. The bold young man had really read his theology to some purpose. His private letters, moreover, showed him to be very witty. He was still young. He might some day learn the error of his ways.

The fact was that, as so often happened, my father's keen human sympathies had been at work, qualifying his controversial *animus*. His undying love for Father Newman, who had first sent him Father Ryder's pamphlet, had also been doing its part. A correspond-

ence which began mainly in the desire for explaining
theological issues and saving waste of time in controversy had grown more intimate and more personal.
Ryder, as he often told me, was amazed to find the
real W. G. Ward, as shown in his letters, so unlike
the embodiment of relentless logic and dogmatic posi-
tiveness which his theological articles had made him
appear.   In this as in other cases a public controversy
had ended with my father in something like a private
friendship.   Ryder's subsequent pamphlets were far
gentler in tone.   And in his last published letter to
my father he wrote : ' You must allow me to thank
you publicly for what the public does not know—the
chivalrous good humour of your private letters to one
who was publicly your foe.'

That their relations had become friendly and even
familiar is clear from the few letters from Father
Ryder which my father preserved.   It was his habit
to burn all letters he received, and these must have
survived accidentally or for purposes of theological
reference.   An occasional touch of pleasantry, almost
of jocosity, enlivened their correspondence, even before
the public controversy had ended.   In the course of a
letter complaining of the expense of publishing theological pamphlets Father Ryder writes : ' I wonder
whether a rejoinder in verse would sell, entitled, we
will say, " Ward's Reformation in Six Cantos [1] ; or,
Pighius Redivivus"?'   And when my father com-
municated to him his intention of giving a very brief

---

[1] This refers, of course, to the well-known book, Ward's *Cantos on
the Reformation.*

summary of the controversy at its conclusion, Father
Ryder wrote on May 17, 1868 : 'It relieves me to
hear that your summary will be so short. As to its
probable effect on me, I can only say that I hope we
shall be able to swallow and be swallowed after our
kind good-humouredly, like the excellent little fishes
in " Ethel's Book of Angels." '

In the following years we heard of Father Ryder
chiefly as the regular intermediary between Father
Newman and my father. The final estrangement
between these two, owing to the opposite lines they
had taken on the question of the proposed oratory at
Oxford, had led to their direct correspondence practically ceasing. But my father's feeling for his former
leader remained to the end the strongest of his life,
and indirect communications took place through Father
Ryder. When the 'Grammar of Assent' appeared
an old point of sympathy between Newman and my
father as to the true philosophy of religious belief was
revived ; and the latter expressed his pleasure in the
work to Father Ryder, who wrote in reply : 'I am
glad you like the Father's book. I thought you
would. He is pleased to know you like it, and says
it is very good news. I feel sure he would be pleased
if you wrote to him about it '—a suggestion on which
my father acted, bringing the pleasant reply from
Newman which is printed in 'W. G. Ward and the
Catholic Revival.'

At the time of Newman's answer to Mr. Gladstone
in 1874, again, an interchange of still more kindly
letters ensued between Newman and my father, owing

largely to Father Ryder's good offices. I well remember my father's happy smile as he said one day :
'Here is a kind letter from Newman ; at last the old
signature again, "Yours affectionately." '

When Father Ryder's answer to Dr. Littledale
appeared, under the title of ' Catholic Controversy,' in
1881, just a year before my father's death, Ryder thus
replied to his letter of congratulation :

I am very glad you think ' Catholic Controversy' good of
its kind, and I can quite understand that a man of your
hearty theological appetite must feel tantalised by the
presentation of so many sips and scraps, the mere preludes
and frustrations of a meal.   Many thanks for your correction,
the worst blot as yet discovered.   There are several, but I
leave them for friends to find.   I have not yet got over my
initial horror of my child, my irreformable child, but I am
very grateful for any corrections or emendations, which may
avail if ever he comes to a second edition.

Three times a meeting between my father and
Father Ryder was planned, but my father's uncertain
health led in each case to its postponement, and they
never did meet.

My own acquaintance with Father Ryder began
in 1885.   Cardinal Newman wrote me a very kind
letter on reading my book, ' The Wish to Believe,'
and a visit from me to the Oratory was the consequence.   I saw much of Father Ryder on the occasion
of this visit, and came to know for the first time his
striking and handsome presence, which his friends
well remember, and in the course of long talks became
familiar with the exceptional qualities of his conversation—so full of humanity, of humour, of information

derived from wide and varied reading.   It was a personality at once extremely sympathetic and fastidiously
refined—with the refinement of the scholar, and with
something also about him of the great gentleman.
We corresponded a good deal afterwards at intervals.
In the two succeeding years we exchanged views on
the Irish question, which was naturally then to the
front, and which greatly exercised a small dining
society of which the late Lord Emly was president
and I was secretary, our common friend, the late Mr.
R. H. Hutton, being a constant attendant at its meetings.   I have found two letters from Father Ryder
bearing on the subject, the second of which has special
interest as showing the great Cardinal's activity of
mind in extreme old age.   The first letter is dated
February 3, 1886, and runs as follows :

My dear Ward,—I am very glad to see your handwriting
again.   I have given your message to the Cardinal, with
which he was very much pleased.   He spoke of you very
kindly and warmly.   I hope you will not miss an opportunity
of paying him another visit.   I must put off till then fairly
going into these political questions.   On the strength of your
recommendation I have routed out the last 'Spectator.'
Well, I cannot say it evoked my enthusiasm.   I am not sure
that these moderate Liberals are not the most responsible of
all for the present mess.   What does the 'Spectator' want?
It will not have Home Rule ; it shrinks from coercion, and
it denounces the poor late Government for its lack of a
definite Irish policy.   You must not think from this that I
do not care for Hutton.   I like to hear him on literary and
directly ethical points, but on politics he is more Gladstonian
than Gladstone himself, in that which is most characteristic
of Gladstone, namely, the sitting between two stools. . . .

A petition to Rome on the Irish question was planned by our dining society—I forget its exact purport—and we asked the Cardinal's judgment as to its wisdom. This is the subject of Father Ryder's other letter, dated April 14, 1887 :

I have read your letter to the Cardinal. We had a long talk over it. I have seldom seen him more interesting and bright. It ended in his saying that it was impossible for him to give an opinion, except with the draft of your petition before him. My advice to you is to draw up something, bring it down with you, and talk it over.

I find it hard to give you an idea of his talk. He agreed with me in feeling the difficulty of avoiding on the one hand, as you proposed doing, all reflection on A. B., and exhibiting at the same time a justification of what looked at first sight like interference with another's cause. . . . On the whole I think the conversation tended to throw cold water on the project, but I do wish you would come and talk it out ; the Cardinal is in fine form and must be particularly well.

Our petition never came off, but it gave me a good reason for more than one visit to the Oratory. In the following year extreme old age did at last show signs of finally prevailing with the Cardinal, though a wonderful rally in the autumn, after death had been regarded as imminent, is chronicled in the following letter from Ryder, dated November 3, 1888 :

I have a very good account to give you of the Cardinal, from whom I have just come. He is really recovering. The doctors consider the dangerous crisis over, but death has been very near, and it was necessary to give him the Last Sacraments. It was simply weakness, drowsiness and re-pugnance for food, but that in an intense degree. He has been sitting up to-day in his chair, and is now lying dressed upon his bed He is really recovering strength and appetite

I gave him your message, and he talked of you and your wife with much feeling, and charged me to thank you very much.

In the following year ' Lux Mundi ' appeared, and Canon Gore's essay in that volume brought the question of Biblical Criticism to the front. I treated it in a tentative way in an article for ' The Nineteenth Century ' entitled ' New Wine in Old Bottles,' which the Cardinal allowed me to send him in proof. At about the same time a certain Father Bartolo brought out a book on the extent of Papal infallibility, in which a far more liberal view was taken than that of Ryder himself, which had incurred so much adverse criticism at the time of his controversy with my father. Yet Father Bartolo's book had the formal approval of Cardinal Manning. It was indeed a moment of reaction after the very stringent views which had been generally current during the pontificate of Pius IX. The two publications above referred to are alluded to in an interesting letter from Father Ryder to myself dated June 7, 1890 :

The Cardinal had your article read to him, and enjoyed it very much, I am told. I have not read more than Gore's essay out of ' Lux Mundi,' and one other, which I am afraid has not left any impression on my mind. I wonder if you remember enough about my controversy with your father to understand my sensations at seeing a book come out with the enthusiastic approval of the Archbishop which leaves me in the position of an ancient Whig in regard to modern Radicalism. There is no point of mine against your father which Bartolo does not assert and go beyond me. He gives up the infallibility of dogmatic facts and canonisation, etc., and he comes forward like Richard III. between two bishops,

Manning and Hefele. I wonder what old X. thinks, who preached my funeral sermon in 'The Westminster Gazette,' giving me a berth with Luther and Jansenius. If I were mischievous I could make folks' ears tingle, but I content myself with saying, 'Tempus spargendi lapides, et tempus iterum colligendi.' There is a time for uttering big things, and again a time for swallowing them. I am sure in Pius IX.'s time Bartolo would have been on the Index within a month of publication, and 'The Dublin' would have sung his Requiem ; . . . seriously, what a lesson it is against strong language.

The Cardinal died in August, and in the following November Father Ryder was elected his successor as Superior of the Oratory. His reply to my congratulations was very characteristic :

My troubles [he wrote] are mainly as yet in anticipation. At present I am sensible of a mild gratification at having been so far thought well of, abstracting altogether from the consideration of my deserts. I have hitherto been a more or less somnolent inside passenger, and a coachman's seat seems very strange to me. I need all the prayers my friends can spare.

Ryder and I worked hard together, in company with R. H. Hutton of 'The Spectator,' writing letters and articles in defence of Cardinal Newman against Dr. Abbott's attack entitled 'Philomythus,' which was published in the following year. I have quite a multitude of letters on this subject, but their interest is controversial rather than personal. Dr. Abbott's evasions in the controversy aroused the anger of Father Ryder. 'You must simply stand over the shifty man until he confesses,' he wrote. His own treatment of the subject in 'The Nineteenth Century'

was exhaustive and extremely able.   He wrote while
he was at work on it, however, in his usual tone of
self-disparagement :

I ought to have written before to thank you for your
work in 'The Spectator,' '*pro mortuo nostro.*' Please
express to Mr. Hutton the pleasure his articles have given
us.   Your points from Eusebius are just what were needed
to break the force of the rampant aggression.   I see he
avails himself of the dodge which he imputes to Newman, of
indefinite adjournment, but of course more is wanted.   I
am working slowly and clumsily, I am afraid, through the
business with the idea of backing up, to use a cricket
expression.   Probably before I can get done you or someone
else will have done it much better.

A few days later he writes :

I am depressed with the difficulty of being bright and
brief and thorough on such a ponderous dog.

On the anxious problem of our time raised by the
speculations and discoveries of the critical and historical
sciences in their relation to theology he wrote me
many wise things.   His general attitude is summed up
in a characteristic sentence from a letter of 1895 :
'The Church as a wise householder brings forth from
her store things new and old : but the cry of "new
outlooks," "new departures" to my mind suggests the
nervous action of Sister Anne.'

I recall two other good sayings on the same
subject—one in print and one in a letter to myself.
The former refers to the contrast, emphasised in the
words I have just cited, between the normal and
cautious development which the needs of the times
may demand within the Church, and the cry of 'liberty'

and 'progress' which was being raised by the more
advanced 'Liberal' Catholics.   He wrote to this
effect :

The Catholic Church, like every old building, accumulates
dust, and the process of dusting thoroughly and carefully
from time to time is a most necessary one.   But the writers
in question, instead of applying their duster to this useful
purpose, prefer instead to flourish it out of the window as a
flag of liberty.

The other *mot* to which I refer concerned a very
extreme Biblical critic whose conclusions he thought
subversive of all that approved theologians had ever
held or tolerated.   This writer was at the same time a
man of the most exemplary piety and devotion to the
Church.   Ryder thus summed up the attitude : 'I do
indeed deeply respect A. B., and really admire the
reverent *decorum* with which he puts out all the lights
on the altar.'

My imperfect and undeveloped suggestions as to
the formal relations between the Church and advancing
science in the Epilogue to my 'Life of Cardinal
Wiseman' led to some adverse criticism, and I was
very anxious for his opinion, and greatly strengthened
by the favourable verdict expressed in the following
letter on December 17, 1897 :

I have this moment finished 'Wiseman.'   I hasten to
express my view that you have in your final chapter been
eminently successful in handling a most delicate and necessary
subject.   I can understand persons who do not see that you
are *necessarily* occupying for the moment a *non*-Catholic
position, for the sake of directing attention from the one point
of view available, being put out somewhat, but this is their

K

fault, not yours. I cannot understand anyone being so quick
to condemn, and publicly, as Father A. B. would seem to have
been. However, you must not mind a little wincing when
you have to go so near the quick.

His last letter to me on this subject is interesting.
It refers to an able paper on the general situation by
his friend the late Father Blakelock :

I thought you would like Father Blakelock's paper. I
was much interested in it, but had nothing to do with its
concoction. It owes its genesis to the writer, inspired more
or less by Father Bacchus.

Yes, we live in strange times, concerning which I am often
tempted to take up my prophecy.

Don't you think that in the interests of the better sort of
Catholic you ought occasionally to look us up? You were
under promise to come last year, and never came, and this
year is fast waning. Letters on such a complicated situation
do not go for much. You would find Fathers Bacchus and
Blakelock both worth talking to ; and for myself, though an
aged stump, upon which the moss of conservatism is gathering
day by day, I am not without a vein of liberal sap.

K——'s article impressed me most painfully. I honestly
preferred A——'s article. There was a man, a man in a passion,
who was inclined to sell his soul for its gratification. The
other was a *petit maître* with no soul to sell that I could
detect.

I think you should come and talk ; not that both you and
I have not to take heed lest we fall, but that I think we have
both inherited in our measure from J. H. N. a portion of
intelligent patience useful for the times.

You will reproach me, perhaps, that I have not been to
see you as you have often asked me. The simple truth is
that the few weeks I can get away from home are devoted to
my brother and sister. It sounds silly, but I can't bear to
curtail them. I will not miss an opportunity of an intercala-
tion of Eastbourne if it offers, as it may. Meanwhile it is

your duty to come here. I am most grieved at what you told me of X. He is such a good fellow, but I felt he was going too far with the tide. . . . If Mrs. Ward is not sick of congratulations, I should like to thank her for her book,[1] which is a gleam of sunshine in a naughty world.

He paid us a visit at Dorking in the autumn of 1901, and was as delightful a companion as ever. We had much music, which he greatly enjoyed, and when I went to see him at the Oratory in November, and he arrived in the evening after a tiring day at Bishop Brownlow's funeral, he proposed that I should repeat some of the songs he had liked. He was taken suddenly ill while I was actually singing to him—a fact which I mention to explain a reference in one of the two singularly characteristic letters which he wrote during his partial recovery :

I am doing very well, everyone says [he wrote on December 8]. I have been driving out three times last week, and I am going to Mass in the Boys' Gallery to-day. But my weakness is colossal. I could fall down headlong and be swept up into the corner. You are my siren who lured me to destruction by your sweet singing. Mrs. Ward and the children mourn over my bones until by a benevolent fairy I am electrocuted into life—a good subject for a religious comic opera. I find it so difficult to say anything that I say things I should not as though they were justified by the difficulty of saying them. Be prepared for this.

A letter of December 28 told of further progress :

I said Mass on Christmas morning, and for the first time realised what a wretched derelict I was. I have been more or less prostrate ever since, but I am glad I did it. I am not

One Poor Scruple.

really the worse.   I purpose trying again New Year's Day, if
I am allowed.   It felt like a strange rite with no sort of
continuity in the prayers.   I had to be dragged through,
prompted at every step.   My nurse went this morning, and,
God forgive me for an ingrate, I was glad to see her back.
I am valeted so far as is necessary by a retired soldier who
has two medals, a charming fellow, who has been understudy-
ing the part ; standing in the shadow like the second murderer
in a play.   Tell Mrs. Ward I aspire to a prayer of which I
am not worthy.   An old woman was told she must die.   Upon
which she folded her hands and exclaimed, ' O God, back me
up in this job.'

His recovery, however, never advanced much
further.   Of the years of trial before his death I will
not speak.   It is when we reach those years in our
retrospect that I propose rather to turn to the thoughts
in his poems which represent what was abiding in his
Christian faith, in his philosophy of life, in his hopes
for the future—the thoughts of the joy that crowns
suffering, of the life of eternal youth that follows old
age and death.   And these are to be found in the
poems.

Let me first, however, cite one or two of the
slighter ones, which bring their writer before us in his
habit of graceful thought concerning the surface of
life.   The following, on ' Adverse Criticism,' which
was published in ' The Spectator' subsequently to the
appearance of his collected poems, is, consequently, less
well known than the rest :

> What flowers I had in one fair knot were bound.
>   And so I laid them on a public stall,
>   Wondering would anyone take note at all,
> Or taking note, to praise them would be found.

A keen-eyed critic turned the nosegay round,
  Then cried ' No true flowers these!' and let it fall;
  ' Mere weeds that grow against the Church's wall!
And what coarse thread about the stalks is wound!

'Tis true, I fear me, dandelions and grass
  I culled, mistaking them for garden bloom,
And half-believing that they so might pass;
  And now my critic has pronounced my doom.
Half undeceived I shall not grudge my lot
If friends may find one true Forget-me-not.

Another brief poem, one of his happiest short
flights, has found its way into modern anthologies.
It was written as an inscription for a photograph book:

  A book of friends who still are friends,
    With friendship waxing stronger,
  A book of friends that once were friends,
    But now are friends no longer.
  I wonder as I turn the leaves
    What further changes yet may be,
  Or e'er the master bind the sheaves,
    And friends are friends eternally.

He wrote, too, of the friends that are dead, as well
as of those that are estranged, a poem longer and
more serious, called ' Animæ Fidelium ':

      No brightness of the sky
      To tell us where they lie;
      The winds that winnow by
        Make no report;
      Their cradle and their bier
      The earth says, ' They were here,
      But now no more appear
        In their resort.'

Their foot-prints all around
Yet make it holy ground;
The way they went, the sound
    Has died away.
The words which they have writ
Of pathos or of wit
The paper may not quit,
    But where are they?

Ah, vainly still we ask:
It is not nature's task
To tear away the mask
    Where God is hid.
Go, bow your troubled face
Closer in God's embrace,
And let His love displace,
    All fears forbid.

Your loved ones are not gone;
Live but for God alone,
And you shall find your own
    Upon His breast:
Safe in the inner shrine,
Within the arms divine;
They are not grown less thine,
    Because more blest.

Turning to the deeper thought in his verse, I will
cite two poems, and two only, which are truly characteristic. His poet's sense of the joy of life, of the
glory of early memories, of the suggestion of im-
mortality in the dreams of childhood, which Words-
worth has stereotyped in our minds once for all, ever
went very deep with him. His own subsequent
lingering illness adds painful associations to the first of
the two, which is yet too beautiful and real to leave
unquoted, and which recalls Byron's saying that

melancholy is often but the 'telescope of truth.'   I
refer to his poem on 'Old Age,' too long to be given
here in full, but containing the following lines :

> Would to God that I might die
> Ere the light has left the sky,
>
> .   .   .   .   .
>
> Better far to leave behind
> Much I care for than to find
> All I care for passed away,
> With the light of yesterday.
> Let me go, since go I must,
> Ere time's fingers in the dust
> Have writ all my joys as done,
> And the moments as they run
> Only their sad selves repeat,
> With naught of music save the beat.
> When I bid the world 'good-bye,'
> I would greet it with an eye
> For its shifting colours keen,
> Its interchange of shade and sheen,
> The eager green of kindling spring,
> And autumn's russet mellowing :
>
> .   .   .   .   .
>
> When I go, ah ! let me leave
> Here and there a heart to grieve
> For a part of its old life,
> That a comrade in its strife,
> A sharer in its daily mirth,
> Treads no longer on the earth.
> Now and then my name should slip
> Among my friends from lip to lip,
> Coupled with, 'It was his way
> Thus to look or this to say';
> With perhaps a whispered prayer
> That might reach me otherwhere.
> Whilst I live I fain would be
> All there ever was of me,

No fragment of existence merely,
For what I had been cherished dearly,
Whose formal death you scarce deplore
The real was so long before.
Forgive me, Saviour, if I plead
That though Thy pangs were hard indeed,
And all Thy body racked and wrung
Some pains Thou hadst not, dying young.
I know that 'neath the olive's shade,
A secular weight on Thee was laid ;
The bitterness of ages past
Into Thy cup of life was cast,
And all time's miseries yet to come
Wrought in Thy mystic martyrdom ;
Yet scarce was middle age begun,
When Thou hadst all Thy labours done.
The Eternal Years in mortal span
Waxed from the child into the man :
It was not meet that God should wane
From man into the child again ;
And so the feet that Mary kissed
The withering touch of age have missed,
And not a golden hair was grey
Upon Thy Crucifixion day.
High on the crest of manhood's hill
Thou didst Thy ministry fulfil
Winning Thy victory in the light ;
Whilst I upon the slopes of night
Creep shuddering down, no victory won,
Or none that I dare count upon.
Yet if it be Thy will, 'tis best
I so should enter on my rest ;
Piecemeal, as some, Thy martyrs died,
But Thou wert standing by their side.
Oh, stand by me when round me press
The sorrows of my loneliness.

.   .   .   .   .

Methinks myself I pity so,

That so I might myself assure
That one must pity me yet more.
Although too late from wasted soil
To win return of wine or oil,
I know there is another sea,
Unwearied of Love's infinity,
To fill, when other loves depart,
The thirsty hollows of the heart.

I have left to the last the poem which is perhaps in its conception the most beautiful of the collection. The lines just cited remind us of a great trial which he has endured and from which he has now been delivered. The following speak of that youth which he had lost and mourned, and which he has now found never to lose it again. It is headed 'Ecce Nova Facio Omnia.'

There was a summer in the past,
  With leaves that rustled overhead,
Which made as though it meant to last,
  But now is gone and dead.

And in that summer children, too,
  As careless and as kind to see
As any here, as you or you,
  Or any like to be.

And still these children move about,
  Though covered with a quaint disguise,
And strive to light their lamps gone out
  At newer children's eyes.

Now and again in summer hours
  They dream they have their summer back,
And catch amid the trees and flowers
  The ancient sunny track.

'Surely,' they cry, 'this way is best,
　A little further on must be
The home, the voices, and the rest
　Of our lost infancy.'

'A little further on,' to mark
　The footprint of a child that springs,
Spurning the earth like mounting lark
　Upborne on eager wings,

In token that 'mid scenes of earth
　Such quest as ours is all in vain,
Though where God's newly born have birth
　Old times may live again.

Yea, haply where God's angels stand.
　By gift of His exceeding grace,
A little soft familiar hand
　May lead us to our place,

To learn 'mid glories manifold
　No heart of man e'er dreamed it knew,
A joy that shall be new and old,
　From the old things made new.

　　I could wish to have said more, and to have cited
some more of his own words.　But for the present the
above extracts from his poetry, his letters, his sayings,
must suffice.　They give at least, in faint outline, the
picture of the great theologian, the true Christian
poet, the literary artist, whom we have lost.

Photo. Elliott & Fry.

SIR M. E. GRANT DUFF.

SIR M. E. GRANT DUFF'S DIARIES

The diaries of Sir Mountstuart Grant Duff attracted, as they appeared considerable attention. Many of the 'good things' which they contain were extracted by the newspapers as each volume came out, and are known to most people. Readers have been grateful for the racy anecdotes with which the diaries abound and the interesting information about an enormous variety of persons and things which they bring together.

I shall take, however, as the text of these remarks one of the adverse criticisms which have been made on them, as the criticism will help me to indicate what I consider to be a chief element in their interest. The 'Notes from a Diary' have been criticised on the score of superfluity in the material included—the occasional record of bare facts and names—a conversation with A. B., a meeting with C. D. ; or of trifling sayings on occasions when the reader would hope for something more substantial.

The selection from such a diary for purposes of publication must always be partly a matter of personal taste, in which there is no further appeal. But the author's selection cannot be intelligently appreciated by those who do not take in the *raison*

d'être of the publication.   Doubtless any collection
of good sayings, and of anecdotes concerning famous
people, has its interest.   Such collections are rapidly
'gutted' by the reviewers, who put a good mark
or a bad one against each paragraph.   So regarded,
Sir Mountstuart's diary is simply one added to the
books of reminiscences of which each year brings
its store, and of which the following year brings
forgetfulness.   The wisdom of including this or that
anecdote must in that case be tested as it is generally
tested in such a work.   The test is purely literary ;
each saying or fact recorded stands or falls by its
intrinsic interest.

Judged by this standard, Sir M. E. Grant Duff's
volumes, rich though they must still remain, would
undoubtedly admit of very considerable compression.
But this rule of selection appears to the present writer
to ignore one chief source of the value of the work.
The diaries have undoubtedly some of the interest
attaching to reminiscences from contemporary notes.
But they have also a far more special interest.   They
are the authentic and sufficiently complete record of a
mode of life which has been very exceptional.   If the
plan on which they are written excludes the philosophical reflection which characterises the *journal
intime*, if in this respect they remind us rather of the
Journal of Sir Walter Scott than of Amiel, the career
they reveal supplies very valuable material for the
comment of the life-philosopher.   It may be a
paradox to speak of one who finds this world of
such absorbing interest as does Sir M. E. Grant Duff

as unworldly—and yet I can find no word which describes better one of the chief characteristics of the man as exhibited in these diaries. They are the record of the life of a man devoted to the world, lived in a very unworldly spirit. They present to us a career inspired from beginning to end by a quasi-religious cult of all that makes this world really interesting.

At the basis of this cult lies a good deal of the old optimistic Liberalism of the 'fifties and 'sixties, so closely associated with the modern triumphs of physical science. The diarist probably in early years anticipated, like his fellows, a perpetual evolutionary progress in the social as in the scientific order—a progress almost worshipful in itself : ' Let the great world spin for ever down the ringing grooves of change.' But the spirit inspiring these diaries is far wider and more catholic than that of the Huxleys or the Tyndalls. The old schoolmen used to contrast *curiositas* with *studiositas*. Their contrast implied that a man who had the former—the ' curious ' man—dissipated his attention too much to attain to the latter—to the thoroughness of the genuine student. Sir M. E. Grant Duff's career is an object-lesson in the possibility of combining the two. This combination of manifold spheres of interest with concentrated devotion is essentially religious rather than worldly. A veritable thirst for information—not superficial but thorough— on a large variety of subjects, an intense desire to touch at some point all those who have made or are making the history of the world, to learn from them if it might be ; if not, at least to see them or come in contact with their personality—here are two leading traits in the man whom the diaries set before us. With a faith which is not of the world he believes it to be intensely worth while, irrespective of any worldly advantage in the ordinary sense, to be in personal relation with any instance of genius or exceptional acquirement.   What marks the book off from its fellows is less the special impressions left by the wonderfully large historical portrait gallery in the diary, than the overwhelming sense which the 'notes' as a whole convey—that this world is, in the eyes of the diarist, filled to the brim with persons and things which are worth knowing.   And this could not possibly be conveyed by a condensed summary which *only* included the actual sayings or facts of most marked interest noted down by the diarist.   It needed a record of how time was spent month by month and week by week. A summary could not give the life itself, or at best could only give the diarist's own impression of his own life—a very insecure test of what it is for others.   The contemporary evidence of a mode of life of which a main feature was the consistency of its aim could only be imparted by a full selection from the record of facts —the multiplicity of the facts being of the essence of the evidence.

I have spoken of the career as unworldly, and as occupied rather with a multiplicity of interests than in following any one path of life.   This does not, however, imply that the writer was a spectator of contemporary history rather than an actor in it.   His worldly career, indeed, was fortunate enough and distinguished

enough. But instead of the commonplace struggle
for success which is the record of so many an official
career, the steadfastness of purpose of the man of
action is exercised in the life here depicted with a far
wider aim. With a steadiness of endeavour, and a
uniform practicalness in achievement, which would
satisfy the requirements of a Jesuit confessor, each
day was devoted to seeing what was to be seen and
learning what was to be learnt from exceptional and
varied opportunities. There is none of the exclusiveness of the official statesman, or of the professional
man—soldier, sailor, lawyer, doctor—or of the man of
fashion. With all such men their active interest is
apt to centre in a particular group of persons and
events. There is not even the exclusiveness of the
man of speculative intellect or the recluse scholar who
may care little for the mere pageant of the great world.
The interest displayed is universal. Everything that
is a power in the world or that goes to make any
department of its history is included. The zest of a
meeting with Cavour or Gambetta is not greater than
the zest of a stimulating talk at the Athenæum with
Hayward or Kinglake. Men of all creeds, all political
parties, all professions, contribute their share.

Indeed, diversity of pursuit or opinion in his companions appears to give the diarist a special feeling of
piquancy. With something of the temperament which
made Lord Houghton ask Cardinal Wiseman to meet
Mazzini at breakfast, Sir M. E. Grant Duff rejoices
when he finds himself at the Metaphysical Society
between Huxley and Manning. His friendships for

Renan and Madame Augustus Craven were perhaps stimulated by the fact that in Paris they belonged to spheres which intersected at no single point.   And he used to relate with infinite delight how Renan once called to fetch him from Mrs. Craven's house in the Rue Barbet de Jouy, and was by mistake shown into the drawing-room.   Mrs. Craven told him afterwards : ' I entered my drawing-room, and when I saw who my visitor was I felt exactly as though I beheld the devil sitting in my armchair.'   But the perfect manners of the two prevented anything but the most courteous termination of the incident.   With an intense faith, allied to an intense scepticism, Sir Mountstuart held such different representatives of literary and religious activity each to be a factor of supreme interest and importance in the history of the world ; while the circumstance that their ideals were mutually destructive had no effect even in diminishing the sympathy felt for each.

In spite of his extravagance, Comte hit upon an idea in the worship of humanity which, apart from his own grotesque setting, is, I believe, characteristic of many a modern mind.   It is a refuge of those whose faith in any one supernatural creed is shaken by the spectacle which history presents of the rise and decay of each in turn, to worship, in some sense, that stately march of civilisation which moves onwards despite the decay of parties and sects.   To idealise the moving picture of history, past or present, and to aim at filling worthily one of the pages of its record, is a quasi-religious aspiration to many who have learnt to regard any confident hope for what is beyond the present scene as chimerical.

Such we may almost say is the religion of the Grant Duff diaries. It is for this reason that, though so much occupied with the world, the *ethos* of the work is unworldly. It is not worldly advantage, or even worldly glory, which inspires the life of the writer; it is an idealised view of the intrinsic value of the forces creating and developing civilisation. Thus reverently to approach and contemplate these forces and their manifestations becomes a quasi-religious act. And to acquire fuller and fuller information about persons and things, and so enable himself to appreciate more intelligently the varied world in which he lives, is the absorbing occupation of life. A day of botanising in the country is as satisfying as a literary and political gathering at Hampden or York House. Each is an end in itself, a realised picture in an ideal life, wholly unworldly in the absence of *arrière pensée* to personal advantage.

And there are few spheres within which the writer was not drawn. A glance at the index of names shows at once a variety of acquaintance, including a large number of his contemporaries of the first eminence and a multitude of the second or third rank. In England alone the number is very great. A member of the House of Commons from early days, and never out of the House until at fifty he was made Governor of Madras, the political sphere was long familiar to Grant Duff. His chief associates belonged to it, and his intercourse with them was constant. His closest friends

L

joined in forming, in 1866, a breakfast club of twelve members, and the choice was made with such a true instinct as to who were really the 'coming' men, that not only were all of its members ultimately of high distinction, but Grant Duff could note with satisfaction, some twenty years after its foundation, that through four of its honorary members it was ruling India, Canada, Bombay, and Madras.   Grant Duff's connection with the literary world was only less close—if at all less close—than with the political.   Such intimate friends as Lord Arthur Russell and Lord Acton belonged to both.   At the Athenæum and at the dinners of the Literary Society much of what was best in the English world of letters, art, and science was to be found.   The Dilettanti and 'The Club'—the lineal successor of the association made illustrious by Johnson and Burke—added a more varied acquaintance.   These groups naturally included the most prominent men of science, and Sir M. E. Grant Duff was enough the child of his time to have his full share of scientific enthusiasm.   A visit to the Museum with Owen is evidently as inspiring a prospect as any of the interesting meetings recorded in the book.

Thus we see in these notes much of his intercourse with men whom the world recognised, or soon came to recognise.   But of equal interest to the diarist are the many doers of good work, known only to specialists or intimate friends, whom the world at large never knew, and yet who were veritable powers from the quality of their work and their influence on the elect few.   The author of a book on botany, an artist, or sculptor, who does fine though hitherto unrecognised work, a religious leader with few disciples, an unpopular metaphysician whose power is known to the few only, a German scholar, translator of the Sikh Granth for the Indian Government, a German constitutional lawyer, the head of a Brahmin sect—here are characters who pass across the scene in a comparatively short space in the diary; men not belonging in any sense to the great world, some of them never acknowledged by any large public, but each in his way a power in some department of art or learning, and each in consequence stimulating the reverent interest in life of which I have spoken.

But no doubt the cosmopolitan element is a special feature of the diary. Foreign Courts—as that of the Empress Frederick—foreign seats of learning, foreign statesmen and *savants* fill a large space. And the record of travel with close knowledge of the historical associations of its scenes recalls Macaulay's saying that geography is the eye of history. Indeed, the rule of getting all that was to be got from each opportunity is conspicuously exhibited in the notes on foreign travel. The historical associations of each town are known or learnt, the thoughts they have inspired in great poets or prose writers are recalled; and few of the actual things or persons which make it interesting in the present are passed over.

This cosmopolitan element in the diarist reminded the present writer of the reminiscences scattered up and down the works of the late Cardinal Wiseman. There is, indeed, a considerable resemblance between the *grande curiosité* of the two men. Both have the

same wide sympathy which includes the distinguished
students of all countries, as well as the socially and
politically eminent.   Both were actors in life as well
as spectators.   Both were primarily and by nature
observers and students, and yet were called upon to
be rulers of men.

   But it is interesting also to note the wide difference
in similarity.   What was to the English statesman
and colonial governor an object of life, the patient
realising of all possible interest in the civilised world,
was in the Cardinal's eyes either a recreation or a temp-
tation.   The time spent amid the great scholars of many
nationalities whom he saw constantly in Rome was,
he said, the happiest of his life.   Yet it was at variance
with his ideal.   The belief in the Church, which put
all good work on its behalf on a different level from
the mere zest of human life, marked him off absolutely from the type to which the Governor of Madras
belonged.   Without the temperament of the man of
one idea (differing in this respect widely from Cardinal
Manning)—indeed, rather with the temperament of a
dilettante—the faith which had possessed Wiseman
from early childhood gave him a unity of aim which
in the nature of the case could not exist in one who
was without it.   Each man was equally inspired by
the pageant of history as it passed before him ; but
while to one the Catholic Church was but a single
group in the pageant—intensely interesting and
picturesque, indeed, but only one among many—to the
other it was the very centre of all, the one phenomenon
which gave coherence to history, which without it was

a tale signifying nothing ; the ultimate object of devotion, to which all else that had any real value in some way ministered. Indeed, if I mistake not, but for his faith in the Church Wiseman would not have been a man of action at all.

There is a strong sympathy with things Catholic in Grant Duff's diaries. It was further developed by the friendship with Mrs. Craven, which became almost a cult of the beautiful form of refined piety revealed in the ' Récit d'une Sœur.' And one may even hazard a conjecture that—again not unlike Comte—the writer views with regret the fact that for him Wiseman's unity of view and aim is impossible, and would welcome a Church of the future, an appointed guardian of religion and science, the embodiment of a new synthesis, which could have the same dominating influence as the Church of the Middle Ages. However this may be, the comparison between the two men, so similar in their appreciation of the drama of life, so closely in sympathy while they preserve the *rôle* of spectator, and yet poles apart as to the duty of an actor on its scene, is instructive. The change in Wiseman's mode of life when he put aside his studies and literary pursuits at the age of thirty-six, and threw himself into the Catholic movement, the remarkable meditations still extant which show the thoughts—we had almost said the visions—which inspired the change, have no counterpart in the diaries I am reviewing. On the other hand, all that will-power and steady resolve which these meditations represent, which enabled the naturally mobile nature of the Roman student to break with his fascinating life amid friends devoted to studies similar to his own, and steadfastly to work for what he believed to be the great cause, exhibited itself in the other man in the pertinacity with which he adhered to the life of eager and varied assimilation, and devoted himself to its record.

'To its record,' I add—for how many people plan to keep a diary and keep it for a month, or even less! The present writer pleads guilty to persevering less than a week in his only attempt. Some few, perhaps, keep it for half a year; fewer still for a couple of years. Who keeps it for a lifetime? It is one of the achievements which mark off Boswell from other biographers that he persevered in noting down on his tablets Johnson's table-talk. In its own way the perseverance of Sir M. E. Grant Duff is equally remarkable. He far surpasses in this respect Evelyn or Pepys. Boswell's worship of Johnson had in it something of a religion—this was one secret of his perseverance. The secret of Sir M. E. Grant Duff's perseverance is similar. The interest of life, the halo which surrounds history that is in process of making, is to him—I say it again—a religion, and it leads to that consistent pursuit of an ideal which is in spirit essentially unworldly.

My object in the above remarks has been not to give any account or criticism of the entries in the Grant Duff diaries, but rather to suggest that background—the spirit, character, and intention of the work, and of the life it records—against which the entries appear to me to stand out in a truer and more

significant light.   I am endeavouring also to help the
reader to see the figure that is presented in the diaries
as a whole.   For the very character of individual
entries prevents them from completely accomplishing
this object by themselves, because the self-revelations
and philosophic musings which mark the *journal
intime* are (as I have already remarked) of set purpose
excluded.   The record is objective—of persons, places,
things, sayings—and hardly ever subjective—of impressions, opinions, reflections.

It is interesting for the Catholic reader to observe
the very special fascination exercised throughout the
Life by things and persons associated with Catholicism.
There is something of the spirit of Matthew Arnold
in the references to this subject.   We see it as early
as the visit to Rome in 1851.   The Princes of the
Church gathered together in the Sistine Chapel arouse
a crowd of historical associations ; and a day spent
with the Abbot of Subiaco is thus noted :

The lights were out in Santa Scholastica ; the abbot had
paid us his last visit, the monks had all gone to their cells,
and the corridors were empty and silent.   The moon looked
over the hilltops into the quiet little cloister below our rooms,
and half lay in light and half in shadow.   I thought over the
last few hours, our visit to Sacro Speco (the cave of St. Benedict), the triple chapel of the noble monastery which covers it
the road winding up to hermitages among the mountains, the
roses famous in legend for the serpent with crushed head on
their leaves.   The spell of the Middle Ages and of the Roman
Church was on everything—no, not on everything, for I
knew, though I could not hear it, that the Anio was dashing
below, changed in name, not in character still the river the
heathen poet knew it, still the ' headlong Anio.'

Scattered up and down are many records of special interest to Catholics. A few taken almost at random from one of the volumes may suffice as specimens. It is interesting to know that when the late Lord Coleridge heard Ravignan preach, he said it had 'opened to him a new chapter in the human mind'; interesting to read that Gladstone said of Newman's influence at Oxford when at its height, 'there has been nothing like it since Abelard lectured in Paris'; interesting to learn that when the diarist met Gambetta in 1878, Gambetta expressed an emphatic opinion, from his personal knowledge of Leo XIII., that, though he was likely to be more conciliatory in manner than Pius IX., he would make no substantial change in the policy of the Papacy ; interesting to read of Carlyle's estimate of St. Columba—'a thoroughly Irish nature, like any of the people who are shouting Justice for Ireland'; interesting to be told of Carlyle's intellectual respect for and ethical disparagement of the Bollandists ; interesting to get many characteristic glimpses of Newman, Montalembert, Döllinger. The friendship with Madame Craven, and the devotion to every page of the 'Récit d'une Sœur,' stand on a footing in some sense higher than any other sentiments in this life, so varied and so filled with worship of the ideal.

But if we wish to have first-hand evidence of the most habitual characteristic of the man, to cite in the writer's own words the sentiment which most con-tinuously characterises these pages, we cannot do better than turn to the concluding paragraphs of the second instalment of the diaries.

When Mr. Grant Duff was appointed Governor of Madras, his friends gave him a dinner before he left for India. The gathering included a number of men of the first distinction, unusually large even on such an occasion. It was a fitting tribute to one whose friendships had been so much to him. And the Governor-elect gave an address, passages from which should be preserved as specimens of happy and unlaboured oratory. The spirit in which he ever regarded his friends and acquaintance, how his intercourse with them had formed a chief part of his life, is testified in simple and felicitous terms at the conclusion of the discourse.

After reviewing the features in his career for which he is specially thankful, he thus continued :

All these are considerable helps and comforts, but I have one which is greater than any, that all my life I have lived amongst the kind of men who are represented by those I see around me to-night. When I first went up as a boy to Oxford, I promised myself that I would do my best to live with those who were superior to me in character, or intelligence, or in knowledge, or in all three. I have, like most people, broken a great many promises I have made to myself, but that one never. I have always endeavoured to have friends, my attitude to whom was half affection and half admiration. It is no light thing to part from such friends, even for a time. It is no light thing to give up such a constituency as I have had ; to say good-bye to the Athenæum and the Literary Society and the Dilettanti and the Breakfast Club, and to those Saturday to Monday gatherings, whether at Hampden, or Knebworth, or York House, which I owe to the kindness of many friends whom I see around me, and to that of many more of both sexes whom they represent. It is no light thing to forego that bath of new ideas which a single day's travelling brings to one who, living in London, has always studied to keep up frequent and close relations with friends on the European continent. . . . I owe much gratitude to those who organised this gathering, in that they have given me an opportunity of expressing my feelings to each and all of you, and they have done me a further service in preventing its assuming the character of a political demonstration. The persons amongst whom I am going to live know perfectly well my political connections and antecedents, but few of them can know anything about my private life, and as *Noscitur a sociis* is a good proverb in all parts of the world, I cannot imagine that anyone could take a better introduction to all that is best in India than by carrying thither the approbation and good wishes of such a gathering as this, comprising as it does so much that is most distinguished and most powerful in so many departments of English life. To all, then, who are here present I return my sincere thanks, and not less to some who are not here present, but who have in various ways expressed to me their goodwill ; and among these to Mr. Gladstone, to Mr. Forster, to Mr. Lefevre, to Mr. John Morley, to Lord Coleridge, to Sir James Stephen, to Mr. Morier, to the Master of Balliol, to the Dean of Salisbury, to Sir Henry Maine, to Mr. Augustus Craven, to Mr. Matthew Arnold ; and last, not least, to that distinguished man, the most famous ecclesiastic who has lived in our times, one whose name naturally arises to our minds when it is a question of the 'Parting of Friends,' and who wrote to me the other day to wish me everything that is *bonum, faustum, fortunatumque*, in the great office which I am going to undertake. . . . Of course there is a certain risk : no one goes to work in the tropics at fifty-two without incurring a certain risk. Lord Napier and the Duke of Buckingham returned ; Mr. Adam and Lord Hobart did not. I hope, of course, and you hope, that I shall draw a favourable number ; but in all such cases we can only fall back upon the famous words :

> If we do meet again, why, we shall smile ;
> If not, why, then this parting was well made.

To say that I shall watch with deep interest the fortunes of those here present would be to use an absurdly inadequate expression. Every educated Englishman will do that, for there is a great part of the history of England, for a good many years to come, collected round this table. What I wish to express is something much more intimate and affectionate which I think I had better not try to put into words. One thing at least is certain, that, whether I come back with my shield or on my shield, I shall have done all that can be expected of me if I have brought no discredit to such a company of friends.

LEO XIII.

THAT a period of fifty-seven years—from 1846 to 1903 —should be spanned by two pontificates is an event quite unparalleled in the history of the Catholic Church. Two successive pontificates of unusual length marked the epoch at which Charlemagne laid the foundations of the Papal States ; but, taken together, the years of Hadrian I. and Leo III. amounted to but forty-three. The two papal reigns of our own time marked, as did those other two, a vital change in the fortunes and position of the Roman See. They began with the dream of Pius IX. that he was to be the head of a federated Italy—a dream shared not only by Gioberti and Rosmini, but by Giuseppe Mazzini. They have witnessed in the end the abandonment of all hope for the restoration of the temporal power in its old form. Both pontificates have been marked by a development of centralisation in the Church. To this the dogma of 1870 has contributed. And the enormous increase in the number of Encyclical letters and the more constant and active guidance of Catholics by the Papacy have been an unconscious witness to the same tendency. This has been a not unnatural culmination of a movement among Catholics which was aroused ninety years ago by the trumpet-call of Joseph de Maistre's ' Du Pape.'

Broadly speaking, it may be said that Pius and

POPE LEO XIII.

Leo have seen the foundation of the new society which
has finally taken the place of the Christendom formally
inaugurated by Hadrian and the earlier Leo. That
Christendom has died very hard; but it is dead.
The revolution of 1793 was the mortal wound. Its
traditions and institutions long survived the changes
of the sixteenth century. But few of them now
remain. Governments are almost universally anti-
Christian; or at best officially non-Christian. Catholics
are an international party, as were the Christians in the
Roman Empire of the third century. De Maistre's
conception of Ultramontanism as a principle of union
among them has definitely taken the place of the older
Gallicanisms and Febronianisms which long witnessed
to the remnant of national Catholicism, the heir to
the national Churches of mediæval times—deferring,
indeed, to the Papacy, but each Church having a large
measure of independent life, and each representing the
religion of its own State.

I propose here briefly to review the outlines of the
career of the remarkable Pontiff Leo XIII. who for
twenty-six years ruled the Church, and to offer a few
suggestions as to the intellectual and ethical character
revealed in the long series of his Pontifical Acts from
1878 to 1903.

Vincenzo Gioacchino Raffaele Luigi Pecci—to
give him his full list of names—was born at Carpineto
on March 2, 1810. He came of a family of good
position residing at Carpineto, but originally from Siena.
The father of Vincenzo—the head of the family—was
a colonel in the army of Napoleon I.

Early in life the future Pope showed signs both of character and of ability. He and his brother Joseph began their education at Rome, and passed, a year later, to the Jesuit College at Viterbo, where they greatly distinguished themselves. A friend of theirs, Monsignor Carmine Lolli, who went to Viterbo to see the boys, reported thus of them in a letter to Carpineto : ' If the Lord gives them life and health, they will be an honour and a glory to themselves, to their family, and to their country.'

In 1824 Leo XII. handed over the Collegio Romano to the Jesuits, and in that year the two brothers Pecci were enrolled among the students. Vincenzo devoted himself at first to philosophy and rhetoric. Like his great contemporary, Cardinal Newman, he failed to take his degree with special distinction, owing to a breakdown of health—although he had been selected as one of the disputants at the public philosophical debate in the Church of St. Ignatius. Vincenzo was not at first a student for the priesthood, but in 1825 he finally resolved to become a priest. The public jubilee of that year made a great impression on him, crowds of pilgrims flocking to Rome to render thanks for the restoration of peace after the Revolution and Napoleon's wars. He had several opportunities of personal intercourse with Leo XII., for whom he conceived an enthusiastic admiration. These events doubtless combined to strengthen the ecclesiastical bent of his mind.

At the Accademia dei Ecclesiastici Nobili he received his preparation for a diplomatic career, and in

1837 was appointed Referendary to the Congregation of the Segnatura. Among his earliest patrons was Cardinal Sala, who employed his services in one of the congregations concerned with the administration of the Papal States. Another of his early friends was that able prelate, Cardinal Lambruschini, Secretary of State to the Pope; and owing to the joint influence of these two cardinals Vincenzo was appointed shortly after his ordination, at the age of twenty-eight, to a critical mission as Apostolic Delegate at Benevento.

Benevento had been a very den of brigands. The banditti who were expelled by the Neapolitans took refuge in that province, and had been so far left almost unmolested by the Pontifical authorities. The Neapolitans naturally complained, and a strong man was needed on the spot to act with energy and decision.

These qualities the young Pecci showed, according to the expectation of his friends. He directed the action of the Pontifical troops, and, and having informed himself of the haunts of the brigands, promptly captured the leaders, and, to calm the minds of the inhabitants, paraded the prisoners, laden with chains, in the streets of the city.

The Delegate's troubles, however, were not at an end. Smuggling on a large scale was another of the disorders with which he had to deal, and among its chief patrons were many of the nobility and landowners. To the stress and anxiety caused by the constant warfare carried on for many months before the smugglers could be brought to justice must be ascribed the serious

illness which terminated Monsignor Pecci's connection
with Benevento.

Monsignor Pecci's next appointment of importance
was at Perugia.   The Carbonari and other secret
societies, at that time so powerful a force in Italy, had
been especially active in Perugia.   In 1841, therefore, Gregory XVI. nominated Pecci Apostolic
Delegate and Civil Governor of the town.   The
Pontiff wished to pay a visit to Perugia in person
at the outset of the Delegate's mission.   The only
means of approach in those days was a steep mule-
path, and Pecci signalised his own entrance on his
office and the Pope's visit by an act of almost
Napoleonic vigour.   He gave orders that a carriage
road should be constructed in twenty days—the time
available before Gregory's arrival.   This was done,
and the Pope entered the town by the new *via*, which
was named the Via Gregoriana.

The success which attended Monsignor Pecci's
attempts at reorganising the public service and the
whole administration at Perugia led to his appointment
a few years later to the vacant episcopal chair of that
city.

But meantime, in the beginning of 1843, Monsignor
Pecci received a summons to Rome, and was informed
at his first audience with Gregory XVI. that he had
been named Nuncio at Brussels.   Monsignor (afterwards Cardinal) Fornari, an old professor at the
Collegio Romano during the student life both of Pecci
and of the English Cardinal Wiseman, had just
resigned the nunciature in that Court, and his former

pupil was to succeed him. Monsignor Pecci was consecrated bishop *in partibus infidelium* on January 27, by Cardinal Lambruschini, in the Church of St. Laurence in Panisperna, the title he chose being that of Bishop of Damietta. In March he sailed from Città Vecchia to Marseilles, and reached Brussels on April 11. It was while Nuncio at Brussels that he first made acquaintance with Queen Victoria, on occasion of a visit paid by her to the Belgian Court.

Pecci's success as a diplomat at Brussels was as complete as that of his earlier career. And it was here also that he first showed those marked academic tastes of which he subsequently gave so many proofs as Pope, interesting himself greatly in the educational institutions of the country, notably the University of Louvain.

On January 19, 1846, Gregory XVI., very shortly before his own death, promoted Pecci to the episcopate of Perugia. King Leopold wrote to the Pope the strongest expressions of esteem for the outgoing Nuncio, and regret at his departure. His letter was answered by Pius IX., after his accession to the Pontifical throne, in terms which, to the initiated, intimated that Pecci was reserved as a cardinal *in petto*: 'Monsignor Pecci. . . . will feel *in due time*,' he wrote, 'the good wishes of your Majesty in the same way as if he had remained in the career of Nuncio.'

Pecci entered Perugia as its bishop on July 26, retaining, as an ex-Nuncio, the title of archbishop. Like his brother bishops, he was made to remember the Revolution of 1848. He passed some weeks in prison, and was forced to endure without means of redress the plunder of his monasteries and his churches.

Many anecdotes survive in his diocese as to his active interest as archbishop in ecclesiastical education. He founded the Academy of St. Thomas Aquinas for theological discussion among his clergy, and few things delighted him more than taking part in a *disputatio*, conducted in mediæval form—a thesis being expounded in Latin, and the chief disputant defending it against all comers ; each argument, however developed and illustrated, being ultimately thrown into the form of a syllogism, with major, minor, and conclusion duly expressed.

As bishop he showed the same activity and the same tendency to exercise close personal supervision and direction in all departments which he had shown as Delegate, and was to evince later on as Pope. Like Haroun al Raschid, he loved to learn for himself the state of things in his own dominions, and would attend lectures *incognito*, or visit the parish churches to satisfy himself as to the efficiency of his priests. On one occasion the Professor of Latin (Monsignor Brunelli), coming in late for his lecture, found the Archbishop seated in his chair expounding Cicero. On another occasion, learning that a parish priest was in the habit of paying a substitute while he absented himself from Monday to Saturday, the Archbishop betook himself in person to the church and did duty for the substitute, to the effectual discomfiture and alarm of the incumbent on his return.

The Archbishop was an early riser and a hard worker in many departments, devoting himself to literature as well as to his special ecclesiastical duties.

He was created a cardinal in the Consistory of 1853. In 1859—when the policy of Napoleon III. and Cavour foreshadowed the loss of the patrimony of St. Peter—he addressed a letter to Pius IX., in which he protested in the strongest language against ' these impious efforts to despoil the Sovereign Pontiff of his dignity and independence ; setting revolt and schism against the great principle of Catholic unity.'

He won the respect even of the Piedmontese invaders by the dignity of his attitude, and was never (it is said) betrayed, even under the provocations of that time, into rash excess in his protests. Nevertheless, he effectually marked his disapproval of the policy of the House of Savoy when occasion permitted. The Government desired, as far as possible, to gain the control of educational institutions—ecclesiastical and lay. In the principal lay college of Perugia they nominated their own professors. Leo XIII. met this move by an act as effectual as it was beyond reach of criticism. He announced that he withdrew his patronage from an institution for the conduct of which he was no longer responsible, and he had his arms removed from the gateway of the college. No remonstrance with the Government would have been as effectual. The parents immediately withdrew their children and the State professors had to address empty benches. Again, when the Piedmontese captured the ecclesiastical seminary, the

Archbishop opened the doors of his palace to the priests, who could there no longer be molested without a direct invasion of the episcopal premises.   His biographer quotes the testimony both of Liberal writers and of Catholics as to the reputation he acquired for energy, firmness, and moderation.   Here are the words of a Liberal writer : ' With respect to the Italian authorities, and in times of great difficulty, he maintained an attitude above all taint of party, so that the civil power, respecting his dignified character, sought always to mitigate the arrangements concerning his diocese.'

One of the threads which he was to take up in his Pontificate may be traced to the days of his episcopate at Perugia.   In the Lent of 1877 the Archbishop issued a pastoral on the labour question which anticipates largely the celebrated Encyclical ' Rerum Novarum.'   It was welcomed by the democratic party for the strong sympathy with the people which it evinced :

The modern schools of economics [wrote Cardinal Pecci] have considered labour as the supreme end of man, whom they take into account as a machine of more or less value, according as he aids more or less in production.   Hence the absence of consideration for the normal man, and the colossal abuse that is made of the poor and lowly, by those who seek to keep them in a state of dependence in order to grow rich at their expense.   And even in countries which have the reputation of being the foremost in civilisation, what grave and repeated complaints do we not hear of the excessive hours of labour imposed on those who must earn their bread by the sweat of their brow?   And does not the sight of the poor children, shut up in factories, where, in the midst of their premature toil, consumption awaits them—does not this sight provoke words of burning indignation from every generous soul, and oblige Governments and Parliaments to make laws that can serve as a check to this inhuman traffic? And were it not for Catholic charity, which, with its asylums and various institutions, never ceases to provide relief to their misery, how many of these children would nowadays be left without protection, and abandoned to themselves by their fathers and mothers, whom the frenzy of labour drags from the domestic hearth? Oh, most beloved children, when we see these things, or hear them related by organs that are above suspicion, we are impotent to contain the feeling of indignation which is ready to burst forth against those who are of opinion that the destinies of civilisation should be entrusted to the hands of these barbarians. And they call this encouraging progress. But there is still worse to be said : this labour without measure, which exhausts and wears out the body, is at the same time the ruin of the soul, from which little by little it cancels all traces of resemblance with God. This rage of keeping men riveted down to matter, steeped in it, absorbed by it, benumbs all intellectual life in these wretched victims of labour, flung back into paganism. All that which can ennoble man, and make him heir to heaven, as God wishes he should be, fades from their sight and is forgotten, leaving only in exchange animal instinct, thenceforth intolerant of any curb. In the presence of these beings—prematurely exhausted by heartless avarice—we ask if, instead of making progress, these adepts of a civilisation without God, and outside the Church, are not rather driving us many centuries back, to those sad times when so great a part of the human race lay crushed in slavery, and of which the poet sorrowfully cried : ' The human species lives only in a few.' (*Humanum paucis vivit genus.*)

Cardinal Pecci had in 1878—the last year of the pontificate of Pius IX.—reached the age of sixty-eight—a time when most people regard active life as ending or ended. He was universally respected in his diocese and out of it. One mark of Papal approval which was to have unforeseen consequences was his recent appointment as Cardinal Camerlengo, a position involving ordinarily no onerous duties, but all-important at the death of the Pope, as the Camerlengo is then almost what a chargé d'affaires is for a vacant embassy, and performs during the inter-regnum most of the administrative duties of the vacant Pontifical See.

The present writer was in this year an ecclesiastical student at the Collegio Inglese in Rome—one of the colleges founded by Gregory XIII. in the reign of Elizabeth for the education of English Catholics, and the alma mater of many distinguished English-men, from Edmund Campion to Cardinal Wiseman. Pius IX. was nearer ninety than eighty, and he was infirm. But he had lived so long that we felt that he might well live on indefinitely. The exceptional feeling of veneration for him, and the love which his singularly sympathetic personality instilled almost at first sight, are still remembered by many. Public events have seldom aroused stronger personal feeling than did the long spoliation of the temporalities of the Papacy from 1859 to 1870. We younger men loved Pius and hated Victor Emmanuel. I treasured the one word I received from the lips of Pius—it was one word of one syllable, and no more. We were received in audience in December, 1877, and as he passed me, carried in his chair, looking scarcely alive, I asked in customary form for ' Benedizione, Santo Padre, per me e per la mia famiglia,' and the Pope turned and

looked at me, raising his hand in blessing while he
acquiesced, the 'si' being spoken with the still deep
and sonorous voice which he kept until the end.

I have said that we loved Pius and hated Victor ;
and while I treasured the blessing and the 'si,' I was
as ready as the other collegians to break the laws
of good manners when the 'Usurper' was concerned.
The King was always anxious as he drove in the city
to get a salute from a priest or cleric, and we used to
go close to the royal carriage and raise our hands as
though to doff our hats. The King's hat was off in a
moment, and the college boys' hands got no higher
than their foreheads, as, with their heads still covered,
they returned his gracious smile with a blank stare.
This was the most we could do to make the man, who
was in our eyes no better than a highwayman, smart ;
and we did it with joy.

One day in January, 1878, our *camerata*—as the
group of collegians walking together was called—spent
the day at one of the country houses of the college—I
think at Magliana. We saw signs of excitement in
the city (as we returned), groups of people talking of
something evidently of exceptional interest. We
soon heard what it was—the King had been suddenly
taken ill. He had the malignant fever known as the
perniciosa. There was no chance of recovery. Then
we learnt what made a deep impression on us. It
was a real or supposed fact—one, at least, which we
had often heard and never doubted—that Victor
Emmanuel had a superstitious dread of sleeping in
the Quirinal, the former palace of the Popes, lest he

might die there, and that he consequently always repaired for the night to a house outside Rome. Now it was in the Quirinal that he was stricken down, and he was too ill to be removed. To the best of my memory he was dead in twenty-four hours, and Padre Ghetti, who lectured to us thrice a week on moral philosophy, implied in his discourse on the following morning, with some glee, that if the King had had the best of it in this world, the Pope would beyond doubt have the best of it in the next. The King had received from Abbate Anzino (I think that was his name) the last ministrations for the dying and a blessing from Pius IX., whose words, 'Usate tutta misericordia' were repeated everywhere.

I remember distinctly that the King's death led someone to tell us of a prophecy made in the previous autumn by a holy anchorite in the Campagna, to the effect that 'early in the following year Rome would see two great coffins'; and, like many others, I thenceforth confidently expected the Pope to die soon after the King—as he did in the event in the following month. Cheap tickets had been issued to Rome from all parts of Italy, with a view to ensuring the presence of large numbers of Italians in the city for the King's funeral, and making it an opportunity for a demonstration and for cementing the disjointed and heterogeneous elements in the new kingdom of Italy. Many who profited by these tickets were still there when Pius died, and Rome was, therefore, unusually crowded. We went twice to St. Peter's to see the body of the dead Pope laid out, in bishop's vestments, the mitre

of the Bishop of Rome on his head, which his fore-
runners had worn so long, and not the tiara—a
development of the later Middle Ages.   He was laid
out in one of the side-chapels, and his face was plainly
visible, rather dark in colour, like bronze, but in
expression beautiful and peaceful after all the years
of trouble.   There were tears shed and many prayers
said.   A rough Garibaldian got in, however, among
the devout crowd, and—it was the only jarring note I
remember—having worked his way close to the iron
gates of the side-chapel, said in a loud voice, ' E meno
malo che sia morto ' (' Small harm that he is dead ').
He was with difficulty rescued from being lynched by
the crowd.

At the Requiem in the Sistine Chapel I listened
for the first time to the wonderful Papal Choir, which
had not sung in public since the entry of the
Piedmontese in 1870.

Cardinal Pecci now assumed the reins of office,
and within a week we heard that the Camerlengo had
made an immense impression on his fellow-cardinals
by his judgment and ability.   Soon came the Conclave,
and in the days which preceded it Cardinal Manning
stayed with us at the English College.   Then he
joined his brethren in the Vatican, the windows of
which were barricaded, according to the tradition of
centuries, to prevent the possibility of any communication between the Conclavisti and the outer world.

As is well known, if no Pope is elected at a particular meeting of the Cardinals in conclave the voting
papers are burnt, and the smoke visible in the Piazza

di San Pietro—the *sfumata*—is a sign for all to dis-
perse. We went each time at the appointed hours,
and by some mistake the papers were burnt after the
election had actually taken place—at the second or
third meeting of the shortest Conclave on record. We
therefore returned to the English College, and I was
taking my siesta when Giovanni, the old College
servant, who had been there since the rectorate of
Cardinal Wiseman in 1836, burst into my room, nearly
drunk with excitement, and cried out, 'Cardinale Pecci
—Leone decimo terzo.' In ten minutes we were all
again in the huge Piazza di San Pietro. Then came
a long pause. Since 1870 the Pope had never come
beyond the Vatican walls into the balcony outside
St. Peter's. The blessing 'to the city and the world,'
'urbi et orbi,' had ceased. Would the new Pope
break this rule? 'Yes,' it was confidently said. After
long waiting, however, 'no' was circulated, and we
crowded into St. Peter's itself. Unless my memory is
at fault the rumour changed again, and we once more
went outside into the Piazza before finally, after some
two hours of waiting, we again entered the Basilica,
and the Pope, erect, tall and thin, never seen hitherto
by most of us, appeared in his white cassock on the
inside balcony and was received by an outburst of
cheering and cries of 'Viva il Papa-re.' Then in
clear and silvery voice, equal to the demands of a
moment of tension and enthusiasm, he chanted the
Pontifical blessing, and we finally dispersed.

The golden opinions won by the Camerlengo were
kept by the Pope. True there was some grumbling.

'A new broom' growled some of the old officials.
But the strong will and intellectual (though not philosophical) force of the Pontiff were soon generally felt
and respected. The difference between himself and
his predecessor was expressed thus : ' Pio nono tocca il
cuore : Leone tocca la mente ' (' Pius touches the heart,
Leo the mind '). I remember the sense of sweetness
and firmness which he conveyed to me in my first
audience, when he spoke to me at some length under
the impression that I was a son of John Henry
Newman, whom he doubtless supposed to have married
in early life like many another clergyman. The bad
Italian of the priest who presented me was responsible
for the mistake.

Leo XIII. ascended the Pontifical throne in the
very year (1878) when modern Socialism was beginning to be a formidable power, and when its
occasional alliance with Nihilism and Anarchism
suggested a danger to the stability of modern society,
the extent of which it appeared impossible to measure.
The two attempts on the life of the German Emperor
and the first endeavour to assassinate the King of
Italy came in the year of the new Pope's accession,
and the same year was marked by Bismarck's stern
measures of repression against German Socialism.

The new Pope, in his first Encyclical, published a
month after his election, struck the keynote of a policy
from which, in spite of many discouragements, he
never departed. The 'Inscrutabili,' published on
April 21, reviewed the ills of modern society, and
traced them in the main to features in the policy of

modern legislators which weakened the authority of the Church. 'This legislation issued,' he wrote, 'in contempt of the episcopal power, in hindrances to the exercise of the ecclesiastical ministry, in the dissolution of religious orders, and the sequestration of the property whereby the priests and the poor were supported.' Striking in this, his first Encyclical, the same note which predominates in the great Encyclical of 1902, on 'the evils of the times,' he deplores the false Liberalism of modern Italy, the secularisation of public institutions, the evil liberty of teaching publicly every kind of system of religion and morality, and the systematic invasion of the right of the Church to educate the young in those principles on which the stability of society depends. 'That is certainly not to be reputed the perfection of civil life by which all lawful authority is boldly despised; nor is that to be deemed liberty which . . . thrives (miserably and disgracefully) on freedom in gratifying evil desires, and on the impunity of crime and the oppression of those who are the best citizens. It is sin that makes people miserable.' Had not the authority of the Church been neglected and repudiated, 'the civil power would not have lost that august and sacred dignity which it bore, which was conferred on it by religion, and which alone makes the condition of obedience worthy and noble in man.'

That the civil power derives its sacredness and its hold on the hearts of men from religion, and that no mere legislation can take the place of that early moulding of the character and of instilling the duty

of obedience, on which the willing observance of all
laws that are enacted depends, was, perhaps, the
leading idea developed by the Pope during his long
Pontificate.   The best laws are of no avail if they are
not kept.   The best judiciary system is useless if
judges are corrupt and witnesses perjured.   In the
absence of general respect for truth and for law the
wisest and strongest rule must fail.   Thus the civil
power, he said, has urgent need of the spiritual.   For
the Governments of the time to war with the Church
is short-sighted policy.   The Church may suffer for
the moment.   In the long run civil society suffers, and
its rulers find their own power weakened.

The Encyclical, 'Quod Apostolici,' of the following
December, condemning Communism and irreligious
Socialism, was a further practical application of the
same principle.   Give the Church liberty, he pleaded,
and she will have the power as well as the will to
co-operate with the civil government in averting this
new danger to society.

This systematic appeal was year after year perse-
veringly renewed and applied in detail, in spite of the
discouraging fact that the rulers of the State themselves
in many cases failed in any way to aid his efforts.   In
some cases Leo XIII. was successful in gaining the
attention of Governments and in affording them substantial aid ; and in some cases he was not.   The
persecution of the Church in Germany—consequent
on the Falk laws of 1873—was at its height at his
accession.   The Pope urged a compromise for the
benefit of Church and State alike.   He urged

the German bishops to make some concessions to the
State, as in the case of notifying ecclesiastical appoint-
ments to the authorities.   He repeatedly pressed on
the German Emperor and the Iron Chancellor the
wisdom of coming to terms with the Church.   Bismarck, as is well known, formed a high opinion of
the capacity, good sense, and far-sightedness of the
Pontiff, and the modification of the Falk laws began
almost at once.   From the date of the first Papal
letter to the Emperor (December, 1882) onwards
the success of the Pope's policy became more and
more manifest.   The high-water mark was reached in
December, 1885, when Bismarck emphasised before
the world his respect for the Papacy by asking Pope
Leo to arbitrate between Germany and Spain in the
dispute as to the ownership of the Caroline Islands.
Doubtless that they should be awarded to Spain was a
foregone conclusion, and Bismarck was partly actuated
in his appeal to the Pope by his desire to retreat with
dignity.   Still, the effect of the Chancellor's action in
notifying before all Europe the value he attached to
the moral power of the Papacy was great.   The Falk
laws had by this time been so far modified that little
remained to fetter the liberty of German Catholics.
The Pope wrote a letter in January, 1886, urging the
Prussian bishops to support the Government, and he
conferred the Order of Christ on Prince Bismarck.
The present Kaiser has carried on the policy which
Bismarck's latter days inaugurated.   He has again
and again gone out of his way to do honour both to
the Church and to the Pontiff.   The state visit to the

Vatican in 1903—when William was saluted in the Piazza with the cry ' a second Charlemagne '— marked the triumph of Catholic patience under the Kulturkampf and of Leo's policy of firmness and conciliation.

A similar policy to that pursued by the Pontiff in Germany, of pleading for the liberty of the Church, urging the beneficial consequences of such freedom to the civil government itself, and at the same time exhorting Catholics to active loyalty, was carried out in Belgium. In April, 1880, the Pope protested against the proposed abolition of the Nunciature by the Liberal Government, and against its attacks on Christian education. In August, 1881, he exhorted the bishops to avoid unnecessary quarrels with the State. The position of the Holy See in the Belgium of to-day, as contrasted with its position in 1880, is perhaps one of the most remarkable landmarks of Catholic progress during his Pontificate.

In Ireland the efforts of the Papacy were perhaps less successful. From the letter to the Irish bishops of December, 1880, to the condemnation of the Plan of Campaign and boycotting, the Papal influence was on the side of law and order. But the forces to be dealt with were complex and powerful. The Persico mission accomplished but little at the time. Yet many who are in a position to judge trace the diminution of the alliance between some of the clergy and the forces tending to political disorder to the line taken by Pope Leo at that crisis.

In France the Papal action in things political

was specially marked. From the Encyclical to the French bishops, 'Nobilissima Gallorum Gens,' of February, 1884, to the Encyclical of February, 1892, 'to the Bishops and Faithful of France,' there was a constant and consistent enforcement of the exhortation to Catholics not to identify the cause of the Church with the cause of Royalism, to be good citizens, loyal to the Republic, and to bring home to the Government the fact that to persecute the Church weakens the State. We know the sequel. Persecution was for a time less virulent than it had been in the days of the Ferry laws. The *esprit nouveau* of M. Spüller was talked of; the tone of respect for the Church introduced into French politics by M. Brunetière in the 'Revue des Deux Mondes' had its counterpart in a growing reverence for religion among the intellectual classes. But the Government, far from echoing the sentiments of the most intelligent French opinion, has carried out—latterly with unparalleled virulence— the policy of the anti-Christian Freemasons. It has hardly a thinker or journal of eminence on its side. The creation of the *ralliés* asserted a great principle, and won sympathy from many moderate men. But as a practical policy it has hitherto not succeeded. The Catholics have been divided into two camps, and have thus lost in organisation; while the governing power has been in the hands of fanatics, whom no policy of moderation will conciliate. Nevertheless, Leo's counsel was a step towards inculcating on Catholics that attitude of liberality and patriotism which once made Montalembert such a power in the

Chamber, and which is the only attitude which can
ultimately win for Catholics any permanent influence
in the affairs of the country.

The various appeals of Leo XIII. on behalf of the
liberties of the Church—to the Sultan in 1879, to the
Emperor of China in 1885, to the Emperor of Japan
in the following May, and to the Emperor of Russia,
as ruler of Poland—may be briefly referred to (space
allows no more) as examples of the wide vigilance of
the Pontiff.

The Oriental Churches early claimed a special
solicitude on the part of Pope Leo, and as early as
May, 1879, he was enabled to secure from the Sultan a
recognition of rights and liberties among the Armenians
which had been infringed. Various minor schisms
among Chaldeans and Armenians were, moreover,
adjusted, and in December, 1880, Antonius Hassan,
Patriarch of the Armenians, was raised to the car-
dinalate.

Allied with this interest in the Eastern Churches
was the wider dream of reunion. The confirmation of
Oriental rights and recognition of a degree of autonomy
among the Oriental communions in 1894 bore no
great practical fruit. But it was the public manifestation of a great thought. And this aspiration for the
reunion of the Churches was eloquently expressed in
a letter published in the same year with the truly
Papal address, ‘ Principibus populisque universis,’ on
the high ideal of unity in the faith.

In the same connection must be recorded the
letter of 1895, ‘ Ad Anglos,’ which also marked a

spirit of charity and conciliation towards those external to the Papal communion. This letter probably bore permanent fruit, although doubtless the complex state of the ecclesiastical world of England was not fully understood by the Pope. The Pope's action could under no circumstances have led to practical negotiations for reunion. And what was won by the subsequent pronouncements on the constitution of the Church (the 'Satis cognitum'), and on Anglican orders (the 'Apostolicæ curæ'), in rescuing the original appeal to the English from misunderstanding, will probably prove in the long run equally important, even though the immediate irritation produced by the Brief on Anglican orders may have been, however inevitably, detrimental. No practical prospect of reunion was defeated by the publication of these later documents, for such a prospect had never existed.

The number of new hierarchies established during the Pontificate deserves a special word. In Scotland a hierarchy was formed in 1878; in Bosnia and Herzegovina in 1881. In 1884 the Archbishopric of Carthage was created in the East Indies; and another in Japan in 1891; in Mexico, in the same year, the hierarchy was reconstituted. In Brazil new dioceses were erected in 1892, and Wales has been within the last years of the Pontificate made first a vicariate and then a diocese.

The movement of centralisation begun by Pius IX. was continued by Leo XIII., but his activity was rather concerned with discipline than with doctrine. It may be plausibly maintained that no formal utterance, generally regarded by Catholic theologians as infallible, has emanated from the Chair of Peter since 1870; but in guiding the policy of Catholics throughout the world (in matters in which Catholic interests are concerned) Pope Leo XIII. was very active, Encyclicals and Briefs being, as in the days of his predecessor, very numerous, and not, as at an earlier time, exceptional events.

Another movement in the direction of centralisation was the further multiplication of the colleges in Rome which train the future priests of many nations. To those already in existence Pope Leo added the South American, the North American, the Armenian, and the Spanish.

Leo XIII. was eminently a patron of letters, and paid that close attention to ecclesiastical education which would be expected from his antecedents as a bishop. He founded universities at Fribourg, at Baltimore, at Ottawa, and showed special interest in many others.

His most noteworthy act in reference to clerical education was the celebrated Encyclical 'Æterni Patris,' on the study of the philosophy of St. Thomas Aquinas. This Encyclical was for a time applied in a somewhat restrictive sense. By degrees, however, the largeness of the doctrine of Aquinas also had, inevitably, its effect in broadening a method of philosophy which in many modern scholastic manuals had lost its original elasticity. Those who are familiar with the writings of Monsignor Mercier of Louvain [1]

[1] Now Cardinal Mercier.

will appreciate the possibilities of breadth and profound thought which have been realised by some leaders of the neo-Thomistic movement, and which have won appreciation among German and French thinkers outside the Catholic Church.

The encouragement of historical studies by Leo XIII., and his liberality in throwing open the Vatican Library to students, Catholics and non-Catholics alike, will be remembered as characteristic acts of the Pontificate. 'If Scripture history had been written on party lines,' he is reported to have said, 'we should never have heard of Judas among the Apostles.'

The questions of civil marriage and the family life, of the relations between seculars and regulars in England and elsewhere, the propagation of the faith in heathen countries, Cardinal Lavigerie's crusade against the African slave traffic, the civil power of the Papacy, Christian education, were all among the subjects of his multifarious utterances.

The adjustment of the education difficulty in Canada was perhaps as skilful and successful an enterprise as any which has marked the Pontificate. The task of thoroughly investigating the question in the country itself was entrusted to Monsignor Raphael Merry del Val,[1] and the decision of the Pope was based on his report. By a Papal pronouncement in which a rhetoric which satisfied the justly and deeply indignant feelings of the more *intransigeant* of the Canadian bishops was united with the practical measures of compromise which the Catholic Premier, Sir Wilfred Laurier,

[1] Afterwards Cardinal Merry del Val, Pontifical Secretary of State.

demanded, religious education was secured for as many as possible. A more uncompromising policy would not only have deprived large numbers of Catholic training, but might have created a schism among Canadian Catholics which would have been most serious in its consequences.

And if this negotiation may be regarded as one of the most skilful of his reign as concerning a particular locality, and from a point of view in some sense diplomatic, the Encyclical of 1892 on the social question was perhaps the most widely important act of the Pontificate, and has exercised the greatest moral effect. That ever-growing movement of the Catholic democracy—in Austria, in Belgium, in Switzerland, in Italy, in France, in Germany—which has at times and in places been dangerous in its alliance with forces of disorder, was drawn under Papal and religious influence by an Encyclical of singular wisdom and moderation. The utmost sympathy with the troubles of the labouring classes, and the recognition of their claim to an adequate remuneration as valid in justice, and not merely as an appeal to Christian pity, was combined with the firmest rejection of utopian Socialism and condemnation of the spirit of insubordination.

And in this connection came another great international spectacle, when the Pope and the German Emperor combined to sanction and approve the congress on the labour question at Berlin in 1889, which included delegates from all nations.

The last three years of Leo's Pontificate witnessed several important utterances—the Rescript to

Cardinal Richard of December, 1900, on the Congregations, beginning, 'Au milieu des consolations,'
the 'Graves de communi' of January, 1901, on social
democracy, the Encyclical on 'The Evils of the Time
and their Remedies'—the great Pontiff's will and
testament, issued in 1902, the year of his jubilee
celebrations. With solemn pathos the Holy Father
depicts in this remarkable Encyclical the sufferings of
the Church, and the share of her ministers in those
Beatitudes which promise a reward for the endurance
of present sorrow and injustice. In language suggestive of that used by Cardinal Newman he describes
the war of the age in which we live on truths the
most sacred, the inroads of secularism on our daily
life, and the failure of the boasted progress of civilisation to take the place of that religion which it has
despised and persecuted. The Encyclical is an earnest
plea, not against modern progress, but against the
forgetfulness of the laws of nature and society which
has accompanied it. It is only so far as it is the foe
to religion that the modern movement is decried.
We are (the Pope says) to welcome and use 'the
advantages which flow from education, from science,
from civilisation, from a wise and peaceful liberty.'
But liberty has passed into licence, and has questioned
the truths on which the life of society depends. And
science has not known its place, but has tried, with
ludicrous unsuccess, to be a substitute for religion.
' Man has been able to subdue matter, but matter has
not been able to give him what it does not possess.
To the great questions which concern our highest

interests science has given no answer.' Comfort and
material civilisation are dearly bought at the cost of
lost hope, lost ideals, lost coherence of principles, the
loss of the realisation of the necessary laws of social
life. 'A law of Providence confirmed by history shows
that man cannot strike at the first principles of religion
without sapping the foundations of social order and
prosperity.' To the vindication, then, of these old
and simple truths—truths of common-sense which the
eccentricity of modern thought has forgotten—he devotes himself; to their restoration to true perspective,
which undisciplined discussion and an exaggeration of
the place occupied by science in the scheme of true
wisdom had destroyed. The Pontiff asks that his
message may be listened to not by Catholics only,
but by all who have at heart the interests of the race.
'May it be received as the testament which, standing,
as we do, so near the gates of eternity, we wish to
leave to the people of the earth, as a presage of the
salvation which we desire for all.' This Encyclical is
perhaps the most touching of the whole Pontificate
and breathes in every page the unearthly wisdom
of the Christian Church. It is the fitting farewell of a
great Pontiff to the people of Christ at the termination
of a memorable reign.

Let me now say a few words on what I must
account the most significant feature of the whole
Pontificate. Leo XIII. was in his early years hailed
as a Liberal Pope. He was to come to terms with the
modern movements and to abandon effete mediæval-
isms. On the true nature of his so-called Liberalism I

shall speak directly ; but any expectation among men
of the world that he would place in the background the
directly spiritual arms of the Church, or its spiritual
claims, or its spiritual aims, in favour of the weapons
and standards of diplomacy, has been absolutely
falsified.   Running parallel with the acts I have
attempted to summarise is a long series of devotional
utterances and admonitions, and nothing is more
apparent throughout the Pontificate than that the
weapons to which the Pontiff has really trusted are
prayer and devotion.   Belief in ' the foolishness of the
Cross,' the simplest faith in that Power which is
beyond our small capacities and comprehension, which
is not of the world, has been in his Pontifical ' Acts '
the mainspring of hope, even where the methods
of diplomacy have been employed.   That the faithful should grow in devotion to the Rosary, that
they should join the Third Order of St. Francis,
that they should lead Christian lives—these are the
means on which the Pontiff ultimately relies for the
success of the Church in the contest with its foes.
No one who reads the remarkable utterances which
have appeared throughout his reign can fail to be
struck by this fact.   Devotion to St. Thomas Aquinas,
to St. Alfonso Liguori, to St. Bonaventure, to St.
Vincent of Paul, to St. Francis of Assisi, but, above
all, to the Sacred Heart of our Lord and to our
Lady—these are the subjects on which the Pontiff
breaks away from diplomatic reserve and shows the
simplest faith and devotion.   The saintly piety of the
' De Jesu Redemptore ' of 1900, and of the singularly

beautiful Encyclical on the Blessed Eucharist, ' Miræ Caritatis,' issued in 1902, reveals the inner character of Leo and the true secret alike of his own trust and of his power over others.

In estimating the results of Leo XIII.'s Pontificate, we must remember—what is obvious once it is stated —that in the last resort the whole of the power of the Papacy rests on its moral influence. Even in the palmy days of Hildebrand and Innocent III., when Popes deposed monarchs and claimed the widest temporal dominion, such claims were only effected in virtue of the prevailing popular faith and sentiment. It was the dominant faith of the age, and its chivalrous and mystical devotion to the See of Peter which made Pepin and Charlemagne eager to support the Papacy with the temporal sword, and to confer on it the dominions which it subsequently held. It was the popular faith in the Papacy which made an interdict in the reign of King John a veritable and effectual punishment to the English people instead of an idle form. The Papal suzerainty over Ireland would never have been yielded in an age when the moral power of the Papacy was less than it was in the time of our Henry II. The temporal power of the Popes, as well as their spiritual power, has ever depended ultimately on the moral influence they have exerted on the faith and reverence of Christendom. And, consequently, it is especially the case with the Papacy that in, estimating the success of a Pontificate, the weights and measures consist largely of impalpable but very real moral considerations. To be a great soldier like

Julius II., or a great scholar like Benedict XIV., is not
necessarily to be a great Pope.   The achievements of
such Pontiffs may be more definitely describable or
ascertainable, may have less of apparent failure, but
they do not, save very indirectly, tend to the restoration of the Papacy to its rightful pre-eminence.   Had
Pius IX. succeeded—as Mazzini once hoped—in
reorganising the Papal States on a new basis, as the
ideal Liberal Pope he would have been a great
political figure.   But it is questionable whether he
would have won influence as deep as he actually secured
at a time of misfortune and failure.   Not, indeed, for
the world at large—which he defied in wrathful indignation—but for Catholics, Pius IX. was a great Pope,
greater than Leo XII., Pius VIII., or Gregory XVI.,
though he lived to see himself robbed of the temporal
power which his predecessors had enjoyed.

In reviewing the very different career of his
successor it would be misleading, then, to measure his
success entirely by the success of the enterprises on
which he set his heart.   A great missionary aims at
converting his hundreds of thousands of souls.   He
does not succeed in doing so; but it is the moral
energy which expressed itself in an infinite aspiration
which actually wins for him his influence, as a spiritual
force, on the minds of men.   Noble aspirations and the
unflinching advocacy—through discouragement—of
high and unworldly principles may be a great power,
and may prove in the long run to have been so even if
each enterprise in which they are manifested fails.
The world gains the moral tonic attaching to the self-

revelation of a character and purpose consistently great.

> Great is the facile conqueror,
> Yet haply he who wounded sore,
> Breathless, unhorsed, all covered o'er
>   With blood and sweat,
> Sinks foiled, yet fighting, evermore,
>   Is greater yet.

It would be unnecessary to apply such thoughts literally to a Pontificate so rich in actual achievement as that of Leo XIII. But the two questions must be kept distinct—the direct aims which he actually achieved beginning at a time when the Papacy, however powerful among Catholics, was an object of hostility and contempt to the outside world; and what his strenuous efforts indirectly accomplished, even through the most unsuccessful enterprises, in raising once again the moral power of the Papacy among the nations, and securing respect and influence for it even among its enemies.

Leo XIII. used at one time (as I have said) to be called a Liberal Pope. This statement is only true with very great reservations, which I shall shortly attempt to indicate. But he was a Pope with those wide and large conceptions of policy which involve great liberality of mind and exclude the bigotry belonging to a narrow purview. The thought of Dante's Papa Angelico, the magnanimous Pope, the friend of science, who was to bring enlightenment and peace to all, must often have dwelt in the mind of one who so loved the age of Aquinas and Bonaventure.

An English writer of power and penetration, no friend to Catholicism—the late Mrs. Oliphant—wrote thus of him a few years back : 'It is touching and pathetic to divine in the present Pope something of that visionary and disinterested ambition that longs to bless and help the universe, which was in those dreams of the mediæval mind prompted by great piety and love that is half Divine. . . . There would seem to be in his old age (which makes it impossible if nothing else did) a trembling consciousness of capacity to be himself a Pope Angelico, and gather us all under his wings.'

At a time when the Papacy was decried by the dominant Liberal party as the incorrigible enemy of the great movement of progress, which was advancing with God-like step, carrying all before it ; within a few years of the Syllabus which had been hailed as the definitive divorce of the Papacy from modern civilisation, Pope Leo had the courage to assume at once the attitude of a great Pope, the friend and guardian of modern civilisation, denouncing the anarchic principles which threatened society, and urging civil rulers to defend religion and the Papacy as the indispensable bulwarks of social order against the revolution. Thus, as we have seen, he began by the unsparing denunciation of anti-social Socialism in the 'Inscrutabili' and the 'Quod Apostolici,' and in the very first years of his Pontificate he had convinced the greatest statesman in Europe, and the head of the greatest Protestant Power, that to persecute the Catholic Church and alienate the Papacy was contrary to the interests of

civil society. The repeal of the Falk laws and the
Papal arbitration in the Caroline Islands are very
noteworthy. It was to the few men of insight that
the Pope had necessarily to look for recognition, at
a time when average opinion was marked by intense
bigotry; and the prompt response of Bismarck to
Pope Leo's overtures was the best means of forcing
on the European mind a new attitude of attention and
respect towards the Papacy.

But doubtless, in these and other critical junctures,
the contrast between the largeness of conception
and aspiration with the limited results secured is
striking. Leo dreamt of himself as the great peacemaker among the nations; the *rôle* of arbitrator was
assumed but once, and in a dispute in which justice
was not really in question. He dreamt, too, of making
peace between labourer and capitalist in all countries.
He has written wisely and beautifully on the subject
in the 'Rerum Novarum.' Very striking have been
the consequent manifestations of loyalty to the Holy
See in the labour pilgrimage. And a strong impetus
has been given by his action to the Catholic social
movement in France and Belgium. But of the idea
of the great international peacemaker in this matter,
as in that of war between the nations, a suggestion
was realised and no more—in the address to the
Pope from the Congressists at Bienne, and the con-
vocation of the Congress of Berlin.

Once again, he has spoken on many occasions
beautiful words concerning the reunion of the Churches.
That he might, like Papa Angelico, be the means of

healing all schism has been a dream second in vivid-
ness to none.   But here again only a faint suggestion
has been realised—a few petty schisms in obscure
regions adjusted, and autonomy granted to the remnant
of Greek Churchmen in communion with Rome, for
which few cared.   Again, he urged that in every land
Governments should defend the liberties of the Church,
and maintained that they would promptly reap their
reward in the loyalty and devotion of Catholics.   And,
doubtless, in Germany he largely succeeded.   In
Belgium, too, the present state of things—in spite of
recent drawbacks—on the whole justifies such a claim.
But elsewhere Governments have often been deaf or—
much worse—Catholic people have been intractable.
Leo gained little from the French rulers, in spite of
the *esprit nouveau* of M. Spüller.

We have had, then, the spectacle of a very great
ideal—something of the ideal associated with Papa
Angelico—pursued with absolute insistency and consistency, winning occasionally emphatic victories, more
often remaining only the spectacle of an ideal retained
with faith and courage amid a civilisation which refuses
to admit of its realisation.

And now we come to consider the epithet, ' A
Liberal Pope,' often applied to Pope Leo, especially
in the early years of his Pontificate.   It is curious
enough that this epithet came to be applied greatly
from the contrast between the attitude of Leo XIII.,
face to face with modern civilisation, and that of his
predecessor ; and yet it is probable that Pius IX. had
more of genuine Liberalism in his composition than

his successor. Liberalism in great Catholic leaders has genera.ly involved both an intellectual attribute and a temper of mind. Intellectually it has involved a real belief in liberty as a factor in true progress, and a means of attaining to truth or justice. The temper of mind it normally involves consists in sympathy with modern civilisation and sanguineness as to its future. In the domain of politics, Montalembert and Lacordaire are classical instances in our own age. They both had a genuine belief in the principles of 1789—in free speech and the other freedoms—as great factors in progress, and as elevating the dignity of human society. Their sympathy with the victims of unjust oppression, of narrow tyranny over mind or body, fused itself with an almost transfiguring delineation of the rights of all to equal justice—which is the inspiring truth underlying the Liberal theory—and a youthful hope that such rights could be effectively realised. That each man has a right to be heard, that truth and justice are best secured by the free and outspoken expression on the part of all of their views and claims—these are the typically English elements in the Liberal view.

And in more intellectual departments we have similar characteristics. The sympathy with modern scientific, critical, and historical methods goes hand in hand with the jealous safeguarding of the absolute freedom necessary for their effective prosecution. To stifle any fresh truth, however dimly or inaccurately expressed, is, from this point of view, to lose a ray of light which, perhaps, will not again be granted. The utmost freedom is required, not as giving any authority to the various arguments, but because it is only by ventilating conjecture that it is gradually converted into something more accurate and ascertained.

I do not think that either the Liberal theory or the Liberal temper of mind, whether in the intellectual or in the political sphere, was characteristic of Leo XIII. If we except a certain constitutional sanguineness, which has led him to make light of difficulties, he was rather a Conservative than a Liberal Pope in temper and in belief. Sanguine and conciliating in method, indeed, he was. Liberalistic or confident in the tendencies of the age he was not. He never had the belief in liberty, as such, which led Pius IX., in 1846, so nearly to accept the partial alliance of Mazzini. He never had the belief in free criticism in history or Biblical research which characterised a Döllinger or a Bickell. His wish to come to terms with modern civilisation was quite of a different kind. It was rather of the kind indicated in his Encyclical on Human Liberty. There was no disposition to idealise the tendencies of modern civilisation. On the contrary, civilisation was ever regarded by him as having in most important matters deteriorated. Yet that was not, in his judgment, a reason for despairing of it. In its present imperfect state, then, we must fully accept its conditions in order to improve it. We must use the modern liberties—our ultimate ideal being largely to get rid of them.

Pius IX. began with a certain sanguine trust in the more generous features of modern Liberalism. Disappointment led to reaction, and made him the *intran-*

sigeant opponent of all that savoured of Liberalism. Leo never idealised Liberalism, and, consequently, he was kinder to it. There was never in his utterances any enthusiasm for the sacred rights of liberty, or even much appreciation of the value of liberty in the search for truth. His constant denunciations of free discussion have not been tempered by any recognition of its indispensable necessity in certain fields of inquiry. Truth was ever referred to by him as the possession of the Church, not only in the sense in which all Catholics so regard it, but almost without qualification—without direct contemplation of that important work of correcting its analysis and defining its limits in relation to advancing secular knowledge, which needs free discussion for its successful accomplishment. How little liberty, as such, has been valued by him in philosophy may be seen from Leo's policy in reference to Thomism—his tendency to treat it as the last word in philosophy, rather than merely as a profound and admirable work of the human reason at a certain epoch. How little liberty, as such, was valued by him in Biblical criticism is seen in his letter on the study of the sacred Scriptures in the early 'nineties. But the wisdom of the statesman, who knows that to rule effectively the ruler must often tolerate what he does not approve, that you must be conciliatory and considerate if you hope to win conciliation and consideration—these are of the essence of Pope Leo's policy. The dreams whose disappointment turned Pius IX. into something of an *intransigeant* had no place in his successor.

Perhaps no clearer indication of Pope Leo's attitude

o

in this respect can be found than in two of the most interesting acts of the later years of his Pontificate— the letter to Cardinal Gibbons on Americanism, and the formation in 1901 of the Commission on Biblical Studies. We find in the letter on Americanism the utmost sympathy for the peculiarities of national character, and the recognition that adaptation of ecclesiastical usage to the times is indispensable. On the other hand, we find a deep sense that the faith ' given to the saints ' was given them for all time, and a consequent conviction that a civilisation which is whittling it away is so far on the downward path, not the upward ; that accommodation, though it may well be an unfortunate necessity, is not likely to be a movement towards higher ideals ; and that a Liberalism which makes light of such considerations—which tampers with Christian doctrine or waters down Christian ethics in deference to the Time Spirit—may sap the very foundations of the Church.

But admirable and convincing as are both sides of this view of the situation, it does not deal at all with the deeper problem, which has been in the minds of those whose imprudence and excesses are justly condemned. That the advance of secular knowledge—of criticism, science, and philosophy—has in the past greatly modified the form and intellectual expression of religious thought ; that a similar modification is always taking place ; that the attempt so to modify it is constantly, in its earlier stages, opposed by ecclesiastical authority—these are facts or suppositions of deep significance to many minds. And the resulting problem—how to combine loyalty to the ancient faith and to ecclesiastical rulers with fidelity to advancing science and increasing knowledge—is a very real one. It is one whose direct treatment, perhaps, in its nature stands outside Pontifical utterances. At any rate, the letter to Cardinal Gibbons did not contemplate it.

Yet perhaps the letter does indirectly help the solution of a problem with which it does not directly deal. The practical wisdom of the Pontiff helps us, perhaps, in a question which it was alien to his mind to contemplate speculatively. For it rebukes excesses on either side—the fossil conservatism of formalists not less than the innovation which tampers with the ancient faith. At the same time, by its significant silences it leaves ample scope for the two tempers of mind which the Church ever allows for: the mind which is alive to the outlook suggested by the advance of knowledge, and the mind to which the Christian revelation is so absorbing as to shut out all lesser lights, as the smaller planets become invisible in the full blaze of the sunlight. To do much more than this—to treat in detail a problem which must wait for the discussions of theologians representing both tempers and the researches of specialists before it can be solved—would no doubt be practically impossible, even if the special genius of the late Pope had led him to attempt it.

Still more remarkable as an illustration of Pope Leo's special temper and gifts has been his treatment of the question of Biblical studies. The Encyclical published nearly ten years ago was distinctly conservative in tone.   It showed little or no familiarity with the problems which modern criticism has made so urgent. The Pope's standpoint was, naturally, that of the contemporaries of his earlier years, in days when the Higher Criticism was regarded as pure rationalism in the hands of Strauss, Bauer, and Volkmar.   But the extraordinary openness of his mind to a new situation, so far as its practical necessities are concerned, was evidenced towards the end of his reign in the formation of a Pontifical Commission, of which nearly all the original members were Biblical critics keenly alive to modern criticism, and entirely opposed to the extremely conservative attitude on Biblical subjects which the earlier Encyclical was popularly supposed to favour.   It was understood that facts were brought before the Pontiff which convinced him that a wider outlook was necessary than that contemplated in his earlier pronouncement, and, with an adaptability truly marvellous in a nonagenarian, he placed on foot a comprehensive inquiry, committed in the first instance to those who are identified with the best work in critical specialism rather than with the preoccupations of conservative theological views.   That the Pontiff personally was conversant with critical problems practically unknown to his generation is not to be supposed.   But his simple eye for the welfare of the Church, his saintly sympathy with those souls whose troubles were not his own, and his statesmanlike realisation of the actual difficulties of the situation, here, as in other cases, prevailed.   And the old man of ninety charged younger thinkers and scholars with the task of dealing comprehensively with the needs of an age whose intellectual atmosphere was so unlike that in which his own mind had been formed.

Leo XIII. had certain qualities which at times made his friends anxious. The great sanguineness and the occasional utopian schemes which he conceived suggested the fear that he might attempt to realise the impossible. His incessant activity led to some alarm lest his reforming zeal should be too regardless of precedent. But in the long run his singleness of aim and the sense of fact belonging to true statesmanship won the day and determined his course. Dreams or prejudices may have existed, but they never practically and permanently misled him. His dreams of reunion with the East and with England have been smiled at, but his critics cannot point to any rash act to which they led him. His ideal of a universal reign of Thomistic philosophy alarmed some able Catholic thinkers, but it was not, in the long run, pressed to practical excess. His sympathy with Christian democracy was in his public utterances carefully safe-guarded. In the matter of Biblical criticism, if he did not fully appreciate the situation intellectually, his practical action was in course of time guided by the real needs of the hour.

I can hardly doubt that history, which will unques-tionably rank him among our holy Pontiffs, will also allow that he steered the bark of Peter with judgment and wisdom in a very troublous and difficult time.[1]

---

[1] The above Essay was written in 1903 as an obituary.

THE GENIUS OF CARDINAL WISEMAN
A CENTENARY ADDRESS [1]

It is a pleasure and an honour to be asked to speak of Cardinal Wiseman in this place and on this occasion. This is one of those representative Catholic gatherings which he so keenly loved, which brought before his vivid imagination the greatness of the Church universal. It is a memorable anniversary in the history of the Church in England ; and it is associated especially with the fortunes of Ushaw College, the home of his boyhood, to which his devotion was deep as it was lifelong.

But how, in the brief space which such an opportunity affords, can I deal at all adequately with a career of which the most obvious characteristic was the multiplicity of the objects which claimed the attention of a busy and devoted life? To do so is hardly possible. But, on the other hand, it is hardly necessary, for that career is probably in outline known to most of those who are here. It will be enough, then, if I briefly remind you of the main fields of Nicholas Wiseman's varied activity, of the several

[1] The address here printed was delivered, at the invitation of the President of Ushaw College, on the occasion of its Centenary Celebration in July 1908.

Walker & Boutall, ph.sc.

Cardinal Wiseman.
Ætatis (c.) 48 from a miniature after
an oil painting at Oscott by J. R. Herbert, R.A.

pictures of the man which we may form at the different stages of his course : and I shall then endeavour to give some unity and point to the lesson which his life and work may teach us by noting certain distinctive traits of character and intellect in the great Cardinal, which were visible in every one alike of the tasks to which he set himself, and which showed him to be one and the same man in so many aspects and in such different surroundings.

We may picture him first, already a distinguished man, at the early age of twenty-six—the time 1831 to 1835, the place the city of Rome. He was then Rector of the English College in the Eternal City. His ' Horæ Syriacæ' had won him a European reputation as a philological and Syrian scholar. This book, though slight in bulk, dealt with studies then familiar to only a few. And it appeared to be the first work of one who promised to be a really great Orientalist. Such authorities as Lachmann, Tischendorf, Tregelles, Scrivener, and one who lived long in the neighbourhood of this college, at Durham, Bishop Westcott, in their writings cite Wiseman's authority on matters of philology as weighty and in some cases as conclusive. The Germans—ever on the alert to discover a man of learning—at once noted the great promise shown by the young ecclesiastic and his cosmopolitan antecedents. The late Lord Houghton used to quote from a German reviewer who hailed Wiseman on his first appearance, describing him with one of the wonderful German ' portmanteau ' words as ' an-in-Spain-born-from-an-Irish-family-descended-in-

England - educated - in - Italy - residing - Syrian - scholar.'
For ten years he acted as the Curator of the Arabic
department of the Vatican Library and was the intimate
friend of the learned Cardinal Mai.   He was not only
a scholar of eminence, but became from his attractive
social gifts one whose society was sought by other
eminent men of learning—residents in Rome or visitors,
of different religions and various nationalities, such
men as Bunsen, Tholuck, Abel Rémusat, and many
another.   We see him at the climax of this portion of
his career when he delivered in Cardinal Weld's
rooms in Rome, in the spring of 1835, before the
intellectual *élite* of residents and visitors in the city, his
celebrated lectures on 'The Connexion between Science
and Religion.'

But mere learning did not satisfy that deeply
religious and apostolic spirit, even though it afforded
an opportunity of pointing out, as against the disciples
of the eighteenth-century scoffers, the compatibility of
true science and the Catholic religion.   Mr. Scrivener,
who hailed Wiseman's achievements in philology as
so 'precocious,' lamented them also as 'deceitful,' for
the English Rector early deserted what to Scrivener
was all-important for what was to a mere scholar
visionary and unreal.   It was not enough for Wiseman
to lead a life devoted to secular learning, pointing out,
by the way, that to be a true man of science was
consistent with being a true Catholic.   He wished to
do something more positive for religion—to win souls
more directly to the Church.   If the first picture of
him, then, is that of the distinguished man of learning,

the second is that of the Christian and Catholic apologist.

His work as an apologist was the second phase of his life—the time 1836 to 1839, the place still Rome as his headquarters, but with visits of critical importance to Munich, Paris and London. And this second phase arose out of the first. Among the men of learning with whom he became associated in the first period of his career were Frederick Schlegel, who visited Rome; the eminent German Professors Döllinger, Phillips and Möhler, with whom Wiseman used to stay at Munich on his way from England to the Eternal City; Montalembert, Lacordaire and Lamennais, whom he often met on the celebrated occasion of their visit to Rome in 1830 and saw later in Paris. Two of these men—Lamennais and Döllinger—awaken sad thoughts, for they were not in the end true to their early promise. But in those days all of them were in different ways fired by the hope of a great triumph for the Church, to be won by a new apologetic couched in the language of the age, making use of its culture, showing how that culture could find its true place and its true expression in Catholic Christianity. The age was to be purged of the remnant of eighteenth - century scepticism by the development, under Catholic influences, of its own best thoughts and aspirations. As the climax of the previous phase of his career had been the lectures in Cardinal Weld's rooms in Rome, so the most noteworthy incident of this was another course of lectures —the discourses on the Catholic Church delivered in

the Sardinian Chapel in London, of which echoes
reached Newman while still an Anglican at Oxford,
and which were hailed by him in 'The British Critic'
as making for the influence of the Catholic ideals of
the Oxford Movement.   In these lectures Wiseman
appealed to Schlegel, de Coux, Bautain, Stolberg and
others—each a typical and eminent man of his age,
who had each found in the Catholic Church alone what
their different lines of thought needed for full realisation.

The lectures were thus delivered under the inspiration drawn from the Catholic revival in Germany and
France.   He desired to extend this Catholic movement
to his own country.   He compared notes with Möhler,
author of the 'Symbolik,' at Munich while on his way
to England to deliver his lectures ; and in Paris, where
he also halted, he heard Lacordaire preach some of
his great *Conférences* at Notre Dame.   The addresses
begun at the Sardinian Chapel were continued at
Moorfields, and the crowds attending them were
immense.   The attention not only of the Puseyites,
but of more liberal thinkers, was arrested, and many of
them were among Wiseman's hearers, including Lord
Chancellor Brougham, who was present at nearly every
one of the lectures.

The third picture of Wiseman is of an English
bishop—the time 1839 to 1845, the place Oscott, of
which he had been appointed President.   He was now
devoting his attention above all things to the Tractarian party, the leaders of which were his neighbours
at Oxford—incessantly endeavouring, by firmness and

sympathy combined, to bring Newman and his friends to the fulfilment of their Catholic aspirations in submission to the See of Peter. And this work, again, arose naturally from the phase which preceded it, for the apologist was concentrating his attention on those whom he had most hope of winning. Together with O'Connell, he had founded ' The Dublin Review ' on the crest of the wave of his successful lectures of 1836. And from the time when, in 1839, he was made President at Oscott the main work of the ' Review '—of which he was himself one of the editors —was to deal with the problems raised by the leaders of the Oxford School. In that very year, 1839, Wiseman wrote the article on the Donatist schism, of which Newman's contemporary letters show, even more plainly than the retrospect in the ' Apologia,' that it was the turning-point in the change of his attitude towards the Apostolic See.

The climax of this phase of Wiseman's career was the memorable scene when Newman presented himself at Oscott in November, 1845, to receive confirmation at the hands of his ancient foe in controversy, now his Bishop, giving up his sword, and with the simplicity of a child placing his future in the hands of the Catholic prelate.

And now we come to the fourth, and last, picture of Wiseman, as the founder of the revived Church in England, the first Cardinal Archbishop of Westminster —the time 1850 to 1862, the place chiefly London, but with an activity which extended to all England. We see him first as the object of an outburst of Protestant invective without parallel in the nineteenth century, the author of that wonderful *tour de force*, the 'Appeal to the English People,' which covered half a sheet of 'The Times' and was written, almost without an erasure, in the space of three days ; the restorer, in England as of the Hierarchy so, too, of the religious orders ; the man who welded together into one polity the old Catholics and converts, the English and immigrant Irish —all this achieved not, indeed, with perfect success, but with a power of initiation and sympathy and a concentrated energy which none of his contemporaries could have approached. We see him surveying the different churches which under his auspices replaced the old Mass-houses of the persecuted 'English Papists.' We see him then in company with Augustus Welby Pugin, their architect, sniffing the air, as it were, with satisfaction at all that had been so successfully accomplished for the Church in England and for the 'greater glory of God.' We see him within the convents of England, and surrounded with the religious women in whom he took so deep an interest, and by the school-children whom he loved. We see him at a State function, revelling in the ceremonies of the Church, which he declared that he enjoyed as a girl enjoys her first ball. We see him at the Synod of Oscott, in 1851, listening to the stirring words of John Henry Newman on the 'Second Spring' of the Church in England, or at the Malines Congress discoursing to the prelates of other countries, with whom, as a true Catholic cosmopolitan, he was so thoroughly at home ; or pontificating at the Moorfields Cathedral, or preach-

ing on a memorable occasion at the London Oratory,
when the admirable conduct of a great ecclesiastical
function overcame him on the spot, and turned an
intended rebuke of certain reported indiscretions into
a sermon of enthusiastic praise and congratulation.

Here we will leave him, and of the last sad years of
suffering and illness—from 1862 to 1865—we will
recall no more than the fact that they were crowned
by a beautiful death. His thoughts went back at the
end with a touching wistfulness to his early days, spent
at Rome and Monte Porzio under the shadow of the
Apostolic See. The services of the Church still gave
him all the old happiness. And when the last solemn
rites for the dying were administered, over which the
portrait of Pius IX. hanging in his room appeared to
the onlookers to preside, the scene left an ineffaceable
picture on the minds of all who were present. His
faithful secretary and nurse, Father Morris, has handed
it on to all of us in his well-known book on the Cardinal's last illness.

And now I will ask, What is it that stands forth in
the four pictures I have indicated of Wiseman, at four
different stages of his career, which marks him as, in
each of them, one and the same man? We have to
consider, I repeat, first the Catholic *savant*, the Rector
of the Collegio Inglese, surrounded at Cardinal Weld's
rooms in the Palazzo Odeschalchi by eminent and
learned men of different religions and nations, listening
to his words with interest and respect; next the
apologist, who joins hands with Lacordaire and
Frederick Schlegel in depicting Catholicism and

Christianity as necessary to the modern world, and defending it with the arguments which appeal to a new age ; then the English Bishop at Oscott, who devotes all his sympathy to the Tractarians of Oxford, and urges them onwards to find the logical issue of their position in the visible Catholic Church ; and, lastly, the Cardinal of Santa Pudentiana, the first Archbishop of Westminster, who founds anew the religious orders in this country and restores a hierarchy and gives a constitution to the English Catholic Church.   What was there in these very different *rôles* which spoke of the man who filled them as one and the same ?

Two qualities I note especially—one, the deep unwavering faith which not only his Ushaw training, but his long residence in Rome, near the tombs of the Apostles and amid the relics of the martyrs, in Rome, the appointed guardian of Catholic dogma, was so well calculated to fix and foster ; the other, a very remarkable inborn power of imaginative sympathy, which I trace in part to his Irish descent.   I may, perhaps, add a third quality, which reminds us again of his Ushaw days, for at Ushaw he was a boy.   I mean the boyish hopefulness and love of enterprise which distinguished him to the end, and is visible in each of the great tasks he accomplished, giving animation and direction to the joint work of faith and sympathy. These qualities were very marked and interacted closely with one another.

First, as the Catholic *savant*, associating with non-Catholic *savants*, winning the regard and friendship of such men as Bunsen, the learned Prussian diplomatic

Minister, and his friends, and of so many others. It was the very firmness of his faith, based on the rock of Peter, what I may call his Catholic backbone, which allowed him to give such full play to his sympathy in his intercourse with such friends ; which enabled him, without fear of having his own standpoint shaken, to enter heartily in imagination into the point of view of the contemporary men of learning, to study their thoughts, to understand their language, and to use it himself when it was necessary. It was, on the other hand, his gift of imaginative sympathy which enabled him to share their thoughts and language with so much success. He was so confident that in the end scientific investigation and discussion, if fairly conducted, would lead to nothing incompatible with Catholic faith that he entered into the discussions of the day fearlessly, freely, frankly, sympathetically. There was nothing (in the invidious sense of the word) 'sectarian' in his attitude. He was not suspicious of the learned inquiries of non-Catholic *savants* because they were not his brethren in the faith, when the real love of truth and of science was apparent in their labours. He was not afraid of joining them in the laborious furthering of their investigations on the neutral *terrain* of secular knowledge. And while this attitude gave the common platform so necessary for co-operation and mutual understanding, his boyish sanguineness, by making him hope, perhaps, for results which were unattainable, for coincidences between new discoveries in the sciences and Christian tradition, at all events more signal and decisive than time has yet brought, gave also a keenness and zest and success to his efforts which they would not otherwise have had. His hope for the impossible widened the range of the possible.

Again, as a Catholic apologist, in the more directly apostolic work, which he began in 1836, we see the same qualities. Schlegel, Joseph Görres, Möhler in Germany; Lacordaire, Montalembert, Rio, Ozanam in France; Manzoni in Italy, touched a chord in which faith, sympathy and hopefulness for the age were combined. The wide sympathy—which was the most distinctive of Wiseman's three qualities and that which enabled his faith and hope so greatly to influence others—is apparent at the very outset of the lectures on Catholicism delivered in the Sardinian Chapel in 1836. He traces the various aspects of Catholicism which had recently won over to the Catholic religion so many of the great minds of the Romantic Movement—how Phillips of Munich had come by the road of historical research and generalisation; how Stolberg and Frederick Schlegel and others had found in Catholicism only the religion which satisfies the needs of man; how de Coux had been led to the Church by economic science, and Adam Müller by the social studies provoked by the events of the French Revolution. And Wiseman's power of sympathy with each of these minds—of himself treading in imagination each of the paths they had followed—was shown also in his own lectures by the choice of just the class of considerations which he felt to be within the comprehension of his hearers in London itself. Thus we have the remarkable spectacle of a man whose mental training had been mainly in scholastic Rome, who was especially familiar with a method of apologetic largely fashioned by the great schoolmen of the thirteenth century, throwing himself by force of imaginative sympathy into the lines of thought which were influencing men in the nineteenth century. He showed how 'all roads lead to Rome,' and how the best thought of his own time could lead there as effectually as that of any other time. Here again, then, we have the combination of faith and keen sympathy. And in this case also, if we read his lectures and letters, we feel that the great results he actually attained could scarcely have been won but for a boyish hopefulness, which dreamt of results of the Catholic revival, in which he was taking his part, in its effect on the thought and beliefs of Englishmen—nay, even of Christendom—which one of a colder nature would have at once pronounced to be utopian, and while doing so would have failed entirely to win the actual success which Wiseman achieved.

It was the same with the Oxford Movement. 'There can be no doubt whatever that without such a view of the Catholic Church and her position as we obtained from "The Dublin Review"'—so wrote one of the Tractarian leaders to Wiseman—'we Oxford people should have had our conversion indefinitely retarded, even had we at last been converted at all.' While the old-fashioned English Catholics were suspicious of the good faith of the Tractarians, and held that the long-recognised groove of apologetic ought to

P

suffice for them if they were sincere, Wiseman, with
generous tact and sympathy, threw himself into their
position and their mentality, appreciated their difficulties, and by this very sympathy with them made
his replies intelligible, persuasive, convincing.   Here,
again, his hope for immense results—for what was
spoken of as the 'conversion of England'—was an
inseparable part of the great wave of imaginative
sympathy with which he actually succeeded, by the
conversion of Newman and his allies in bringing the
movement to a termination which the bulk of English
Catholics had openly laughed at as an impossible
dream.

And as Cardinal Archbishop he showed the same
faith and sympathy and hope.   His faith and hope
were shown by the largeness of the enterprise he
undertook and by its persistent and successful accomplishment.   His sympathy was apparent in the manifold works it involved.   He vehemently disclaimed,
in regard to the conduct of one of his undertakings,
the 'reproach of belonging to a party.'   And the same
sentiment applied to all.   His faith was ever firm and
deep, never narrow or partisan.   His sympathy was
universal—with every good work, every new religious
congregation, every monastic or conventual order.
Each had its place and its vocation.   The late Father
Whitty, speaking of this trait in his character, once
said that as a national poet expresses the distinctive
genius of his nation, so Wiseman's temperament represented the many-sided genius of the Church herself—not of Church authority alone, but of the rich

and varied life which the Church displays in her saints, in her religious orders, in her theological schools, in her great social workers. The same spirit is visible to the very end of his life, and it is nowhere more manifest than in the inaugural address to the Accademia of the Catholic Religion in 1861, which is, perhaps, the last of Wiseman's great public utterances in which his full powers are apparent, untouched by a trace of the hand of illness. ' He has done a great work,' wrote Newman at the time of Wiseman's death, 'and has finished it. Of how few men' (he adds) 'can this be said.' He had not, indeed—again in this last phase—done all he dreamt of; but indomitable energy and hopefulness had enabled him to accomplish what in this world of imperfection was very wonderful, and would have been impossible, one may fairly say, to any of his contemporaries.

Let me now add one word on the lesson which I think we may learn, in our own time, from the characteristics of Nicholas, Cardinal Wiseman, on which I have dwelt. We are now in the presence of perils which he himself never suspected. It would be obviously impossible on an occasion like this to survey the many trials and troubles of the Church in our own day. But I will name two dangers which are likely to increase as time goes on, and in which I think that Wiseman's union of faith, sympathy and hopefulness are especially called for. I speak of the intemperate excesses of the democratic movement, which have issued in the danger to society presented by Socialism

as we see it in Italy and Germany and elsewhere, and
the anti-Christian theories which are being broached, in
the name of historical criticism, by those who devote
themselves to the study of the historical origins of
Christianity.   The former concerns us all ; the latter
is felt especially at the universities, where historical
and Biblical studies are of necessity pursued in detail ;
and I found on the occasion of an interesting visit to
Louvain, that the problems which these subjects raise
were exercising the best minds of that great centre of
Catholic learning.   The peculiarity of both these
dangers is that they often present themselves in a
form which cannot be successfully resisted by indis-
criminate attack.   Not all that the advocates of these
modern movements urge is false and anti-Christian.
The democratic movement owes much of its influence
to a generous resentment of real wrongs, which the
people have endured in the past and still endure in
modern civilisation.   The critical and historical movement, however extravagant some of its manifestations,
embodies also, as we all know, scientific evidence for
facts which are being ascertained in the course of the
systematic study of history—facts which are at variance
with some long-standing traditions.   Here, then, while
courage and hopefulness are especially demanded by
the great difficulties which have to be surmounted,
there is a very special call for Wiseman's gift of
sympathy as well as for his faith.   Without his faith
unproven theories, subversive of Christianity, may be
adopted in the name of science.   Without his sympathy
with the discoveries of the age justice may not be done

to what is true in modern research, and we may thus fail to face and meet the real difficulties which genuine scientific study already presents to many thinking minds and will gradually bring home to many more. Excesses and extravagant theories can be effectively met only by granting what is true and proven and dissociating this from what is false and fanciful. And the case is, I suppose, somewhat parallel with the democratic movement—its wild theories and its just grievances and demands. Wiseman did not live to cope with either of these problems. But in regard to the difficulties presented by the advance of the positive sciences his spirit, as I have described it, is represented with absolute fidelity by another great Cardinal, who saw the situation in which we now are almost prophetically fifty years ago ; and even at the present hour, perhaps, a Catholic can hardly need or imagine a more trustworthy guide as to the application of the double spirit of understanding sympathy and Catholic faith to this problem than he will find in Cardinal Newman's lecture, written in 1855 and published in the second part of the ' Idea of a University,' entitled ' Christianity and Scientific Investigation.'

The lecture is so helpful and so suggestive that I could wish to give some account of its drift. But as this cannot be, I can only hope that those whose minds are exercised by these problems of the times, and who are not familiar with it, will read it carefully for themselves.

On the second question, we have in recent years an equally remarkable exhibition of the same temper of

sympathy and faith from a still higher authority in the
great Encyclical of Leo XIII., the 'Rerum Novarum.'
This study of the social question, so full of sympathy,
so firm in Christian principle, will, I cannot doubt, long
stand out as an almost ideal application of that Catholic
spirit which was so prominent in Cardinal Wiseman's
work to one of the hardest problems of our own
times.

I have a further reason for speaking here as
I have done of this special combination in Cardinal
Wiseman of faith and sympathy, over and above the
fact that in reading his letters and works they seem to
me to stand forth as the very essence of his genius
and character.   For this combination, so necessary for
our own country, where Catholics have to influence and
win the ear of many whose antecedents and habits of
thought are so unlike their own, characterised, in
different ways, both the men of whom Cardinal Wiseman has spoken as especially helping him in his own
boyhood at Ushaw.

Dr. Newsham—first his teacher and afterwards
his lifelong friend, so long one of Ushaw's most
honoured Presidents—had in certain departments in a
very marked degree Wiseman's own gift of sympathy.
With the solitary exception of Wiseman himself, the
Oxford converts of 1845 found in no born Catholic so
much understanding sympathy as in Dr. Newsham.
To this fact I can cite at least the testimony of my own
father, confirmed by significant words of Cardinal
Newman.   And if I were to point to a single English
Catholic who, in the first half of the nineteenth cen-

tury, had addressed the English public with absolute success, compelling respect by the scrupulous impartiality of his statements and fidelity of his research, avoiding controversy where it was unconvincing or merely irritating, and consequently ever weighty and successful when he felt argument to be really in place, I should name another Ushaw man and early friend of Wiseman, the great Dr. John Lingard. 'Lingard has never been found wrong.' These words formed the brief but eloquent tribute of one who was, perhaps, the most universally learned of modern historical critics—the late Lord Acton. To the splendid work done by this distinguished son of Ushaw, and to its powerful, though indirect, help to the cause of the Catholic Church, the late Dr. Russell of Maynooth bore eloquent testimony when this College was celebrating its Jubilee fifty years ago.

And the thought of this celebration reminds me that to the four pictures of Cardinal Wiseman with which I began my remarks I ought, in conclusion, to add a fifth—the time July, 1858, the place this very College of St. Cuthbert at Ushaw. There and then we may picture him, still in the height of his powers, surrounded by dear friends who are with us no more —Newsham, Tate, John Gillow, and many another— entering with as much zest and eagerness into this festivity of boys and young men as he had into the greatest and most public enterprises of his life. We see the boys under his guidance rehearsing his play, 'The Hidden Gem,' written by him for the occasion. We see him teaching the College choir the Jubilee

Ode, of which he was also the author. We see passed round for inspection the medal of Cardinal Allen, the founder of Douay (the parent College of Ushaw), with an inscription in honour of the occasion—again the work of Cardinal Wiseman. If the other pictures I have suggested show Wiseman a greater and more prominent actor on the scene of life, none shows him a happier man. 'Almost from the dawn of reason to the present hour,' he wrote a little earlier, 'my connection with Ushaw has been unceasing, and in its comfort to me unvarying.' Even for his sensitive spirit all that was associated with Ushaw told for happiness. In his Jubilee Ode, amid its bright thoughts of the present, he turns for a moment to the remembrance of those sons of Ushaw who had gone to their reward, whom he pictures as still sharing from the world behind the veil in the Festival of Alma Mater. The last stanza but one begins :

> Hush, good spirits fill the air,
> They come our joy and love to share,
> Great Lingard, Gibson, Gillow, Eyre.

The inexorable march of time has now taken Nicholas Wiseman himself into that august company. And the living sons of Ushaw—among whom I am proud to count myself one—may well turn their minds, as he did then, to the mighty dead, and think of Wiseman in company with others who loved Ushaw with such deep devotion, above all, his dear friend, Charles Newsham, as looking down on this great gathering with a sympathy even deeper and truer that he had when his cheery voice was heard in the ambulacrum fifty years ago, and his genial presence cast a sunshine on all about him. And, if he shares our rejoicings, can we doubt that it is to him a special happiness to see the President's place filled by a prelate [1] whom he well knew and valued in life, by one who has so much of his own large-hearted spirit, one to whom Durham Cathedral taught the faith of its Catholic builders, and whose conversion was among the offerings to the Church of the great movement which was so long Wiseman's especial care.

Let this, then, be our last thought within these halls of the great scholar, apologist, Bishop and Cardinal, that as he was the son of Ushaw as a boy, and her constant and devoted friend through life, he is still with us as truly as he was at our Jubilee fifty years ago; that he watches her fortunes with even greater power than of old to help his *Alma Mater*— his affectionate sympathy still what it was of yore, the steadfast faith and old hopefulness turned into certain knowledge of future blessings in store for her, so long as Ushaw is true to the great traditions of her past.

[1] The reference is to Dr. Wilkinson, Bishop of Hexham, and President of Ushaw.

JOHN HENRY NEWMAN

AN ADDRESS [1]

WHEN I was asked to speak in this city of the great man who for some ten years reigned supreme over the best intellect and character in Oxford, I felt that it would be natural that I should refer especially to the part he played in what is popularly known as 'The Oxford Movement.' I might briefly remind you of the main historical features of the Movement, and give some description of John Henry Newman as the central figure in the drama. To do this would be to give the story of a party ; and it would be to repeat the narrative he has himself given in the 'Apologia.' I prefer, therefore, to speak of certain ideas developed by him in his exposition of the programme of the Movement which were something better than principles of party action. They were ideas never fully understood by all his followers, possessing an intellectual and spiritual depth not belonging to any party. They gave him influence over many who never joined the Tractarian party at all. Newman devoted himself to controversy and

[1] This Address was delivered at Oxford, by invitation of the University Extension Committee, at the summer meeting of 1907. The first three quarters is here printed exactly as it was delivered. In the last part some changes and additions have been made.

Photo. Barraud.

CARDINAL NEWMAN.

became a party man from the practical necessities of the case; but the mental attitude which made him adhere to the Oxford Movement, and which he brought to its interpretation, belongs not to controversy or to party, but to that search for truth in which all candid and deep thinkers have a natural fellowship. There are sections of the 'Arians of the Fourth Century' and of 'Tract 85,' the University Sermons on 'The Theory of Religious Belief,' and the essay on the 'Development of Christian Doctrine'—though some of these writings were occasioned by the controversies of the hour—which deal with thoughts on a different intellectual plane from those of the more controversial tracts, including the famous 'Tract 90.' And it is these thoughts which are of permanent interest now that the lapse of sixty years has blurred old party divisions, and reconstructed the schools of thought which in our own day claim to inherit the past.

In order to appreciate adequately the nature of Newman's deeper thought and its influence at Oxford, we must first remind ourselves of the position he held there in the eyes of his younger contemporaries at the height of his power, about 1838, and speak of some of the qualities to which it was due. Let it be remembered that he held no university or college office. He had long ago resigned his Oriel tutorship. His familiar intercourse was with only a few intimate friends. What the public knew was the wonderful Sunday evening sermons at St. Mary's, of which he was vicar, the occasional lectures in Adam de Brome's chapel and elsewhere, some of which were afterwards embodied in 'Tracts for the Times,' and the Tracts themselves. Such were the slender instruments through which the genius of the man made itself felt.   How great and how universal his influence, both intellectual and moral, became we have been told by many witnesses.   The estimates of Dean Lake and Dean Church are probably well known to you all.   They speak of his influence on the flower of young Oxford as unlike anything that had ever been known in the University before ; and testimonies quite as strong have been supplied to us by men whose theological views were, or became, widely different from those of Newman himself.   Mark Pattison and Principal Shairp of St. Andrew's have borne witness as whole-hearted as that of any Tractarian disciple to the influence of the man, and have recognised its power for good.   Dean Stanley, Matthew Arnold, and James Anthony Froude have used words of almost equal significance.

'His sermons,' says Dean Stanley, 'did not belong to provincial dogma, but to the literature of all time.' ' Those who never heard him,' wrote Principal Shairp, ' might fancy that his sermons would be about Apostolic succession, or the rights of the Church, or against Dissenters.   Nothing of the kind.   You might hear him preach for weeks without an allusion to these things.   What there was of High Church teaching was implied rather than enforced.   The local, the temporary, and the modern were ennobled by the presence of the catholic truth belonging to all ages that pervaded the whole.   His power showed itself chiefly in the new and unlooked-for way in which he touched into life old truths, moral or spiritual, which all Christians acknowledge, but most have ceased to feel.' [1]

The essential breadth and reality of his thought, then, led to an influence which extended to those who were then or later theological opponents, as well as to his own adherents.

And the impression left by his social personality in Oxford is, similarly, one of breadth and of the genius which appeals to all :

Newman's mind was world-wide [writes Mr. Froude in his recollections of those days]. He was interested in everything which was going on—in science, in politics, in literature. Nothing was too large for him, nothing too trivial if it threw light upon the central question, what man really was, and what was his destiny. . . . He could admire enthusiastically any greatness of action or character, however remote the sphere of it from his own. Gurwood's 'Despatches of the Duke of Wellington' came out just then. Newman had been reading the book, and a friend asked him what he thought of it. 'Think?' he said; 'it makes one burn to have been a soldier.' . . . Keble had looked into no lines of thought but his own. Newman had read omnivorously, and had studied modern thought and modern life in all its forms and with all its many-coloured passions.[2]

So far Mr. Froude ; and to Newman's directly religious influence on the University Principal Shairp has perhaps given the most definite and direct testimony. After speaking, in the Essay from which I have quoted above, of the high moral ideal pervading the youth of Oxford in the 'thirties, he writes as follows :

[1] See Principal Shairp's Essay on Keble in his 'Studies in Poetry.'
[2] 'Short Studies,' iv. pp. 278, 279.

If such was the general aspect of Oxford society at that time, where was the centre and soul from which so mighty a power emanated ? It lay, and had for some years lain, mainly in one man, a man in many ways the most remarkable that England had seen during this century, perhaps the most remarkable the English Church has possessed in any century— John Henry Newman. The influence he had gained, without apparently setting himself to seek it, was something altogether unlike anything else in our time. A mysterious veneration had by degrees gathered round him, till now it was almost as though some Ambrose or Augustine of older ages had reappeared. He himself tells how one day, when he was an undergraduate, a friend with whom he was walking in an Oxford street cried out eagerly, ' There is Keble,' and with what awe he looked at him. A few years and the same took place with regard to himself. In Oriel Lane light-hearted undergraduates would drop their voices and whisper, ' There's Newman,' as with head thrust forward and gaze fixed as though at some vision seen only by himself, with swift, noiseless step he glided by. Awe fell on them for a moment almost as if it had been some apparition that had passed. . . . What were the qualities that inspired these feelings ? There was, of course, learning and refinement. There was genius, not, indeed, of a philosopher, but of a subtle and original thinker, an unequalled edge of dialectic, and these all glorified by the imagination of a poet. Then there was the utter unworldliness, the setting aside of all the things which men most prize, the tamelessness of soul which was ready to essay the impossible. Men felt that here was

> ' One of that small transfigured band
> Which the world cannot tame.'

Such testimonies might easily be multiplied. But these will suffice to remind us what was popular sentiment concerning John Henry Newman in the Oxford of that time.

Among the characteristics to which Newman owed

his personal charm, which was in its sphere as great as his deeper spiritual influence, I would name the extraordinary delicacy of all his senses and perceptions. The very tone of voice in which he read the prayers conveyed this quality and is in the memory of many still living. Old men, speaking at an interval of half a century, have recalled to me, almost with tears, the delicate intonation of Newman's reading at St. Mary's of Collect or Psalm, the felt perception of its beauty, the dramatic though most untheatrical effect of spiritual reality which it conveyed. Principal Shairp speaks in his Recollections of the 'silver intonation' of Newman's voice as he read the Lessons. ' It seemed,' he adds, ' to bring new meaning out of the familiar words. Still lingers in the memory the tone in which he read "that Jerusalem which is above is free, which is the mother of us all."' It was the same with his preaching :

When he began to preach [says the same witness] a stranger was not likely to be much struck, especially if he had been accustomed to the pulpit oratory of the Boanerges sort. Here was no vehemence, no declamation, no show of literary argument. I believe that if he had preached one of his St. Mary sermons before a Scotch town congregation they would have thought the preacher a 'silly body.' The delivery had a peculiarity which it took the new hearer some time to get over. Each separate sentence, or at least each short paragraph, was spoken rapidly and with great clearness of intonation, and then at its close there was a pause lasting for nearly half a minute, then another rapidly but clearly spoken sentence, followed by another pause. It took some time to get over this, but when once done the wonderful charm dawned on you. The look and bearing of the preacher was as of one who dwelt apart, and although he

knew his age well, he did not live in it. . . . Subtle truths
which it would have taken philosophers pages of circumlocu-
tion and big words to state were dropped out by the way in
a sentence or two of the most transparent Saxon. What
delicacy of style, yet what calm power, how gentle, yet how
strong, how simple, yet how suggestive, how homely, yet how
refined !

The impression of delicate perception of which
Principal Shairp speaks as conveyed in the tone and
the language had its counterpart in Newman's whole
sensitive equipment. His taste was in the highest
degree delicate, and he chose the wines for the Oriel
cellars. His exquisite sense of literary form was
universally acknowledged. His love for music was
acute, his appreciation of its beauty intense. When,
after some years of abstinence, he played the new
violin which was given to him by his friend Dean
Church, he described in a letter to the donor how he
shed so many tears over a quartette of Beethoven that
he could play no more. I remember myself, at the
funeral of the Duchess of Norfolk in the London
Oratory, when he was nearly eighty-six years old, the
sweet tone and the accuracy of intonation in his singing as he chanted a few phrases of the Absolution—a
curious contrast to the unmusical sounds emitted by
his colleagues, old men indeed, but not by any means
as old as he. There was a parallel stamp of keen
perception and refinement in his conversation. ' Prosy
he could not be,' says Mr. Froude ; ' he was lightness
itself—the lightness of elastic strength.' His perfect
sense of the fitness of things was part of the same
quality. There is, unquestionably, an unconscious

analysis of himself in his description, in the 'Idea of a University,' of the bearing of the true gentleman, who 'has his eyes on all his company,' who 'is tender towards the bashful, gentle towards the distant, and merciful towards the absurd'; who 'can recollect to whom he is speaking'; who 'guards against unseasonable allusions or topics which may irritate'; who 'is seldom prominent in conversation and never wearisome.'

The sensitive temperament, which was so apparent in voice, manner of speech, and personal bearing, went with a piercing appreciation of what was beautiful and happy in the world around him and in life. Readers of his letters gain from them an impression of that veritable poet's nature to which 'the earth and every common sight' seemed ever 'apparelled in celestial light.' When the daughter of an old friend was born on the Feast of the Transfiguration, he wrote to her father: 'I earnestly pray that the festival on which she was born may overshadow her all through her life, and that she may find it good to be here until that time of blessed transfiguration when she will find from experience that it is better to be in heaven.' And he himself appreciated with accuracy and delicacy all that could make it 'good to be here.' He cherished in his memory the smallest incidents in his child life, and loved early associations and friends with a clinging affection. In his old age he spent whole weeks in transcribing notes and documents in which past days were minutely recorded: at the very desk he had used as a boy of eight. Yet, along with his keen sense of all that was beautiful and winning in the world around

Q

him, and in his own life on earth, he at the same time
stood in a sense aloof from it all—a pilgrim whose
true home was elsewhere.

For these delicate perceptions, keenly alive to
possibilities of pleasure, were overshadowed by a
deeper sense—by the warning voice of conscience
within him, which spoke to him unmistakably of
human sinfulness. This did not destroy the lightness
and brightness of his nature, but it left in him a strange
duality of consciousness, which appears in a remarkable
letter written in 1822 :

As to my religious opinions [he wrote to his mother], if
they made me melancholy, morose, austere, distant, reserved,
sullen, then indeed they may be a subject of anxiety ; but if,
as I think is the case, I am always cheerful, if at home I am
always ready and glad to join in any merriment, if I am not
clouded with sadness, if my meditations make me neither
absent in mind nor deficient in action, then my principles
may be gazed at, and puzzle the gazer, but they cannot be
accused of bad practical effects. Take me when I am most
foolish at home and extend my mirth to childishness, stop
me short and ask me then what I think of myself, whether
my opinions are less gloomy ; no, I think I should seriously
return the same answer that I shudder at myself.[1]

This duality of consciousness had, I think, its
counterpart in his character. Some of the qualities
I have noted above are essentially those belonging to
the temperament of an artist. Yet this last extract
reminds us that he had also the severe and unbending
conscience of the saint. The artistic temperament

[1] See Miss Mozley's 'Letters and Correspondence of J. H. Newman,'
vol. i. p. 59.

goes, ordinarily speaking, with waywardness and incon-
sistency of action. The mental nerves are, as it were,
exposed and at the mercy of the keenly felt pleasures
or pains of the hour. Effort is generally made only
on intermittent impulse. Uncongenial effort involves
almost unbearable torture. Men of this stamp are,
therefore, mostly moody and fitful in their work. With
Newman, on the contrary, intensely deep conscientious-
ness led to that life of consistent effort which is more
often led by those who are less keenly alive to the
joys of life and the attractions of sense. His artistic
perceptions never carried him away. He utilised them
for the good cause, but kept them under control.
Though, as I have said, he tasted the wines for his
college, yet he was no wine drinker. 'He had not in
him,' says his relation, Miss Mozley, 'a grain of con-
viviality.' And this combination symbolised the man.
He tasted with discriminating delicacy of the whole
world of sense, but he did not drink of it. Even from
his beloved music, the most spiritual pleasure of the
senses, he fasted, never playing his violin for eleven
years after he had joined the Catholic Church.
Wonderful master though he was of style in writing,
in early years he avowedly kept a restraining hand on
all desire for literary effect, and he studied above all
things clearness and simplicity in his style. He never
wrote for fame, always from duty. He remained to
the end, as I have said, a pilgrim to whom this earth,
which he so keenly appreciated, was a foreign land.
Yet the sensitiveness to pain which ever goes with
sensitiveness to pleasure was apt to make the path

of duty at times a veritable martyrdom.   And this
appeared especially at the great crisis of his life in the
'forties.   The tenacious love and keen feelings which
caused Oriel, Oxford, the Church of England, the
friends of his youth to weave so many associations in
his memory and soul, tendrils round every fibre of
him, made it a veritable death-struggle to tear himself
from them.   He describes in the 'Apologia' the agony
the separation cost him.   He speaks of the years which
he spent in retirement, from 1842 to 1845, as 'a deathbed.'   No metaphor could be more significant than this
one which he himself uses.   The farewell sermon at
Littlemore, in 1843, on the 'parting of friends,' which
was interrupted by the sobs of those whom he was
soon to leave, shows all his weariness, and the bitterness of the struggle that was passing in him; and in
an unpublished autobiographical note he has left it on
record that ever since he 'set his face towards Rome'
the pain was so great that the whole expression of his
countenance changed.   Such was the effect of the
strain of stern duty acting against the grain on an
artistic temperament of almost unequalled sensitiveness.
Before that time he used (so he told his friends) to
walk through the Oxford streets with his lips parted
and a smile on his face.   Ever afterwards his lips
were set and his expression gradually became more
and more severe.   One day in 1847, walking with his
friend, John Bernard Dalgairns, of Exeter, in the
Vatican Gallery, their attention was arrested by a
stern and forbidding-looking statue of Fate.   Dalgairns
said, 'I am sure I know that face,' and suddenly turned

to Newman, adding, 'Of course it is you.' The words brought home to him, Newman used to say, the change of which he was already partly conscious.

Newman's pursuit of the path marked out by conscience at the cost of so much suffering brings home to us that there is tragic pathos as well as true poetry in 'Lead, kindly Light.' He ever followed indeed, what he believed to be a Divine light, but it was distant and often dim. It was descried by conscience, and gave him only at moments that secure sense of reality which could bring perfect peace. 'The night is dark, and I am far from home'—this was his constant feeling as duty beckoned him onwards. But he faithfully followed the 'kindly Light,' at the cost often of more suffering than it is given to most men to be capable of enduring. The combination of the pains of a deathbed described in the 'Apologia' with the 'blessed vision of peace' referred to in the epilogue to the Essay on Development—written at the moment of his religious change—represents this union of happiness in duty, recognised as rightly attaching to its performance, but only now and again realised, and intense suffering ever pressing and ever present.

Let me here note in his intellectual view of things a quality parallel to the duality in his nature of which I have spoken. I refer to his intense sensitiveness to and candid recognition of all facts, however perplexing and apparently inconsistent, in this complex world, of which we know so little, and yet his deep conviction that they had their place in the designs of

an overruling Providence.   He attempted no forced
reconciliation of the two beliefs.   He neither ignored
nor tampered with facts to make the world more
intelligible, nor did he doubt the Providence they at
times failed to disclose.   His delicate senses were part
of a wider equipment, giving him a keen sense of the
reality of all that came before him.   His own phrase,
'the illative sense,' which he uses to designate the auto-
matic action of our rational nature whereby all facts
are felt and weighed, and the mind led on to its conclusion from premises of which it is only partially
conscious, brings home to us this analogy between his
intellectual and his sense perceptions.   His consciousness of sin was part of this sensitiveness to all reality
—it meant a keen sensitiveness to the voice of conscience, and to the witness it bore to God's existence
as ruler and judge.   Both classes of fact—outer and
inner—were intensely real to him.   Yet the facts of
the outer world seemed often to defy all explanation
on the part of the Christian Theist.   Here again
he sought for a Light 'amid the encircling gloom.'
He was keenly alive to the facts of history, and the
apparent absence of God from His own creation
which those facts often seemed to show.   He speaks
of this in a passage in the 'Apologia' too famous
for me to quote.   He was keenly alive to the facts of
psychology, and to those characteristics of the human
intellect which make atheism possible and enable
clever writers to make it plausible; and Huxley
declared that he could compile a primer on infidelity
from Newman's writings.   Yet there was a deeper

fact than those recognised by Huxley's naturalism,
and it is brought to light in conscience. His own
sense of sin, and of the presence of God as revealed in conscience, kept unmistakably present for
him a Divine light for the rays of which he often
sought in vain in the world around him. Like Tennyson, he found the most cogent evidence of God's
presence not in the outer world, but in the moral order
and the heart of man. That God had marked out in
His providence an appointed course for his own life
was from the very first Newman's unwavering conviction. And so his search amid the darkness, the
' encircling gloom ' of the world, was double—a search
for visible tokens of the God of his conscience, and a
search for the Light which should define and make
clear his own path.

The qualities, personal and mental, to which I
have referred affected his career and influence, and
entered into the nature of his adherence to the Oxford
Movement. The great hold that he gained on young
Oxford was due, in the first instance, to the extraordinary psychological insight shown in the sermons at
St. Mary's. It was the delicate hand with which he
played on the minds of his hearers, searching out the
true sources of human motive; his faithful delineation
of the facts of human nature and human life, coupled
with his unwavering insistence on religious duty, which
gave him so strong a hold on all who listened to him,
quite irrespective of their theological convictions.
Men trusted one who read and told them their own
half-conscious thoughts. Men believed one who saw

so truly the world we live in when he spoke to them of another world.   His acute sensitiveness, again, to the general character of the facts added to our knowledge by modern science, and by the more careful and candid study of history, led to the phase of liberalism in theology which was the prelude to his Catholic development—for he shared with such friends of the liberal camp as Blanco White and Whately the conviction that the traditional Anglican theology as it stood was not adequate to modern knowledge, still less to the flood of scientific discovery which new methods portended.   He was then for a time more or less identified with the intellectualists, of whom the two above mentioned were his intimate friends—with the school whose successors were known as Broad Churchmen. And the conviction on which this alliance rested was never changed in him—the conviction, namely, that such traditional opinions as embodied pre-scientific and inaccurate conjectures needed careful revision in view of the circumstances of modern knowledge.   What did change was his sense of the relative importance of different truths in their bearing on religion, and his appreciation of the peculiar conditions regulating theological science — a science which concerns a world so largely beyond the sphere accessible to reason and scientific method, in which, consequently, the reforms effected by the human reason may be so easily mistaken ones.   Here again his accurate sense of the facts of human nature corrected the theories of liberalism.   He tells us that the occasion of this change was illness and bereavement—the death of his beloved sister Mary and his own serious illness in 1828. Thrown thus afresh upon religion for comfort and support, he came to feel that intellectualism, or what he called theological liberalism, however much of incidental truth its pursuit might lead to, had an inherent tendency, as a temper of mind, to diminish the sense of the importance of the most fundamental religious truths, and even of their reality. Mere intellectual speculation in fallen man generally fails (he held) to reach, either by way of justification or by way of disproof, what is highest. The dialectical method represented by Whately or by the Cambridge school, however serviceable in its place, was on a plane different from those perceptions of the conscience, or, for that matter, of the artistic sense, which are man's highest intuitions and among his greatest possessions. The 'happy guidance of the moral sense' was necessary, lest reason should go astray both in its assumptions and in its conclusions. Moreover, by its attitude of self-sufficiency, the dialectical temper tended in some instances to a form of what is now called Agnosticism, to the rejection as unknowable of all that was beyond its own sphere.

Turning to the pages of the Church history of the early centuries to which his attention was directed when he consented to write his book on the Arians in 1828, he saw presented in it the story of the Christian community intent on maintaining against would-be innovators and reformers—the intellectualists of each age—the truths which had been handed down to it, which were first discerned by spiritual or

prophetic genius, or given by Divine revelation.   He
traces in his work the principle involved in the gradual
imposition of creeds and dogmatic definitions.   They
were expressions in human language, designed to
preserve against the rationalists, or heretics, the
mysterious divine truth, and the Christian spirit which
was so closely bound up with that truth.   The Christian
Church was, then, the instrument of preserving for
mankind far greater wisdom and knowledge than the
acquirements of its members at any given time represented.   The shortcomings of individuals might impress their stamp on portions of its theological literature;
the jealous conservatism with which they had held the
truths of which they were guardians might be extended
beyond its lawful sphere, yet it is only by such
fidelity in transmission that the truths we owe to
Divine revelation in the past can be kept for us.   He
gained, in short, the idea of the Church as a great
instrument for preserving the highest spiritual knowledge of the race.   The voice of conscience was made
commanding and articulate in the doctrine of Theism
which her ministers taught; and dogmatic definition
gave to the Christian creed the definiteness which
was needed for its permanent effect on character.
Soon after he had begun his work on the Arians he
wrote as follows in a letter to his mother :

Listen to my theory.   As each individual has certain
instincts of right and wrong, antecedently to reason, on
which he acts, and rightly so, which perverse reasoning may
supplant, which can then be hardly regained, but if regained
will be regained from a different source—from reasoning, and
not from nature—so I think is the world of men collectively.

God gave us truths in His miraculous revelations, and other truths in the unsophisticated fancy of nations scarcely less necessary and divine. These are transmitted as the wisdom of our ancestors through men, many of whom cannot enter into them or receive them themselves, still on from age to age, not the less truths because many of the generations through which they are transmitted are unable to prove them, but hold them either from pious and honest feeling, it may be, or from bigotry or prejudice. That they are truths it is most difficult to prove, for great men alone can prove great ideas, or grasp them. Such a mind was Hooker's, such Butler's, and as moral evil triumphs over good on a small field of action, so in the argument of an hour or in the compass of a volume would men like Brougham, or again Whately, show to far greater advantage than Hooker and Butler. Moral truth is . . . transmitted by faith and by prejudice. Keble's book is full of such truths, which any Cambridge man may refute with the greatest ease.

This line of thought had a close affinity with that of such traditionalists as Bonald and Lamennais in France.[1] In England it had engaged the powerful intellect of Coleridge. Burke had sown the seed in the eighteenth century; and it is interesting to compare with the letter of Newman which I have just cited Burke's vindication of the value of prejudice in his 'French Revolution':

We are afraid [writes Burke] to put men to live and trade each on his own private stock of reason, because we suspect that the stock in each man is small, and that individuals would do better to avail themselves of the great bank and capital of nations and of ages. Many of our men of speculation, instead of exploding general prejudices, apply their

[1] I say a 'close affinity'; but the 'University Sermons' make it plain that even in his Anglican days Newman did not hold with the excesses of traditionalism which were condemned by the Holy See.

sagacity to the discovery of the latent wisdom which prevails in them. If they find what they seek—and they seldom fail—they think it more wise to continue the prejudice with the reason involved than to cast away the coat of prejudice and to leave nothing but the naked reason. Because prejudice with its reason has a motive to give action to that reason and affection which will give it permanence. Prejudice is of ready application to the emergency. It previously engages the mind in a steady course of wisdom and virtue, and does not leave a man hesitating in the moment of decision sceptical, puzzled, and unresolved. Prejudice renders a man's virtue his habit, and not a series of unconnected acts. Through just prejudice his duty becomes part of his nature.

Newman would, I think, in 1833 have accepted every word of this quotation; and we have here the secret of the apparent paradox that Newman considered that in becoming a party man, in accepting party prejudices and practical schemes, in identifying himself even with what was accounted the stupid party, he was really gaining in that breadth and depth of view which is commensurate with a full recognition of the facts of life and of human nature, more especially in its dealings with the unseen world. Whately asked him to meet at dinner a party of the 'two-bottle orthodox,' in order to bring home to him how un-intellectual was the camp he had chosen. Newman saw the humour of the situation, yet held his party principles to be both deeper and broader than the liberalism of Whately's allies. The breadth of what Newman called 'liberalism' was a spurious breadth, not taking account of the whole of human nature, almost ignoring theoretically what is deepest in it. What human reason could not reach and completely analyse was ignored or rejected by it. Church principles, on the other hand, supplied at all events a line of orientation towards the inaccessible heights.

Readers of the 'Apologia' know the story of the journey to Greece and Italy with Hurrell Froude which immediately followed the completion of the work on the Arians. It was then that Newman had most strongly on him the sense of a mission for the future, a sense which haunted him in the delirium of his illness in Sicily. He came home just at the time when Keble was marshalling the forces of the Church party to a great battle with liberalism, and preached his sermon on National Apostacy. Bishoprics were being suppressed, and the Church treated as a mere tool of the State, while the most vigorous party of theological reformers, with Arnold and Whately at their head, were advocating views which seemed in Newman's eyes to lead logically to the destruction of the principle of faith. In the Church movement, then, Newman saw the great hope for the preservation of the Christian inheritance. The liberalism which it opposed was shallow in its intellectual principles and shallow in its utilitarian policy. The Erastianism which dominated it judged of utility by the standards of an unbelieving State. Its projected intellectual reforms measured theology by the standards of human science. They left out of account in what they planned to correct or abolish, the imperfections inevitable in a science of Divine things built up of human notions. The liberals destroyed the tares with the wheat, for they assumed a power which our intellect does not possess, of accurate discrimination in a sacred tradition whose sources were mixed and obscure, partly Divine, partly human. ' Liberalism' Newman defined as ' the exercise of thought upon matters in which from the constitution of the human mind thought cannot be brought to any successful issue. Among such matters,' he adds, 'are first principles of whatever kind, and of these, the most sacred and momentous are especially to be reckoned the truths of revelation.'

The apparent narrowness of High Church principles meant, then, in Newman's eyes a truer breadth than that of the liberal school. It meant tenacity to a sacred tradition which liberalism would lose. That tradition was believed by all Christians to include a Divine revelation. And if it also included popular beliefs due to the superstition or ignorance of an unscientific age, it was far beyond the power of the rough-and-ready intellect of the day to discriminate at once and precisely between the human and the Divine. The tradition must, therefore, be dealt with tenderly and reverently.

Moreover, the traditional teaching represented facts, and not fancy theories. It embodied what has actually grown out of the Apostolic revelation, and what has been unconsciously moulded by actual use and tested by experience. New creeds, new catechisms, had all the weakness of *a priori* schemes. Who could tell how they would work, what they might eventually be found to have kept, what to have lost, of Christianity as Christ gave it to us? Real

intellectual breadth included caution, for breadth was
not synonymous with speculative adventurousness. Its
true function consisted in the continuation of that
process of adapting the expression and practice of
Christianity to the needs of contemporary life which
the records of Church history show in the past. The
intellect which is sane as well as broad aims at adding
a stone or many stones to the building of religious
thought, and eliminating what has become clearly
unstable or untrustworthy, supplanting what was based
on imperfect secular knowledge by the corrections
which modern research enables us to supply. But to
aim, as the liberals did, at complete theological recon-
struction was to mistake the essential nature of dogma
as revealed and to make light of the invaluable ac-
quisitions of past experience. The Christian Church
was, then, to Newman narrow only in the sense that
she was tenacious of Christian tradition, lest she might
lose what was Divine in it ; and that her doctrines were
definite. And they were definite, not as pretending
adequately to describe in their definitions what was
infinite, but because human nature needs definite
conceptions of truth for its support and for practical
action, even though they be inadequate in respect of
the mysteries above human comprehension. Both in
his 'Arians' and in his University Sermons he compared this definiteness to that of the five senses. Our
five senses represent to us but aspects of the reality
of things known to God ; still, their definiteness is what
makes them effective in placing us in relation with
truth, and valuable in action. Sensible things are, to

use his phrase, economic representations of a reality. So the Church afforded an economic representation of the Divine truth contained in the Christian message. She wove together in the long course of her consistent organic life, in her dogmas, her rites, her liturgy, in the lives of her great representatives, the saints of each generation, a great fabric—theology, liturgy, devotional traditions, hagiology—appealing to the imagination of man as well as his intellect, and enabling him to make vivid and definite for his own life that unseen world which unaided human nature recognises so faintly and so uncertainly.

Such was the Church catholic in Newman's eyes as early as 1833; and he gradually came to believe that it was the failure to preserve this ideal, the assertion against this ideal of the sufficiency of the individual private judgment in religious knowledge, which had led to the great separation of England from Rome in the sixteenth century. Therefore, the very philosophical principles which had made him a High Churchman perforce made him a Roman Catholic. He saw in the story of the Arians and in the story of the Monophysites the same types, the same principles at work, as in the story of Protestantism. On the one hand there were the heretics of history—the clever critics who attempted to rationalise dogma on the principle of individual choice and definition which the very word 'heresy' conveys. On the other hand there was the firmness of Rome, 'peremptory and stern, resolute, relentless,' which took its stand on the tradition of the ages, and refused to tamper with what it had received

as definite truth in deference to human speculation.
This same antithesis was visible to him in the England
of the sixteenth century. To preserve, then, the ideal,
religious and philosophical, of the Church catholic
which he had gained in his study of the Fathers became
for him to recognise that, with whatever intellectual
and even moral faults and imperfections among its
members, the Church in communion with the Holy
See was the Catholic Church. It was the Church
appointed to preserve for all time in definite forms
the revelation committed to her by Christ.

This ideal, which contains the philosophical essence
of Newman's religious position, reappears again and
again both in his Anglican and in his Catholic works.
It is perhaps most effectively presented in a lecture
seldom quoted, which he delivered in Dublin, in 1859,
to the School of Medical Science at the Catholic
University. His central contention in this lecture is,
that while the facts to which physical science appeals
are unmistakable and unforgettable, the truths, on the
other hand, on which theology is based, whose real
home is in another world, need for their effective assertion on this earth 'a concrete representative of things
invisible.' The Church thus becomes the normal protection of human nature against an agnosticism to
which physical science by itself is apt to lead. He
writes as follows :—

The physical nature lies before us, patent to the sight,
ready to the touch, appealing to the senses in so unequivocal
a way that the science which is founded upon it is as real to
us as the fact of our personal existence. But the phenomena

R

which are the basis of morals and religion have nothing of this luminous evidence. Instead of being obtruded upon our notice, so that we cannot possibly overlook them, they are the dictates either of conscience or of the Faith. They are faint shadows and tracings, certain indeed, but delicate, fragile, and almost evanescent, which the mind recognises at one time, not at another—discerns when it is calm, loses when it is in agitation. The reflection of sky and mountains in the lake is a proof that sky and mountains are around it, but the twilight, or the mist, or the sudden storm hurries away the beautiful image, which leaves behind it no memorial of what it was. Something like this are the moral law and the informations of faith, as they present themselves to individual minds. Who can deny the existence of conscience? Who does not feel the force of its injunctions? But how dim is the illumination in which it is invested, and how feeble its influence, compared with that evidence of sight and touch which is the foundation of physical science! How easily can we be talked out of our clearest views of duty! How does this or that moral precept crumble into nothing when we rudely handle it! How does the fear of sin pass off from us, as quickly as the glow of modesty dies away from the countenance! And then we say, ' It is all superstition.' However, after a time we look round, and then, to our surprise, we see, as before, the same law of duty, the same moral precepts, the same protests against sin, appearing over against us in their old places, as if they never had been brushed away, like the Divine handwriting upon the wall at the banquet. Then perhaps we approach them rudely, and inspect them irreverently, and accost them sceptically, and away they go again, like so many spectres—shining in their cold beauty, but not presenting themselves bodily to us for our inspection, so to say, of their hands and their feet. And thus these awful, supernatural, bright, majestic, delicate apparitions, much as we may in our hearts acknowledge their sovereignty, are no match as a foundation of science for the hard, palpable, material facts which make up the province of physics.

Such is our knowledge, fitful and imperfect, in its hold on us of the truths whose home is in another world. We need an institution in *this* world to represent their interests and bring them home to our memory and imagination, to make them as real to us as the truths belonging to the world of sense itself. It is the Catholic Church which performs this function.

That great institution, the Catholic Church [he continues], has been kept up by Divine mercy as a present, visible antagonist, and the only possible antagonist, to sight and sense. Conscience, reason, good feeling, the instincts of our moral nature, the traditions of faith, the conclusions and deductions of philosophical religion, are no match at all for the stubborn facts (for they *are* facts, though there are other facts besides them)—for the facts which are the foundation of physical science. Gentlemen, if you feel, as you must feel, the whisper of a law of moral truth within you, and the impulse to believe, be sure there is nothing whatever on earth which can be the sufficient champion of these sovereign authorities of your soul, which can vindicate and preserve them to you, and make you loyal to them, but the Catholic Church. You fear they will go, you see with dismay that they are going, under the continual impression created on your mind by the details of the material science to which you have devoted your lives. It is so—I do not deny it; except under rare and happy circumstances go they will, unless you have Catholicism to back you up in keeping faithful to them. The world is a rough antagonist of spiritual truth: sometimes with mailed hand, sometimes with pertinacious logic, sometimes with a storm of irresistible facts, it presses on against you. What it says is true, perhaps, as far as it goes, but it is not the whole truth or the most important truth. These more important truths, which the natural heart admits in their substance, though it cannot maintain—the being of a God, the certainty of future retribution, the claims of the moral law, the reality of sin, the hope of supernatural help—of these the Church is in matter of fact the undaunted and the only defender.

Even those who do not look on her as divine must grant as much as this. I do not ask you for more here than to contemplate and recognise her as a fact—as other things are facts. She has been eighteen hundred years in the world, and all that time she has been doing battle in the boldest, most obstinate way in the cause of the human race, in maintenance of the undeniable but comparatively obscure truths of religion. She is always alive, always on the alert when any enemy whatever attacks them. She has brought them through a thousand perils. Sometimes preaching, sometimes pleading, sometimes arguing—sometimes exposing her ministers to death, and sometimes, though rarely, inflicting blows herself—by peremptory deeds, by patient concessions —she has fought on and fulfilled her trust. No wonder so many speak against her, for she deserves it; she has earned the hatred and obloquy of her opponents by her success in opposing them.

I have endeavoured to set forth this account of the functions of the Church in relation to the religious instincts of the individual on lines which are not controversial. Newman claimed so comprehensive a thinker as Coleridge as his philosophical forerunner; and men like Dean Church accepted the main outline of his theory, while they could not go with him in finding its realisation in the Catholic Church in communion with Rome. Dean Church, like John Keble, seems rather to have looked to the many Churches in Christendom as forming, in spite of their divisions, that social power whereby religious truth is made definite and operative. Both of them held the narrowness and exclusiveness which characterised the Church of Rome, in their eyes, to be more fatal to her claims than the anomalies and differences existing among her rivals were fatal to a wider and more inclusive conception of the Church catholic.

My concern here, however, is with Newman himself, and I would endeavour in conclusion to point out some of the ways in which his many-sided mind employed itself to the end, often without set purpose, in enforcing and illustrating the general nature of the work before the members of that Catholic Church which he had come to accept as the divinely appointed antagonist against religious negation, and the normal protector of Christian faith.

Popular opinion generally seizes on certain broad lines which, as far as they go, are true ; and there certainly is a truth underlying the popular impression which regards Newman as comparatively narrow and conservative in his Anglican days, comparatively wide in sympathy and liberal after he joined the Church of Rome. The view as sometimes given in detail is false, as popular views usually are. But it represents a truth. In each period his practical policy was one of opposition to the excesses prevalent in those quarters towards which his attention was especially directed. To the liberalising movement in the Church of England he opposed the conservative conception of a Church catholic whose dogma was unchangeable. As a Catholic he opposed that 'violent ultra-party' which, in his own words, 'exalted opinions into dogmas and had it principally at heart to destroy every school of thought but its own.' He opposed those who regarded their own exposition of theology as though it were the only orthodox one. He preached what he called in his ' Letter to the Duke of Norfolk '[1] 'a wise and gentle minimism,' in opposition to those theological writers who 'dogmatised' and 'maximised' and 'stretched principles until they were on the point of snapping '—those whose orthodox zeal against largeness of outlook and variety of opinion had issued in what their enemies termed obscurantism.   To such an attitude he opposed the essential breadth of view which must result from a careful historical survey of the development of theology, with its many orthodox schools of thought, in the past.

If such largeness of outlook and comprehensiveness of view, which had existed in the past, were not possible for Catholics in the present, the very work of upholding Christianity in the modern world, which he believed to be especially theirs, could not adequately be accomplished.   For an exposition of religious doctrine which did not reconcile the truths known to human reason with Christian dogma, which did not separate that dogma from views susceptible of scientific disproof, could not be intellectually influential in the modern world.

I will not here enlarge on this point of view ; but it bred a curious antithesis in his later attitude, as curious as those I have already noted in his earlier.

Mr. Richard Hutton has placed on record the impression left on him by Newman's later writings, that as a Catholic he felt comparatively free and ' unmuzzled'; and there is, unquestionably, a sense of security and consequent freedom in the Catholic works corresponding to the wide conception of the essential nature and possibilities of Catholicism which history had given him. On the other hand, his strong sense of duty towards the society in which he lived and towards his ecclesiastical superiors brought him constantly into difficulties, when he wrote on theology, in the presence of the very conservative standards enforced by certain earnest and zealous men who were at times, like Cardinal Cullen, in a position of ecclesiastical authority. I should say that his own mind and his own views became far more comprehensive as a Catholic. The Church was in his eyes a rock of security for his faith in the supernatural; and a freedom of reasoning, which, apart from such a support, he had felt to be dangerous, was no longer dreaded by him. The tone of exultant confidence which Mr. Hutton notes in his later writings did truly betoken a new freedom of mind. On the other hand, in his actual writings on matters theological, in the definite propositions to which he committed himself, as distinguished from the general attitude and sympathies revealed, he had to take account of many theological opinions which he did not regard as adequate, and which, nevertheless, he desired to treat with respect. He had perforce to treat certain questions with reserve, as he intimates in the 'Apologia.' Before dealing with them more fully and freely he had to make clear to more conservative thinkers the orthodoxy of such freer treatment. He therefore devoted much of his attention to pointing out the scope for reasonable freedom really allowed by the Church, which had ever in the past enabled her thinkers to take account of newly discovered facts. This was an indispensable preliminary condition to securing and exercising the liberty necessary to the discussion of problems which then, as now, were raised by historical and critical research.

He saw that the excessive conservatism of some of his contemporaries was largely due to the fact that the old theological schools at the great universities had been destroyed at the French Revolution, and that modern theologians often lived perforce separated from the world of secular thought, research and science, and so lacked those influences which make breadth and general culture natural and easy. It was his dream to make use of his position as Rector of the Catholic University of Ireland to remedy this defect. The pressure on the Christian thinker of all branches of knowledge, historical, critical and scientific, which a university naturally supplied must effectually prevent the narrowness of general outlook which is almost inevitable where one science is left entirely to determine it. In a most gentle and undemonstrative form, indeed, and with absolute submission to constituted authority, both in utterance and in action, he indicated the necessity of an ever-growing thoroughness in education and in thought among his fellow-Catholics. The Catholic community in every age, indeed, had need of reform, and the unconsciousness of such a need, whether among persons in authority or among the mass of the faithful, had ever been regarded

by the saints as a fault most of all calling for reformation.   The existing defects were primarily intellectual.
They were due to deficiencies in liberal education.
They implied a far less disastrous state of things than
existed in days when the immorality of popes and
clergy was an open scandal.   But the memory of
those days was an undying reminder that, though the
Christian Church was from God, it held its divine
treasure of truth in earthen vessels.

The need for free discussion, both in theology and
in the secular sciences, was insisted on in some of
the lectures contained in the ' Idea of a University,' in
which also the bearing of advancing secular science on
religious opinions long current, yet possibly not well
founded, is dwelt on—notably in the lecture on
' Christianity and Scientific Investigation.'   The work
of individuals in forming the Christian intellect within
the Church in the past, the scope for originality and
creative power in theologians which real theological
thought affords, was spoken of in the last part of
the ' Apologia ' and in the essay on the ' Benedictine
Centuries.'   The freedom of theological discussion
within the Church, to which scholastic theology in its
palmy days actually owed its thoroughness and comprehensiveness in relation to contemporary thought,
is dwelt upon both in the ' Apologia ' and in the ' Idea
of a University.'   But he carefully notes that while such
freedom has been allowed to the experts, restraint has
also been necessary in order to prevent the unsettlement
of the average mind by dangerous speculations.   The
liberality of the Church in the long run towards all

sound and sincere Christian thought is likewise dwelt
on in the last-named work, while her encouragement
of 'a wise and gentle minimism' in what she insists on
as of obligatory belief, is recalled in the 'Letter to the
Duke of Norfolk.' It was more than ever necessary
to emphasise the traditionary habit of comprehensive
discussion in the schools, whereby the harmony
between faith and reason had been effected in the
Middle Ages, because the modern sciences were
creating a fresh and urgent necessity for it. They
were constantly opening out new points of view on
the borderland between secular and religious thought,
and rendering probable new facts, of which the candid
religious thinker must take account.

A work in the same direction, to which he attached
great importance, was making the apologetic arguments
both for Catholicism and for Christianity quite true to
psychological fact—taking full account of the state of
mind of those whom the believer would convince, and
accurately marking the point at which the thinking
mind which accepted these arguments as conclusive
differed from the mind which did not. Here those
who personally knew the heretic or infidel had an
advantage which the dweller in a Catholic community
might lack.

'Your Italian divines,' he wrote, 'whom I sincerely
wish to follow in dogmatics, are not in my mind the
best in polemics. . . . They know nothing at all of
heretics as realities. They live at Rome, a place
whose boast it is that it has never given birth to
heresy, and they think proofs ought to be convincing

which in fact are not.   Hence they are accustomed
to speak of the argument for Catholicity as a demonstration, and to see no force in objections to it, and to
admit no perplexity of the intellect which is not directly
and immediately wilful.'[1]   It was clear that such
treatment was inadequate to the actual facts of human
nature.

He endeavoured, then, in the 'Grammar of Assent'
to bring the argument both for Catholicism and
for Christianity and Theism into closer accord with
psychological fact than were the statements current
in many scholastic text-books.   The work was a
survey of the actual operations of the human mind in
reaching its conclusions on these subjects.

The 'Grammar of Assent' was a fine supplement
to the 'University Sermons' (published in 1843)—full
of psychological insight.   It was in this work that he
first used the phrase 'illative sense' to sum up the
inductive process whereby the human reason spontaneously takes account of *all* the facts of which it is aware,
consciously and semi-consciously, all of which should
have their share in the conclusions drawn.   The part
played by conscience in accepting the assumptions
necessary to the philosophy of faith is more expressly
treated in the 'Grammar' than in the Oxford
Sermons.   But he never worked out in it one very
interesting suggestion in the University Sermon on
'Wisdom as Contrasted with Faith and Bigotry.'
The obvious objection to the illative-sense theory is
that it may canonise prejudice as well as insight.   The

[1] See Abbot Gasquet's *Lord Acton and his Circle* p. xviii.

sub-conscious or 'implicit' grounds of belief (says the objector) *may* indeed be valid and contribute to insight, but they may also be invalid and bound up with prejudice. The line intimated in the Oxford Sermons—that the spontaneous faith of the earnest and devout mind involves, in the reasoning process it really includes, some semi-conscious share in the wisdom of the Christian community, including its seers and its saints, that it finds in this dependence a trustful power which marks it off, as a mere psychological phenomenon, from prejudice—was never elaborated by him, or so exhibited as to accord with the recognised analysis of the schools, with which he concurred as far as it went, while he desired to supplement it.

In all this work we see the quality I emphasised at the beginning of this lecture—Newman's sensitiveness to *fact*. As St. Thomas was the embodiment of the deductive rationalism of the thirteenth century, restrained and tempered by Christianity, so was Newman of the inductive temper of the nineteenth. No fact escaped him. He was keenly alive, as we have seen, to the facts of our spiritual consciousness, their truth and sacredness; to the value also of ecclesiastical tradition and Church authority in keeping all spiritual truths firmly and clearly established in the weak human mind—even apart from their function in imparting the truths of revelation. These facts, psychological and social, were as truly facts as the historical and physical truths brought to light by the sciences. But he was keenly alive to these latter facts as well, and to the general trend of science and criticism, even beyond the details with which he was familiar. He was absolutely candid in his recognition of their results, probable and certain. Few men are equally alive to all classes of fact—religious, psychological, and scientific.

With less spiritual minds than Newman's free inquiry and criticism are apt to beget irreverence, as recent excesses among Christian thinkers have shown. A critical examination, for example, of the genesis and accuracy of certain pious opinions long current among Christians may lead to the carping spirit. It is apt to issue in a real pleasure in overthrowing cherished traditions, and in an *a priori* bias *against* their possible truth. A certain opposition is usually manifest between the critical temper and the devotional and reverent temper, which ought in reality to be united. This is one great difficulty under which religious thinkers labour. The consequence is that two camps are formed—one under the flag of reverence, which shuns the candid searching criticism leading to a growth of exactness in our critical knowledge, the other under the flag of critical research, which lacks caution and reverence.

Moreover, while narrow minds will defend as part of orthodoxy opinions which may be general only because they were *formed* before new discoveries affecting their premises were before the world, the broader and more adventurous intellects, on the other hand, are apt at once to embrace unproven and highly speculative theories, broached by critics and scientists, as though they were the necessary outcome of the new knowledge of our time. Newman's intensely reverent and candid temper protected him from both extremes. He belonged to neither camp. He shared the strength of both. He held that a truly scientific system of thought on religious questions should never be stereotyped as a set of conclusions *only*, but should be always alive to the premises on which it rested, and thus to the bearing on their outcome of fresh facts as being fresh premises; and that true secular science and criticism should be always cautious, separating carefully established facts from conjectures. Conjecture, indeed, had its place in science. It was a means of reaching fact. So, too, repression and conservatism had their place in religious thought. They were often a valuable antidote to over-free speculation, carrying with them a bracing insistence on self-control and self-restraint in intellectual theorising. But on the whole reverent science, wide and bold in outlook yet cautious in decision, was the keynote of his thought:

> Let knowledge grow to more and more,
> But more of reverence in us dwell,
> That mind and soul according well
> May make one music as before,
> But vaster.

If I were to single out one of his works in which this temper is especially apparent, I would point to the 'Idea of a University'—notably to the lectures 'Christianity and Physical Science' and 'Christianity and Scientific Investigation.'

The entire and absolute justice he did to the new

scientific outlook bred confidence. One who could so clearly recognise it, and yet remain so steadfast in his adherence to Catholicism, won a trust from doubters which the slightest want of candour would have destroyed. Difficulties recognised, even though unsolved, may help the troubled mind far more than the most logical synthesis and solution which is not quite true to fact. He ever preferred to leave an apparent contradiction unsolved rather than to advance a half-sincere solution. The ultimate solution would probably consist in the rejection, on the one hand, of the speculative excesses of scientists and critics, and on the other of the pre-scientific opinions of writers on religion. Yet both classes of writers were jealous of interference, slow to recognise their own excesses : and with some reason, for outsiders might tamper with either branch of thought flippantly and dangerously. Neither side would readily abandon what they were disposed to identify with their science itself. Thus patience was needed. And meanwhile, during the time of difficulty and apparent contradiction, absolute obedience to the authority of the Church was the law which he preached in season and out of season.

Let it be observed in passing that, while his keen sense of fact was directed in his later writings to making the organism of the Catholic community intensely alive, and thus in a state to throw off both lethargy and disease, he did at the same time on occasion deal the most telling blows at the enemy. And here again the sense of fact was most apparent and most potent. His lectures delivered at the time

of the ' Papal aggression ' agitation, on the ' Present
Position of Catholics,' which he regarded as the best
written work of his life, not only set right with great
rhetorical effect the actual slanders and misrepresenta-
tions against the Church which in 1851 were widely
current, but owe their subtler and greater qualities to
his wonderful analysis of British prejudice, of the actual
workings of the mind of the prejudiced man—an analysis
which killed the slander at its source by showing that
source to be in an utterly malformed and distorted
mental vision.   His controversial works, then, while
rhetorically his most effective, had also their share in
bringing into play his deeper qualities as a psychological analyst.

All his later works were, in one form or another,
undertaken on behalf of candour and reality of mind,
among those of his own household, and those without
—his fellow-countrymen especially, for whom his
affection was so deep.   He declined a cheap victory
in controversy at the expense of being unjust to the
facts.   He demanded justice for the maligned members
of the ancient Church among its foes, but justice also
for the Anglicans among members of the communion
he had joined.   Yet, when he held the cause of his own
party to be simply that of truth and fair play, he was
unsparing in attack.   Obvious instances of this are
his onslaught on Kingsley and some of the more
satirical chapters in the ' Present Position of Catholics.'
The only one of his works in which he had, I think,
a misgiving lest his controversy was, under pressure
from others, not quite fair to the length and breadth

of the matter in hand—namely, some of the Lectures
of 1850 on Anglican difficulties—is believed to have
been written with less willingness than anything he
ever did.   Thus it is that he who throughout his
life held it a necessity (often so unpleasant) to act as a
party man, preferring the incidental prejudice of a
party which upheld the good cause and worked for
principles representing the highest he saw to the
colourless lower level of those who killed, in their zeal
against prejudice, the higher vision and deeper motive
power of which prejudice was often the sheath—
preferring even bigoted dogmatism to indifferentism
—never lost that underlying width of sympathy which
meant intellectual comprehensiveness.   Any narrowness in immediate policy was—let me say it again—
primarily practical, not intellectual.   It was a form of
concentration, for we cannot take many paths at once.
We take what we hold to be the best, though others
may be good.   And it completes rather than changes
our picture of the man to recall that one of his very
last letters on these subjects, published a few years
ago by Professor Knight, told of his sense of the
unity of aim in many religious hearts, and of his own
hope for some real and solid union among Christians,
which should form a basis of a Christian public
opinion in the future to resist the agnostic tendency
which he dreaded.

Newman was now an old man of eighty-six and a
Cardinal of the Holy Roman Church.   Eight years
had passed since he had delivered in Rome itself his
last great address against religious liberalism or

indifferentism—the celebrated 'Biglietto' speech of 1879, on occasion of his public acceptance of the cardinal's hat.   To write at all was now pain and labour to him; yet, when he heard of the death of Principal Shairp, whose sympathy with him in Oxford days amid theological divergence I have already noted, he began a letter, which his feebleness forbade him to finish, on the thoughts which such sympathy suggested.

Newman writes thus to Professor Knight in January 1887 :

Passing by my personal feelings, I lament the Principal's loss to us on a more serious account. In this day of religious indifference and unbelief it has long been my hope and comfort to think that a silent and secret process is going on in the hearts of many which, though it may not reach its limit and scope in this generation or the next, is a definite work of Divine providence, in prospect of a state of religion such as the world has never yet seen ; issuing not, indeed, in a millennium, but in a public opinion strong enough for the vigorous spread and exaltation, and thereby the influence and prosperity, of Divine truth all over the world. The world may not in the Divine decrees last long enough for a work so elaborate and multiform ; but, without indulging in such great conceptions, one can fancy such a return to primitive truth to be vouchsafed to particular countries which at present are divided and broken up into a hundred sects, all at war with each other.

The words of this letter are written in trembling characters, and it breaks off here abruptly : ' I am too tired to go on [he adds], and I ought not to have begun what I cannot finish.'

In these few parting words, however, we have the

root principle of his teaching in a somewhat developed form.   There is still the wide sympathy, the kinship with all keen and earnest religious thinkers; there is still, on the other hand, a sense of the need for a corporate society, the *Ecclesia* established once for all by our Lord as the champion of primitive revealed truth—a society which will inevitably be composed of persons of very unequal endowments—which acts, in fact, as a social force keeping Christian faith strong and vivid in the weak and vacillating mind of the individual. But there is also the dream that pressure from the foes of Christianity may gradually lead the two classes—the most earnest thinkers and the members of the Church —to become more and more nearly identical.   While in early life he regarded the liberal Christian thinkers as advocating principles which might well lead them in the end to make common cause with the rationalists, in later days he hoped that the wheel would be reversed, and that the sight of naked rationalism and agnosticism, would drive back most sincere Christians to a trust in their deeper instincts and in the Christianity of history, and that this truly Catholic principle should eventually lead large numbers of choice spirits to the Catholic Church.   It was the dream of a Catholic Church representative in its *personnel* of all that was best in religious thought and life.

NEWMAN AND MANNING

THOSE for whom the great representatives of the Catholic and Roman Church have special fascination in the scene of the world's drama often wish that they had lived in the days of Bossuet and Fénelon.   I think that to have lived in the days of Newman and Manning is, from this point of view, equally interesting.   In the mere appeal to the senses, as well as in the deeper qualities of character and intellectual force, it would be hard for a dramatist to create two more striking figures.

In the merely external drama of life the figure of Manning as cardinal was perhaps the most impressive ecclesiastical figure known to his generation, almost perfect in its own kind.   The stately presence, the handsome, refined, and ascetic features, the piercing eye, the unfailing personal dignity, the happy ease in his intercourse with his fellows—these were his most superficial gifts.   Then, again, the power of ready speech and the extraordinary facility of extempore exposition, the stately and eloquent, though not impassioned or poetical, delivery of sermon or oration, in their kind also approached perfection.   And withal there was apparent in his speech and demeanour a mystic sense of representing God's Church on earth, the look as of one who saw a vision, which added

Cardinal Manning

From a painting by G. F. Watts

something of the aspect of prophet or seer—just that something required to complete the ideal presence of the great Churchman.

A public man must necessarily think of the effect of his words on the public mind ; and one who lives before the general gaze incurs something of the same running fire of criticism which a schoolmaster receives at the hands of his boys. Manning was the recipient of his full share of such scrutiny ; and captious critics used to recall, as applying to some of his impressive addresses, Carlyle's saying on his own lectures—that they were a 'mixture of prophesying and play-acting.' But it was the greatest tribute to Manning's personality and character that, even with such criticisms in his hearers' minds, and even allowing for a grain of truth in them, the impressive effect of his addresses was nevertheless irresistible at the moment. The deep earnestness on behalf of a cause held by him to be sacred, the felt spirituality of the man, who was known to lead an ideal priestly life, the superb, if in some directions superficial, intellectual gifts, and equally superb use he made of them, allied with the manner and appearance of the ' sacerdos magnus,' seldom failed to convey the sense of greatness of a certain kind ; and even oracular utterances in conversation, which Mr. Purcell, in his biography of the Cardinal, tries to make us smile at in the retrospect, produced their effect at the time in virtue of the personality of the speaker.

Catholicism in England owes much to Manning. It received from him all that can be gained from a

gifted spokesman, a high character, in many ways
singularly unworldly, an ascetic life, an indomitable
will exercised in the interests of the Catholic Church,
an unrivalled power of attaining the objects on which
he had fixed his mind for the advance of the Catholic
cause in England.   He worked untiringly and successfully for the Catholic schools; he won from the
Government important concessions towards the free
exercise of their religion by Catholics in workhouses,
in industrial schools, in the army and navy.   For
seven-and-twenty years English Catholics had in him,
as their official spokesman, one of the most commanding figures in the country.   Their cause was
pleaded with dignity, eloquence, and a power of
persuasion fully equal to the prestige of the speaker.
His intense belief in and devotion to the Church, and
his readiness to champion its claims, even where they
were unpalatable to his fellow-countrymen, ultimately
won the respect of the bulk of Englishmen, and
greatly diminished the national prejudice against his
co-religionists.   Moreover, this remarkable figure in
public life was also endowed with an unusual gift of
priestly sympathy as a director of souls and as an
occasional counsellor.   His example and his precept,
on the priestly vocation, embodied one of the most
attractive and distinctive ideals of Catholicism.   He
had caught here the veritable spirit of St. Francis
de Sales, and of St. Charles Borromeo under whose
patronage he founded his congregation of 'Oblate
Fathers.'   Let those of the present generation who
would realise for themselves this quality in him find

its reflection in some of the pages of his beautiful work on the ' Eternal Priesthood.'

Yet the historian who attempts to estimate his policy, as well as his virtues and powers, will ask why one who did so much did not do more. The hopes prevalent among Catholics in 1845 and 1850—hopes of a vast increase in the influence of the Church in this country—have certainly not been realised. The historian will note the significant utterances of Manning's later life as to the reasons why the Catholic body had not gained more influence in England ; and he will examine how far the actions of this remarkable man himself in the days of his prime tended to diminish or to increase the causes of failure which he himself ultimately recognised. The time is come when such an investigation may be made consistently with profound respect for a character as to whose earnest devotedness there can be no question.

Let us, then, for a moment consider some features in his larger policy as archbishop. Let us consider his attempts to solve those problems, which needed not merely strenuous will, and skill in attaining predetermined ends, but true perception, from his standpoint as the leader of Catholics in England, as to the needs of the hour, in order to determine the ends themselves. No Crusader ever uttered his ' God wills it ' with greater conviction than did Manning during the years of his prime in his successive projects for the Catholic community in England. His first object was the creation of an effective body of priests. The

clergy ought, he urged, to be Roman in spirit ; insular
and English sympathies were to be crushed ; the type
exhibited in the Italian or French seminaries was to
be reproduced in England, with no infusion of the
literary, cultured ideal of Anglican Oxford. Each
bishop was to have his future priests around him ;
and by means of this direct episcopal influence the
new and ideal clergy was to be formed. This was,
he held, in accordance with the mind of the Council
of Trent. It was part of the Divine plan for the
Catholic Church. Not only Anglican ideals, but the
Cisalpine tendencies of the hereditary Catholics were
suspect. St. Edmund's College, in Hertfordshire—
the lineal descendant of old Douay College, founded
by Cardinal Allen in the sixteenth century—was
supposed still to embody this semi-Gallican, or at
least non-Roman, tendency. The divinity students
were therefore, in 1869, suddenly removed from the
college by a *coup d'état* to which all laws of worldly
prudence seemed opposed. A new ecclesiastical
seminary was forthwith founded at Hammersmith.
All this was carried through by the masterful will of
the Archbishop, in opposition to the views of the most
experienced priests. It mattered not. It was part of
what was regarded in those days, by a section of the
Oxford converts and their disciples, as the inspiring
crusade of the time—the rooting-out of the old-
fashioned English Catholic traditions, then regarded
as far too deferential to the prejudices of the sur-
rounding Protestant world, and the formation of a
new spirit, Roman, ascetic, unworldly, uncompromising,

which should pay no heed to the opinion of a civilisation gradually ceasing to be Christian.

If earnestness and a high ideal could dispense with knowledge of human nature and the prudent forecast of probabilities, and the accurate estimate of existing tendencies, all would have been well. In point of fact we are left to chronicle the acknowledged failure of much that was achieved. Many consider that the old Douay type of priest, at that time surviving and long respected in Ireland, still to be found at Ushaw (the coheir with St. Edmund's of Douay College), might well have been developed in the direction which Manning desired, while retaining at the same time that English character which made it especially practicable for our countrymen. The type was the outcome largely of experience, and had shown that it could wear. The asceticism and Catholic zeal and devotion to the Holy See of a Challoner or a Milner could vie with that of any of the foreign models held up by Manning for imitation; yet Milner and Challoner were products of the old system. Such a development seemed to many to promise more of success and stability than the transplantation of foreign habits. Be this as it may, the experiment was not tried. The old ideal was displaced; and it can hardly be said that the new was realised at Hammersmith. The divinity students are now again at St. Edmund's; and the memory of the Hammersmith scheme is, with most of those who care for such matters, that of a serious injury done to the interests of ecclesiastical education. Many who feel this do not withdraw their respect for the ideal which inspired the promoters of the new movement. Still statesmanship, even ecclesiastical, must be judged by results ; and, so judged, the effort stands in great measure condemned.

So much for the formation and education of the clergy. What of the laity? Cardinal Wiseman, Manning's predecessor, had dreamt fondly of the time when the growth of a liberal spirit in Oxford and Cambridge should open to Catholics the old universities. The time came ; but Manning, whose influence with Wiseman had become paramount, had by that time adopted here also a policy of the pursuit of absolute ideals irrespective of their practicability. For the laity, as for the clergy, he dreaded ' low views,' and the national or English type, and the spirit of 'worldliness.' The cry against 'mixed' education had been raised by Gregory XVI. and invoked for the destruction of the Queen's Colleges in Ireland. But it was capable of being applied in very different degrees, according to local circumstances. In England, where Catholics were a handful and had no university, it had been anticipated by Cardinal Wiseman that their attendance at Oxford and Cambridge would, with due precautions, be tolerated. He had written more than once in ' The Dublin Review ' inveighing against the hardship of the exclusion of Catholics from the universities ; and most people supposed that, when the spirit of the Emancipation Act had extended to the removal of the ban, Catholics would gladly enter them, as they had entered the House of Commons. Manning decided otherwise.

The principle that 'mixed' education was evil was taken up by Manning and applied in an entirely uncompromising form. Here again he acted with the zeal and whole-heartedness of one who was carrying out a Divine mission. To listen to reasons on the other side was to lend an ear to the tempter. With the same indomitable will and power of carrying through a scheme against all opposition which he had shown in founding the seminary at Hammersmith, he obtained from the Roman authorities strong rescripts forbidding English Catholics to finish their education at Oxford or Cambridge. When the absence of higher education for these young men was complained of he founded the 'Catholic University' at Kensington. Here also his action appeared to many to set at naught the laws of prudence. He placed over the new institution a man wholly unacquainted with university traditions, Monsignor Capel. The two real powers among English Catholics in matters educational and intellectual were Dr. Newman, at the Oratory, and the English Jesuits. Manning declined the co-operation of the Jesuits, and made no attempt to secure that of Newman. The scheme was practically still-born. A large staff of eminent professors, including F. A. Paley, St. George Mivart, Barff the chemist, and others equally able, lectured to a handful of undergraduates—their numbers never much exceeded twenty. After a few years the University really ceased to exist, though, like a true Englishman, the

Cardinal would not see that he was beaten; and I believe that the 'Catholic Directory,' years later, gave the name 'Catholic University College' to the learned Dr. Robert Clarke (one of the eminent group of savants who formed the original Biblical Commission in Rome) and about three pupils, who traced the same lineal descent from the Catholic University of England that the Rector of the non-existent Catholic University of Ireland, the late Dr. Molloy, traced from the institution founded by Newman.

These are two salient instances of Manning's larger policy; and they illustrate his character in a remarkable way. A dominant influence in his life, which has not been duly emphasised, was a power of conviction that certain lines of policy were entrusted to him by Providence to carry out against all human wills, and as part of a great battle for the Church against the world, which he pictured in almost Apocalyptic colours. Not a poet in the ordinary sense, he had a strong vein of mystical imagination in this connection. Some genuinely beautiful chance thought as to the due relation of the 'pastor and his flock,' or the fitting attitude of a 'priest according to the order of Melchizedek,' would determine his policy; and he would be absolutely inflexible in carrying it out. His very strength in execution was a consequence of the precarious nature of the original motive—precarious, that is to say, if clear, Divine guidance were not really vouchsafed. It was just because he regarded his scheme as God's will, and as outside the sphere in which human reason or prudence should be consulted, that he would not attend to symptoms of defeat or auguries of failure. Nay, defeat in a good cause was next best to victory. He had maxims which corresponded to this habit of unflinching action. To look back in an enterprise and hesitate as to its wisdom was, he said, to act like Lot's wife. The 'pillar of salt' was a warning for all time. And he would defend what appeared to be the blindest obstinacy by quoting, ' He that putteth his hand to the plough,' &c. Martyrdom for the good cause was to be welcomed. ' Stand and be shot' was the motto he used to hold up to his priests.

This attitude was, in fact, based on the very strong, and again mystical, sense to which I have already alluded, of a battle raging between the Church and the modern world. The wrong which most Catholics held to be inflicted on the Papacy in the Piedmontese attack on the Papal States, and the forlorn condition of his beloved Pius IX., made this congenial picture intensely vivid in his mind. The general view that there was, as there ever is, a battle between the Church and the world is of course indisputable, and the 'sixties witnessed a specially keen conflict between mediæval and modern ideals ; but in Manning this thought assumed a peculiarly mystical character, and it was allowed to dominate his policy in a very literal and absolute manner. Nothing could be more generous and whole-hearted than Archbishop Manning's attitude, apart from all question of its wisdom. From 1865 to 1876 he almost courted unpopularity. The 'Cordati Catholici' were a 'little band.' The world's hand was against them. They must be ready to fight against overwhelming odds and die as soldiers. British Catholics were to be trained as a body of Janissaries devoted to Rome, free from the 'low' traditions of England and Oxford. This element of almost unbridled mysticism has been, as we have said, astonishingly little dwelt upon by those who have dealt with this remarkable man's career. Yet it lies, I believe, at the very root of Manning's character. Few of his letters bring it home to a reader, in a short compass, better than one published by Mr. Purcell, and written to the late Mrs. W. G. Ward, in 1865, from his 'Retreat,' under the direction of the Passionist Fathers, at Highgate, immediately after his appointment as archbishop :

I have in these last three weeks felt as if our Lord had called me by name. Everything else has passed out of my mind. The firm belief I have long had that the Holy Father is the most supernatural person I have ever seen has given me this feeling more deeply still. I feel as if I had been brought, contrary to all human wills, by the Divine will into an immediate relation to our Divine Lord. The effect on me is one of awe, not fear, but a conscious nearness to God and the supernatural agencies and sufferings of His Church.

I have long had a fixed belief that a persecution is impending over the Church. When, I cannot say—whether in our time or not. But I believe it might come any day. I pray God that I may be found in my lot at that day.

I believe I can say that what has come upon me has not raised my pulse one beat; that it has given me no joy or personal gratification. I have lived long for work and little else, and I look upon this as so much work. It has brought me some sadness, for I must lose for ever much of the happiness of a pastor's life, and nearly all my peace and rest.   If anything has consoled me, it is the feeling that, if the Vicar of our Lord trusts me, our Lord does not distrust me.   And if He has not lifted me up for my greater reprobation, He has chosen me to do Him some service in the few years of my time, whether by life or by death.   I feel great joy in the hope that our Lord does not distrust me; and, after all this gall and vinegar I have had to drink, this thought is unutterably sweet.

We may trace a striking resemblance, both in gifts and in limitations, between Henry Edward Manning and another remarkable figure who long occupied a large space in the public eye—his friend William Ewart Gladstone. With both men it was will-power and that side of statesmanship which consists in ability to persuade others, and to carry through a definite policy against all opposition, which were so conspicuous.   Both were, therefore, magnificent and dominating figures in their own day, when the influence of a striking personality could throw a glamour over even impracticable or unwise schemes, and before time, the parent of truth, had made the unwisdom unmistakable.   Both have left as a legacy the memory of great figures and great forces.   Neither has contributed much to the highest wisdom of the world or its well-being.   Both, indeed, lacked the very highest intellectual qualities, though in each case the infinite skill with which they used the powers they had, and, again, the presence of the more superficial and practically useful mental gifts in a state of the highest activity and efficiency, might almost disguise this want. That acute observer, Walter Bagehot, when asked if

Gladstone's was a first-rate intellect, hesitated, and then said, ' No, but an admirable second-rate intellect in a first-rate state of effervescence.' The word ' effervescence ' is less applicable to Manning ; but substantially the verdict on him must be the same. On the other hand, a man is accounted great as an effective power who fills a large space in the world's eye, and who dominates the minds and wills of his fellows ; who has the perseverance and ability to carry out large and difficult designs ; and, so judged, greatness can be denied neither to Manning nor to Gladstone, and was not attained by Bagehot himself, whose merely intellectual powers were certainly far higher in quality.

The resemblance between Manning and Gladstone extends in some degree to the disproportion between the immediate tenacity of conviction and the strength of its grounds. The wiry, persistent effort which enabled each to carry through a project did not necessarily correspond to real depth of belief. It represented will-power rather than intellectual grasp. And the same consequence is visible in both—an ultimate instability of view, the more startling because of the tenacity with which the abandoned view had once been held. Gladstone began life as a Tory and ended as almost a Radical. From being a strong Unionist he became a Home-Ruler. So unexpected and surprising were his mental revolutions that Aubrey de Vere wittily compared them to the knight's move at chess. So Manning, the typical representative of ' morbid moderation ' as Archdeacon of Chichester, astonished Odo Russell, who remembered his past, when he appeared in Rome in 1870 as the typical *intransigeant* of the hour. And the days which saw Gladstone become a Home Ruler saw Manning make a further marked change in his views on the temporal power and on the education of the clergy—the very points on which his earlier attitude had seemed to be almost that of an inspired prophet.

Nor was this mystical element wanting in Gladstone. The strong religious tendency, which nearly led him to adopt the Church as a profession, remained through life, and included the characteristic of which I speak. Everyone remembers the saying of a well-known politician : ' I don't mind Mr. Gladstone playing with three aces up his sleeve, but I object to his trying to persuade me that Almighty God put them there.' Another story illustrative of this peculiarity was current in 1886. Gladstone was said to have written a letter to the late Lord Tennyson, at the end of which he referred to his new Home Rule policy. Tennyson, a strong Unionist, had found some lines in ' Hesiod ' to the effect that ' a man can very easily pull down a political Constitution by tampering with it, but that, if anyone thinks he can do what must be the work of many generations, namely, build up a new Constitution, that man shall fail unless he is inhabited by the spirit of a god.' A friend to whom Tennyson showed these lines remarked, ' I hope they will make Gladstone think.' ' Think ? ' Tennyson replied ; ' yes, they will make him think he is inhabited by the spirit of a god.' Gladstone's answer fulfilled this prophecy. He spoke of having, in consequence of

T

Tennyson's letter, ' cross-examined himself with a deep sense of his responsibilities,' and concluded by saying that at his time of life he should never have attempted anything so difficult and far-reaching unless he had had a clear conviction that it was his divinely appointed work to do so.

The perseverance of Mr. Gladstone at the cost of breaking up his party and losing his oldest friends showed on a larger canvas the same qualities as Manning's disastrous education schemes. The Gladstonian party was formed, but Home Rule was not achieved. So, too, Hammersmith and Kensington were accomplished facts ; but the effective education of Roman Catholic clergy and laity was certainly not advanced.

Just the same gifts were visible in Manning's action on behalf of the definition of Papal infallibility in 1870. The present writer had several conversations with Manning (in 1891) about his action at the Council. He regarded it as the greatest achievement of his life. It was fascinating to see the animation with which the old Cardinal recalled his former battles. ' Come again. It does me good to talk of it. It makes me live in the past,' he said. He related how he and the Bishop of Ratisbon, sitting on the steps of the Papal throne on the Feast of S. Peter and Paul in 1866, made a vow that they would work for the definition of Papal infallibility. He regarded the doctrine as a great weapon for the soldier of Christ in those evil days. Its acceptance was also to be the touchstone whereby the whole-hearted Catholics were to be known from

the half-hearted. He meant to 'fight the battle of
Peter against his enemies' and to vindicate the claims of
the Holy Father, smiting the world with 'high doctrine.'
The definition would throw a halo round the figure of
the Vicar of Christ. Here was the mystical idea, the
motive power; and in its execution he perhaps showed
greater capacity than ever before. Though a foreigner,
and not a perfect Italian scholar—inferior in this
respect to Cardinal Wiseman—he dominated the whole
assembly, and was by common consent the greatest
power in the Council. Ubiquitous and untiring, his
enemies called him 'Il diavolo del concilio.'

The mystic bent in later years concentrated itself
on the people and the poor, especially the poor of
Ireland. There was a distinctly mystical element in
his democratic sympathies, and it was characteristic
of him to say that Moses first made him a democrat.
Let it be added that there was in his love of the poor
and of the people something very winning and tender—
something especially representative also of his own
ideal of the Christian priest and pastor.

He had courted unpopularity in the eyes of the
English world for the first fifteen years of his archi-
episcopate by acting on fixed principles uncongenial
to Englishmen. But in his last years a measure of
popularity came; and it was not unwelcome. His
views on the temporal power and on the type of
clergy needed for the success of the Roman Church
in England, expressed in the famous 'Hindrances,'
indicate so wide a change in some of his opinions that
the critic has in a sense the Cardinal's own sanction

for strictures on his earlier policy.   But it is observable that, while giving the judgment of more mature experience, he seems never to have reflected that it was his own policy which was largely responsible for the failures and faults which he deplores.   He had denounced the type of mind Newman wished to form among Roman Catholics as a repetition of the cultivated Oxford type; yet it is expressly the qualities of the Oxford clergyman which he desiderates in the 'Hindrances.'   Here are his words, in a letter to Monsignor Talbot, written in 1866, the second year of his reign as archbishop:

> I see much danger of an English Catholicism of which Newman is the highest type.   It is the old Anglican, patristic, literary, Oxford tone transplanted into the Church.   It takes the line of deprecating exaggerations, foreign devotions Ultramontanism, anti-national sympathies.   In one word, it is worldly Catholicism.[1]

Against this 'danger' he worked for many years with all his untiring energy.   Yet it is the absence among the English Roman Catholic clergy of these very qualities, which the Anglican clergy possess—of the Oxford literary culture—the absence in them of patriotism and the presence of anti-national sympathies, which he denounced in 1890 as the first of the 'hindrances' to the spread of Catholicism in England.   Here are his remarkable words:

> In 1848 I was in Rome, and read Gioberti's 'Primato degli Italiani.'   In describing England and its religion he says that the Anglican clergy are 'un clero colto e civile.'   As to culture, they certainly have a literary and scientific

[1] Purcell's *Life*, ii. 323.

culture, more general and more advanced than the body of
our priests; sacred science and theology hardly exist among
them. Here and there only, such men as Lightfoot and
Westcott are to be found. Nevertheless, they are literary:
history, constitutional law, and experience in politics, they
have very generally. Moreover, they have an interest in
public affairs, in the politics and welfare of the country.
They are therefore *civiles*. They share and promote the civil
life of the people. It is here that we are wanting, and
mischievously wanting.

The long persecution of the Catholic Church by the laws
of England has alienated the hearts of Catholics from the
public and political life of England. Till fifty years ago they
were legally *ex-lex*. The law is changed, but not the habit of
mind formed by it. ' Ecclesia patria nostra.' Catholics have
not only been alienated from public life, but have been
tempted to think that patriotism is hardly reconcilable with
Catholic fidelity. . . . So long as this habit of mind lasts we
shall never have a civil priesthood; and, so long as our
priesthood is not civil it will be confined to the sacristy,
as in France, not by hostile public opinion, but by our
own incapacity to mix in the civil life of the country.[1]

A commanding presence while he was with us,
Manning has left us a great example of priestly virtue
and ascetic life, of untiring devotion to the Church, of
tender sympathy with the poor. But of lasting
wisdom, the most he has bequeathed is to be found in
his later words, which are at variance with the thoughts
and acts of three-quarters of his reign. On the
Oxford question, however, he remained in theory
firm, though even W. G. Ward wavered after the
failure of the Kensington University. It was left to
Cardinal Vaughan, all unwillingly, to yield to the
wishes of the laity and to undo his predecessor's

[1] Purcell, ii. 774.

work by permitting Catholics to frequent the national universities.

That John Henry Newman was conspicuous in his early days for many of the external gifts which help to make a personality impressive as a public figure we know from the testimony of his Oxford contemporaries. The demeanour which suggested to Principal Shairp a Chrysostom or an Athanasius come to life again ; the musical voice, with its delicate intonations in preaching or reading prayers ; the suppressed emotion, the dramatic instinct which made his sermons, though read from a manuscript, masterpieces in an eloquence quite peculiar to himself—all these made a deep impression on the Oxford of the 'thirties. But as an ecclesiastic in the Catholic and Roman Church Newman was no longer in the same sense a public character. The contrast between him and Manning is for this reason the more complete. He lived a life of retirement at the Oratory in Birmingham, seen and heard only by a few intimate friends. If Manning was essentially the success of the moment in the Catholic Church, ever before the public eye, ever carrying through the schemes he initiated, and yet left comparatively little that was valuable as a permanent contribution either to thought or to the well-being of the community, in Newman the parts were reversed. He was emphatically the recluse, the apparent failure of the moment, the man of the future. It is not too much to say that his life was from the first a succession of apparent failures, each of which won him his opportunity of conferring on Christian thought a contribution, the value of which is now recognised by ever-increasing numbers, whether they accept his conclusions or not. And that value is not only speculative—the value of thought as thought—but concerns the abiding practical relations between Christianity and modern civilisation.

The characteristics of his career of which I speak marked especially the years after 1845. He used to talk jestingly at Oxford—though there was deep pathos mixed with the jest—of his ' floors.' He failed as a tutor at Oriel to impress the undergraduates. There is every reason to think that Lord Malmesbury's picture, in his ' Memoirs,' of Newman's ineffectiveness in dealing with the average undergraduate gives a true impression. The plan which he and Hurrell Froude conceived for exercising quasi-apostolic functions in their tutorship was opposed by Hawkins, the Provost; and Newman was ultimately compelled to resign. The ' Tracts for the Times,' which he inaugurated and edited in 1834, incurred episcopal censure in 1841 and had to be discontinued. As a Catholic, almost his first important work was as Rector of the Catholic University of Ireland. Newman designed this foundation as the university for all English-speaking Catholics. He wholly failed to make it so. For nearly four years after his nomination he was unable to bring the university into being at all. Few even of the Irish bishops could be induced to take any interest in it, except as a party measure against the Queen's Colleges. At its best it was not a success ; and it ultimately ceased to exist, its medical schools alone surviving as a memorial of the attempt.

Newman next endeavoured to guide the policy of 'The Rambler'—that very able periodical known afterwards, in its enlarged form, as 'The Home and Foreign Review'—which, in the hands of the late Lord Acton and Mr. Richard Simpson, impressed Matthew Arnold as displaying more 'knowledge and play of mind' than any other review of the time. Newman failed, however, to keep 'The Rambler' on lines acceptable to the Catholic bishops. He then tried to edit it himself, but had to resign after his second number. He was commissioned to undertake a translation of the Scriptures which was to supersede the old Douay version, but had to abandon the attempt. Twice, in 1864 and 1867, did he plan an oratory at Oxford ; twice was his design impeded by the ecclesiastical authorities when apparently on the verge of completion. The years from 1851 to 1867 were one long record of failure in every practical scheme he undertook, with the exception of the Oratory School, which did not call forth his special powers and was chiefly under the able direction of Father Ambrose St. John.

Yet it is hardly an exaggeration to say that each of his failures of the hour led to a work by which posterity has profited. Had he been absorbed by his Oriel tutorship we should never have had the work on 'The Arians of the Fourth Century,' with its really remarkable historical generalisations on the genesis and *rationale* of creeds and dogmatic *formulæ* ; and it is doubtful if the Oxford Movement, as history knows it, would ever have come into existence. For only one man was capable of blending the philosophy of tradition, conceived on Coleridgian lines and expressed or implied in Newman's 'Tracts' and 'Sermons,' with a practical movement which appealed to Pusey, to Palmer, and to the rank and file of High Churchmen of the new school. The subsequent breakdown of the 'Tracts,' again—another practical failure—gave him a stimulus for one of his works which was for all time—the 'Essay on the Development of Christian Doctrine,' in which, fifteen years before the 'Origin of Species' appeared, the philosophical idea of evolution was so clearly foreshadowed. To the long-drawn-out failure of the Dublin Rectorship we owe alike the 'Idea of a University' and the third volume of 'Historical Sketches,' both full of interest for the years that were to come. The connection here again was causal. To his work for 'The Rambler,' and his consequent experience of the difficulties of combining really comprehensive thought with taking the line desired on prudential grounds by ecclesiastical authority in a time of tension, we owe that remarkable chapter of the 'Apologia,' 'The Position of My Mind since 1845,' the title of which so little conveys its interest and value. The scheme for the translation of the Scriptures led him to prepare an 'Introduction' which traced the development of the religious idea in the history of Israel—a fitting prelude to the essay on the 'Development of Christian Doctrine.' Should this exist in any form suitable for publication, I can hardly doubt that its value will be very considerable.

If the failure of the Oxford scheme had no direct effect in extracting from him any publication for which his admirers are grateful, it at least gave Newman the leisure but for which the 'Grammar of Assent' might never have been written. Moreover, the lines of policy attempted by him without success in action, partially indicated in writing, are just those which the deepest thinkers among Catholics regard as offering permanent hope for the practical success of Catholic thought and action in the future. The addition of the fine and true psychology of the 'Grammar of Assent' to the metaphysics of religious belief in the text-books long current, is gradually being effected in the more cultured Catholic educational centres. The ideal of a university in which all sciences, including theology, should be represented, so as to effect the provisional synthesis which would keep Christian theology abreast of modern knowledge and preserve for education its religious character, remains as an ideal for the thoughtful Catholic, whether the university in which it may be attempted is itself Catholic, like Louvain, or more or less neutral, like Oxford. And, lastly, the idea of development, exhibited in the work which marked his failure as an Anglican leader, while giving an *apologia* for the past, gives also the hope for the future ; for it proposes to reconcile the proud *semper eadem* of Rome with a power in her organisation and theology of adaptation to new circumstances in thought and life. And on this the thinkers and men of science in the Church build their hopes for the age to come.

Indeed, the whole succession of Newman's failures

in efforts designed to subserve education and thought
for his co-religionists had a large share in inspiring a
brief but most important essay of his later years, which
is the sketch of a treatise on the philosophy of an
ecclesiastical polity. I refer to the ' Introduction,'
written in 1877, to a new edition of the ' Prophetical
Office,' republished under the title of ' Via Media.' His
aim in his work at Dublin, in editing ' The Rambler,'
and in his proposed work at Oxford in the 'sixties, had
been to combine real and thorough treatment of the
questions absorbing the thinking world with loyalty to
the existing ecclesiastical authority and to the main
outlines of Catholic tradition. Newman believed the
living organism of the Catholic Church in communion
with Rome to be in its idea the great antidote to
that attitude of negation in religion now known as
agnosticism. In order that it should in reality prove
to be so, two things were required—the recognition of
authority as keeping the organism one, and a body of
theological thought constantly energising, and as well
adapted to the present time as the lectures and writings
of St. Thomas Aquinas had been to the thought of
the thirteenth century. Newman found that this last
requisite must take time to achieve. The freedom
which was necessary for thoroughness and candour
was at that time suspect as playing into the hands of
the enemy. Men like Louis Veuillot were ready to
brand as heretics all who did not agree with their own
version of orthodoxy. Newman as well as Dupanloup
deplored the influence of this extreme school in narrow-
ing Catholic thought. ' Extreme views alone,' he wrote,

'are in favour, and a man who is not extravagant is thought treacherous.' In a certain sense the story of his Anglican life was repeated. In 1841 he claimed liberty to hold Catholic views as an Anglican ; the retort was the condemnation of ' Tract 90 ' by the heads of houses at Oxford and by the bishops. In 1855 he claimed, in a remarkable lecture, freedom of research as a Catholic ; and he soon learnt that the dominant party would not practically tolerate it. Speaking of history, he wrote in oft-quoted words, ' One would not be thought a good Catholic unless one doctored all one's facts.' We have lived to see the days when Leo XIII. directly encouraged among Catholic scholars the utmost candour in historical research ; and the official approval, during his pontificate, of Pastor's history of the Popes showed a widely different temper from that deprecated in Newman's words given above.

It may fairly be argued that the change was largely due to the influence of Newman's own writings. Such changes in policy in high places are from time to time wrought by the gradual influence on thought of a powerful personality. They express at the moment the different views of individual rulers and their advisers. Newman, in his Introduction to the republished ' Via Media,' analysed, with acute perception, the forces at work in the Catholic community which are calculated to bring about adaptations to the requirements of the time, and thereby helped his followers to possess their souls in patience in days when his thoughts and opinions were viewed with suspicion by zealous but narrow men, and even by some of the ecclesiastical

authorities. He likewise traced those forces which
made such opposition and suspicion at times inevitable
in the case of good and necessary work on somewhat
novel lines. Passages from the works of St. Thomas
Aquinas were for upwards of half a century under the
ban of ecclesiastical censure ; in the end his opinions
could claim an authority in the Church second to no
other. Newman points out the conflicting interests in
the work of the Church which explain both phases ;
and his argument, which shows him as the Burke of
the ecclesiastical polity, applies to other religious communions besides the Catholic Church. Christianity is
of course, he says, in the first place a creed. As such
it appeals to the intellect. Theology attempts the task
of analysing its implications and reconciling it with
thought and learning ; and the principle of theology
is truth. But Christianity has been also throughout a
worship appealing to the devotional nature ; and the
Church became, moreover, a polity. The principle of
devotion is edification. A polity needs rulers ; and
expediency is the immediate guiding principle of rule.
What is expedient at one time may not be so at
another ; and different rulers will judge differently of
expediency.

All these three aspects are ever present in any
communion which claims to represent Christianity ;
and the interests of one may at times encroach on
those of another. At a time of civil disorder, when
places of education are broken up, the intellectual
element may suffer from the absence of institutions
devoted to its cultivation. Thus Newman constantly

lamented the dissolution of the Sorbonne as a blow to Catholic theology. Again, free discussion, the pre-requisite of ascertaining scientific truth, and its exact relations with theology, may lead to undesirable contention at a crisis when union of forces is specially desirable ; and then the interests of expediency militate against those of truth. Theology in the large sense may languish while devotion and rule are active. The very presence of danger keeps faith and devotion alive ; and, if anarchy threatens or prevails, the rulers naturally become more absolute and alert. And their action in enforcing positions which are theologically ' safe,' but not necessarily adequate to new problems raised by advancing research and thought, may retard investigations which will ultimately lead to new scientific truth. Thus intellectual interests for a time are injured. At other times the intellectual element may become too active and unruly, as it did early in the thirteenth century ; and the principles of authority and tradition may be too weak to withstand the rationalism which results from such excess. Hence the widespread infidelity in the medi-æval University of Paris. Again, rationalism may seriously imperil the devotional element, which necessarily thrives best in an atmosphere of faith ; or the exclusive presence of devotion, however pure and intense, if it sets at naught the principles of common-sense or the conditions necessary to stable rule, may be disastrous for the Church. Thus, even St. Francis of Assisi needed the wise counsels of official authority to make his great enterprise practicable.

Thus again, when the cardinals, sick of worldliness in high places, brought from his mountain-cell to the papal chair the ascetic hermit who took the name of Celestine V., the total absence in the new Pope of the qualities of a ruler led to hopeless confusion and disaster. The *gran rifiuto* was a necessity ; and the embodiment of masterful rule—not without its attendant defects—occupied the throne of Peter in the person of Boniface VIII.

Thus did the English Cardinal find a philosophy in the history of the Church which brought patience and endurance in the special trials of his later life ; and thus did he reconcile himself to a time when, during the pontificate of Pius IX., his own gifts found little scope in the Church, without ever suffering the ' blessed vision of peace,' of which he speaks in the wonderful epilogue to his work on Development, and to which the ' kindly light ' had led him, to grow dim in his eyes. The 'sixties of the last century were, he wrote, ' a peculiar time.' He constantly regretted that the French Revolution had destroyed the old theological schools, and that they had not been effectively replaced. While original theological thought was largely in abeyance, the Revolution of 1848, and the subsequent Roman crisis, led inevitably to a strong opposition in Rome to the dangers of 'liberalism'; and at such a crisis even the best men may be slow to distinguish accurately the freedom of thought which is essential to the interests of truth from that which would mean insubordination and rationalism.

The triple division in the ecclesiastical polity—

between the interests of truth, of devotion, and of stable rule—was formulated by Newman in 1877 ; but, in fact, his whole life as a Catholic was based on its practical recognition.   His Anglican life from 1828 onwards had been the story of his growing belief that he had found the reconciliation of the conflicting claims of the intellect and the spirit in the historical Christian Church, which had faithfully preserved the Apostolic *ethos*.   It was his sense of the claims of the spiritual nature, stimulated by sorrow, as he tells us in the 'Apologia,' that led him, under the guidance of the Fathers, from an incipient liberalism and intellectualism to join forces with Pusey and the High Anglicans.   The early years of his Catholic life saw the peace and happiness which came from his belief that he had found in the Church, with its Apostolic descent, that spirituality which he looked for.   But from the time when, as Rector of the Catholic University, he had to turn his attention to the intellectual attitude of an educated Catholic, at the very moment when the scientific movement was threatening to destroy in all religious communions so many old landmarks, his difficulties began.

Newman's qualities and his antecedents and his University position at that time marked him out as in many ways just the intellectual leader whom the times demanded.   Yet he soon found that his hands were tied.   It was a truism to the student of Church history —so he urged in the 'Apologia'—that 'individuals and not the Holy See have taken the initiative and given the lead to the Catholic mind in theological enquiry.'   The great men who have formed Catholic theology did not form it as official ecclesiastical rulers, but gained their influence in virtue of intellectual genius, learning, and sanctity. St. Clement of Alexandria and St. Augustine, Albertus Magnus and St. Thomas Aquinas, were instances in point at different periods in Church history. Some who had most strongly influenced theology were, on certain points, accounted unorthodox, as were Origen and Tertullian. Theology ever stood in need of the great thinkers, for it was the product of thought, and not of inspiration. If the Catholic Church was *semper eadem*, it was not, he held, to be expected that this rule of the past should be reversed in the present or the future. Therefore Newman felt that he had himself a work to do in which he might follow the greatest examples in Church history. Like Albertus Magnus and St. Thomas Aquinas, he was the teacher of Catholic youth in a university. This was the very position in which precedent—and he was very sensitive to precedent and tradition—most clearly sanctioned the work of reconciling the truths of revelation and Christian tradition with the new learning and thought of the day. Yet he ever insisted on obedience to authority as the mark distinguishing fruitful intellectual effort for the Church from the freethought which leads to heresy. In this matter he had fallen on difficult times. The influence of Cardinal Cullen in Ireland, quite as much as that of Archbishop Manning in England, was held to favour a policy of absoluteness and *intransigeance* in the intellectual domain. A certain jealousy and fear of the *rôle* of the intellectual leader had, moreover,

U

perhaps been common among those in authority ever
since freethought at the Reformation threatened the
unity of the Church ; and the Revolution, in all its
phases, had renewed and increased this fear.

Thus the troubles of the Church, and the dread in
high places of the excesses of intellectual freedom,
were obstacles in the way of the frankness and candour
and thoroughness in historical and critical research
which Newman's work required. He had to content
himself with indicating its lines with the greatest tact
in his lectures—notably in the lecture on Christianity
and Scientific Investigation. He often referred wist-
fully in them to the freedom of thought allowed in
mediæval universities. Still, though the theological
temper of the moment hampered him in work for which
he was, above all men, fitted, he never swerved
from his rule of obedience, and recognised the justification as well as the cause of a temporary conservatism which might be repressive, in the excesses
of modern free thought.

There can be little doubt, however, that in this and
in his succeeding efforts, feeling urgently the importance of frankly dealing with the vital questions of the
hour, he was disposed on the whole to regard perseverance in the more timid course much as a doctor
would regard the refusal to undergo an operation
which would cure, though at the cost of anxiety and
pain, an otherwise incurable illness. ' In some states
of society, such as our own,' he wrote in the introduction of 1877 to the ' Via Media,' ' it is the worst
charity, and the most provoking, irritating rule of

action, and the most unhappy policy, not to speak out,
not to suffer to be spoken out, all that there is to say.'
Hence he had a certain sympathy with the aims of
Lord Acton in 'The Rambler,' which, in spite of what
he regarded as defects of tone, did make the attempt
to grapple frankly and honestly and with real knowledge
with the science and thought of a new era. Hence
his readiness to go to Oxford and do there some of
the work which he had wished to do in Dublin.
But, with unyielding conviction, he recognised that
the right to decide on the opportuneness of any such
policy lay with the ecclesiastical authorities. Loyal
obedience was due to them, even where their decision
might be opposed to the line he himself judged wisest.

Just as he had instantly stopped the 'Tracts for
the Times' on a hint from the Anglican Bishop of
Oxford, so he resigned the editorship of 'The Rambler'
when he found that its methods were displeasing to the
Catholic episcopate. He twice dropped the Oxford
scheme without a struggle. He plainly said in the
'Apologia' that his hands were tied so far as controversy was concerned. 'I interpret recent acts of
authority,' he wrote, 'as tying the hands of such a
controversialist as I should be.' His respect for the
interests of successful apologetic would not allow him
to undertake it on lines which did not convince himself. His respect for the rights of authority would not
allow him to write on his own lines, when they might
seem to be at variance with what the authorities
judged to be prudent.

The contrast between Newman and Manning is

292 TEN PERSONAL STUDIES

all the more interesting because they to some extent
embody two distinct types of mental character which
we now see widely represented in the Catholic
Church. Each man was fascinated by a type in
conformity with his own earlier life. The Rector of
Lavington and the Archdeacon was drawn to the
Church of St. Francis of Sales and St. Charles
Borromeo—of the pastor of souls, and the guide
of consciences, and of the saintly official ruler.
The study of such historical characters brought out in
Manning a special affinity for the post-Reformation Church, of which they were representatives;
that is, for the Church in action, and in controversy
with those who had rebelled from her authority.
Consideration of deeper intellectual problems, wide
and penetrating thought among Churchmen, was not
the characteristic of the period immediately succeeding
the Reformation. True, these qualities are to be
found a little later in the writings of such divines as
Suarez and de Lugo; while the works of Petavius will
ever stand high as specimens of frank treatment of the
history of theology. But the success of the Counter-
Reformation was due to other gifts in which the Jesuits
specially excelled—ascetic life, ready and persuasive
speech, controversial rather than philosophical ability.
The whole seminary system then introduced was on
these lines. The old mediæval disputations, once
symbols of almost unbridled freedom of speech and
speculation, were reorganised and marshalled to defend
fixed propositions affirmed by the Catholic, denied by
the Protestant. Authority and devotion enjoyed para-

mount influence; intellect was but the servant whose business it was to defend their claims. Manning, with his high ascetic ideals, his enthusiasm for the priestly caste, his ready but not deep intellect, found in this atmosphere an entirely congenial home.

To Newman it was before all things the Church of the Fathers which typified the genius of the Catholic Church. The days when Christian thought was building up theology as the expression of Christ's faith best suited to educated men in view of the controversies of the hour, persuasive to the intellect of Alexandria or of Athens, were the days congenial to the man who had lived his life among thinkers and scholars in Oxford. On the patristic era of Church history, he tells us, his imagination loved to dwell as 'in a paradise of delight.' Theology occupied primarily, not in refuting 'heretical rebels,' but in intellectually interpreting and applying the genius of Christianity, satisfying the deeper thought of its own champions rather than merely scoring immediate successes in argument, was his ideal. The controversial zeal of an Athanasius, indeed, was not uncongenial to him. It had its place in the scheme. If it was militant, it was so in defence of a few great principles and truths. But neither officialism nor organised special pleading on behalf of a number of predetermined intellectual positions, to be preserved because they were in possession, was in harmony with his own peculiar bent of mind.

Newman, I think, found it hard to walk in the theological armour of the mediæval Schoolmen, though

his respect for those great doctors and their work was
profound. The scholastic text-books of his own time
represented an intellectual structure which had been
erected by a very curious sequence of events. The
dialectical mania of the thirteenth century had led
the Schoolmen, at Paris and elsewhere, to formulate
answers to every conceivable question posed by the
roving intellect of the University scholars to whom
Oriental pantheism was familiar as well as Christian
theology. Hence the *nimia subtilitas* to which Leo
XIII. referred on a celebrated occasion as qualifying
the claims of the Schoolmen to imitation by ourselves.
These *responsa* had been used in the lecture-room to
answer inquirers; and some of course dealt with
questions beyond our ken, which were, perhaps, only
answered to quiet the questioners, much as a child
must be satisfied with a definite reply, and clamours
for it in matters on which no really provable answer
is available. In the sixteenth century came the natural
reaction against the resulting over-elaborate and over-
definite structure to be found in some specimens of the
school-theology—against those peculiarities which belonged really to the clever childhood of modern
Western civilisation. Readers of Sir Thomas More's
earlier works will come to the conclusion, from his
words on the subject, that, in the ordinary course of
events, excessive scholastic 'subtlety' was destined to
be thrown over at that time by the more cultivated
Catholics. Be this as it may, the Reformation brought
a panic which made any far-reaching movement of
intellectual reform impossible; and the insistence on

authority as against private judgment led to a new vogue for the writings of the scholastic theologians, so useful, in such a crisis, from their very definiteness and completeness. Thus a system which was the product of an age of almost unbridled rationalism became the bulwark of conservatism.

To Newman's own intellectual temper the method of the Fathers was, as he has told us, ever the more congenial. His psychological subtlety had little in common with the logical subtlety of the Schoolmen. If I am right in maintaining that it was, on the other hand, the genius of the militant post-Reformation Catholicism which Manning represented, we have at once an explanation, over and above his own special qualities and defects, which partly accounts for his successes and his failures. What zeal and ability in an emergency will do, he did, carrying out what appeared to him to be the orders of a God-given authority. This was the keynote of the work done in the post-Reformation Church, when military obedience was as essential to the Catholic divine as energy and capacity in its exercise. Granted that the Council of Trent required Archbishop Manning to found his seminary, none of his contemporaries could have shown more energy in carrying through an unpromising scheme. Granted that there ought to be an English Catholic university under his own absolute control, no one was better fitted to set it on foot. Granted that the definition of 1870 would have all the consequences his imagination pictured, no other Churchman of the day would have carried it through so successfully. In each case the voice of authority, as he interpreted its decisions, was to him the voice of God, and directed and inspired his great capacities in their unswerving and untiring efforts.   But the task of framing the initial judgment as to the wisest practicable policy—the root of lasting and constructive work—is, with a system subject to military discipline, in the hands of very few indeed ; and Manning was not fitted by his qualities, remarkable as they were, to be one of those few.

I have said that Manning and Newman represented two types of Catholicism—that of the Counter-Reformation and that of the patristic era respectively.   It may be asked, How far is the type to which Newman belonged akin to what was long known as liberal Catholicism, represented in England by the late Lord Acton ?   In one point, and in one point only, the resemblance is very marked : namely, that both types urged strongly the necessity of a frank consideration of the drift of the positive sciences and deprecated undue dogmatism in theology.   But the temper evinced in Newman's opposition to the liberalism of modern society, his strong sense of the value of intellectual conservatism as a protection to the stability of the ecclesiastical polity, and his distrust of reason as ever prone in matters religious to exceed its powers—all marked features in his intellectual character—have no parallel in the 'liberal' Roman Catholics.   Newman's temper is far more akin to that of More and Erasmus, who rejected scholastic subtlety and undue dogmatism, but were, nevertheless, filled with enthusiasm for ancient ways and venerable traditions.   Still, he has told us in the ' Apologia ' that he ' enthusiastically concurred ' in the ' general line of thought ' of

Lacordaire and Montalembert ; and the story of his
connection with Lord Acton and 'The Rambler'
shows his deep sympathy with the thoroughness of
research which was one main characteristic of the
liberal Catholic movement. But he ever had a statesman's sense of the wide interval which separates discussion from any definite step forward, not merely in
the official decisions of the Church, but in the finally
accepted and avowed convictions of the theological
schools, and even of individuals.

Moreover, he was keenly alive to the liability of
the human reason to error in its conclusions on the
things of God. He inveighed against those who, like
Louis Veuillot, 'exalted opinions into dogmas.' The
very ground of his opposition to such theological dogmatism was also an argument against the sanguineness—
equally over-confidence—of theological liberalism. All
these considerations weighed in keeping him in the
Church of England long after his reason pointed the
way clearly to the Church of Rome. Still more did
they weigh against the final acceptance of any serious
modification of traditional opinions in the Catholic
Church. There was, then, a compartment in his mind
in which the 'liberal' Catholic would have found a
very congenial atmosphere ; but the whole man, in
action and in practical belief, remained a Father of
the Church. Reverence, conservatism, and the love
of wisdom were his characteristics. He would have
found his kinship in our own day with the learned
Benedictine, who stores up ancient theology as a
treasure of thought, not as an instrument for oppres-
sive dogmatising, whose heart is in the past, while he

keeps abreast of modern criticism, far more than with the typical liberal Catholic, who says strong things against the theologians and against the ecclesiastical rulers, and is sanguine of creating a new theology radiant with the hues of twentieth-century progress.

The modern opposition between liberalism and *intransigeance* is, indeed, an opposition between temporary excesses on either side at a time of transition. So far as the underlying permanent antithesis is between elements reconcilable with Catholicism, it must resolve itself into that between the types which we have styled Jesuit and patristic respectively. The former is the type which rejoices especially in authority and discipline. It is proper to a Church in the state of defensive warfare, which keeps the intellect under military discipline. The latter form of Catholicism is perhaps more general in the Church when she is promoting peaceful civilisation, giving to individual initiative free scope, and encouraging original learning and thought as important factors in her well-being. These two types are largely those symbolised by the two English cardinals. Manning, in spite of his opposition to the Jesuits, belongs unmistakably to that type of Catholicism of which they are the most distinguished representatives, and Newman rather to the type preserved in the Benedictine Order, owning as fellow-creatures such writers as Mabillon and the congregation of St. Maur; though he added an element of active and free speculation more akin to his beloved Augustine, or to the mediæval Schoolmen, than to the calmer labours of the monkish historians.

APPENDIX

THE following is the text of the interchange of letters between Mr. Balfour and Mr. Chamberlain, known as the 'Valentine Correspondence,' and referred to in the postscript to the first essay in this volume :—

4 Carlton Gardens, S.W. : Feb. 14, 1906.

MY DEAR CHAMBERLAIN,—The controversy aroused by the fiscal question has produced not unnaturally an impression, which I have constantly combated, that the practical differences between fiscal reformers are much deeper than is in fact the case. The exchange of views which has recently taken place between us leads me to hope that this misconception may be removed, and with it much friction which has proved injurious to the party.

My own opinion, which I believe is shared by the great majority of the Unionist party, may be briefly summarised as follows :—

I hold that fiscal reform is and must remain the first constructive work of the Unionist party ;

That the objects of such reform are to secure more equal terms of competition for British trade and closer commercial union with the Colonies ;

That while it is at present unnecessary to prescribe the exact methods by which these objects are to be attained, and inexpedient to permit differences as to these methods to divide the party, though other means may be possible, the establishment of a moderate general tariff on manufactured goods, not imposed for the purpose of raising prices or giving artificial protection against legitimate competition, and the imposition of a small duty on foreign corn, are not in principle objectionable, and should be adopted if shown to be necessary for the ends in view or for purposes of revenue.

Believe me yours sincerely,

ARTHUR JAMES BALFOUR

40 Prince's Gardens, S.W. : Feb. 14.

MY DEAR BALFOUR,—I cordially welcome your letter of to-day, in which you have summarised the conclusions that we have reached during our recent discussion. I entirely agree with your description of the objects which we both have in view, and gladly accept the policy which you indicate as the wise and desirable one for the Unionist party to adopt. In endeavouring to give effect to this policy and in defending all Unionist principles any services that I can render will be entirely at your disposal.

I am yours very truly,

J. CHAMBERLAIN.

Mr. Wharton's amendment of March 9, 1904—referred to at pages 3 and 24—proposed formally to approve of the declaration of Ministers that their policy did not include Protection or taxation of food. On learning its purport 112 Chamberlainites held an informal meeting and sent an ultimatum to the Government requesting its withdrawal. Although the amendment had received the sanction of the Government Whips it was thereupon withdrawn.

Mr. Ainsworth's resolution, referred to at page 3, was proposed on March 22, 1905. It embodied a condemnation of Mr. Chamberlain's proposal of 10 per cent. on all imported manufactured articles. Mr. Ainsworth maintained that Mr. Chamberlain's policy "was played out, and that the Prime Minister had won all round." Mr. Balfour saved the Chamberlainites from unmistakable defeat by declining to make the resolution one for the Government Whips or to vote on it, and inviting his friends to absent themselves. The result was that all Chamberlainites abstained from voting, and the resolution was carried with only two dissentients.